PENGUIN BOOKS

THE SPELL OF THE FLYING FOXES

Sylvia Dyer was born in 1928 and grew up in the wilds of Champaran in north Bihar, on a plantation pioneered as an indigo estate by her great-grandfather, an Englishman. She spent ten years of schooling at St Helen's Convent at Kurseong, Darjeeling, was married twice, and widowed both times, to Indian Army officers. There were two sons from her first marriage and a daughter from the second. She now lives alone in Pune and her two surviving children have settled abroad.

W0246885

The Spell of the Flying Foxes

SYLVIA DYER

PENGUIN BOOKS

An imprint of Penguin Random House

PENGUIN BOOKS

USA | Canada | UK | Ireland | Australia
New Zealand | India | South Africa | China | Singapore

Penguin Books is part of the Penguin Random House group of companies
whose addresses can be found at global.penguinrandomhouse.com

Published by Penguin Random House India Pvt. Ltd
4th Floor, Capital Tower 1, MG Road,
Gurugram 122 002, Haryana, India

Penguin
Random House
India

First published by Penguin Books India 2011

10 9 8 7 6 5 4 3 2

The views and opinions expressed in this book are the author's own and
the facts are as reported by her which have been verifi ed to the extent possible,
and the publishers are not in any way liable for the same.

ISBN 9780143065340

Typeset in Sabon by R. Ajith Kumar, New Delhi
Printed at Repro India Limited

www.penguin.co.in

MIX
Paper from
responsible sources
FSC® C047271

This is a legitimate digitally printed version of the book and therefore might not
have certain extra finishing on the cover.

Contents

PART 1

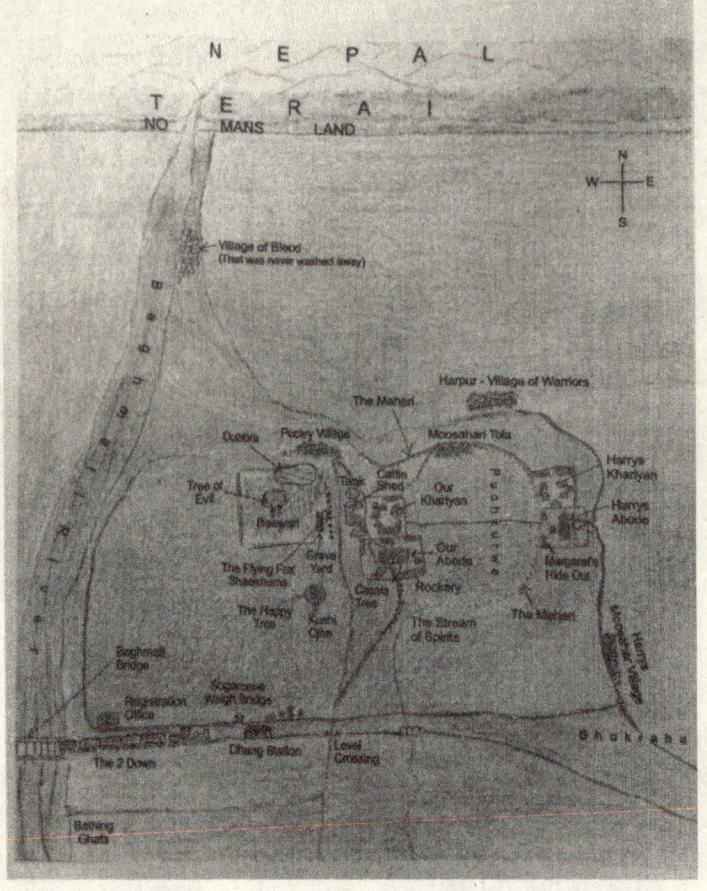

The Flying Foxes

Nobody would ever forget Dhang, though after all these years it seems to me that it never really existed, and was just a long-ago, stretched-out dream. But it was there all right, tucked away at the foot of the Himalaya, in the district of Champaran in Bihar, sharing a common boundary with the 'Forbidden Kingdom', as Nepal was then known. Previously, there had been no boundary at all, just an understanding with the 'Forbidden', for in those days the Terai spread across the brow of India in a belt so dark and dense that people scarcely knew, or cared, where India ended and Nepal began, so engrossed were they in the ceaseless tug of war with the ever-encroaching jungle.

But the British had, as usual, decided the 'where', pushing forward the frontiers in an action that seemed to say, 'People of the hills, live in the hills!' They set up new boundary posts at a desolate spot named Majorgunj, five kilometres north-east of Dhang, and a cemetery to speak for their dead, most of whom had been felled not by the kukri, but by raging tropical diseases like cholera, smallpox and malaria, so the gravestones revealed.

The jungle too was pushed back by determined cultivators, and slowly, very slowly, lush green fields began to appear in progressively widening patches leading to a momentous discovery. The soil of Champaran was capital for the cultivation of indigo, which in those days was the world's only blue dye and regarded as 'Blue Gold'. Naturally it attracted men from the West, adventurous and enterprising men who were looking for a new beginning like my great-grandfather, Alfred Augustus Tripe. That is how it all began.

Slowly the scene changed. Villages sprang up, and shallow embankments that served as demarcation or boundary lines planted with rows of shisham trees. These were quality timber trees known for their strength and durability, and they stood like ramparts against the worst floods of the river Baghmati, which during heavier monsoons went berserk, flowing savagely away with any weakly rooted thing, whether cultivation, habitation or line of demarcation. But the shisham trees, like invincible green sentinels, stood fast, holding their ground against the worst floods, as though it had been decreed, 'Stand fast, and the madness of the river shall not prevail against you!'

The Baghmati wreaked its havoc; yet, as if guided by an underlying sense of fairness, it paid for the damage with the glorious silt it spread lavishly over its transgressions. So in the final count, you loved this river and saw why it was called the 'Baghmati', which means 'Garden Earth'. And you knew that Dhang was the gift of the Baghmati.

And so it was. A land so fertile, locals claimed, that my great-grandfather's walking stick, once left out in the garden, had taken root and sprouted leaves overnight! Men had to be mindful of their walking sticks. It was a tall story, like so many others in the days when people amused themselves with stories, squatting under a wide, shady tree in summer or around a bonfire in winter with the flames spitting cinders at their nonsensical talk. But even Alfred Augustus Tripe, who was a hard-headed, no-nonsense man, used to say that when he touched this soil gold came forth from it. And so it did, in the beginning.

Over this enchanted land the sun rose, touching the tips of the mighty old shisham trees, slowly, almost reverently washing them down with sunlight, a daily head-to-foot ritual like the Hindu bath. They presented a singular appearance of grace and strength, this particular row of trees, since for some reason unknown to us they had been exempted from the yearly pruning that shisham trees were normally subjected to. So their many branches grew out laterally graceful, like the arms of gods and goddesses in serene and benevolent attitudes, hung with streamer-like offshoots and cascades of little coin-shaped leaves.

And just about this time, if you happened to look up, little, black specks began to appear in the brightening sky, taking shape as they drew nearer in twos and threes and fours, moving with the awkward elastic progression peculiar to flying foxes hurrying home from their nocturnal excursions, which, contrary to what some people think, were really quite innocent. They were not blood-crazed Draculas, but merely little foxes with membranous wings, pointed snouts, stand-up ears and clear, vegetarian eyes. Soon, there were scores of them, softly screeching their chaaaans and chiiiis as they flapped about their favourite trees to hang themselves up for the day. Hooked-up, soft, furry bodies with stomachs full of fruit, suspended in the black-ribbed latex of their wings like foxy people in hammocks, getting an upside-down view of the world, day after day, year after year. At sunset they unhooked, unfolded and flew off, the right way up. Verily they had, you might say, a three-hundred-and-sixty-degree view of life that rendered them fairly omniscient creatures. Who knows?

'But why?' we wanted to know. 'Why only this row of trees?'

Mother gazed at them searching for an explanation for something that had never crossed her mind. 'Could it be that since these trees were never pruned, they had so many branches for the flying foxes to hang upon?'

'But then, why were they not?'

She couldn't say. How or why, nobody could say, or even remember. Sukhesar Ojha, one of our oldest retainers and the intellectual among the Brahmins, peering into the mists of time, recalled that even when they were children, the trees and the flying foxes had been there.

'One thing is certain. They were here in the time of your great-grandfather,' he said clearing his throat, as he always did before the delivery of a revelation, while the eyes in his fine-featured brown face lit up with a keen fire. 'Flying foxes,' he said, 'are believed to be a symbol of prosperity; and during that time there was a curious prediction concerning these creatures.'

That day we learned from Sukhesar about the spell of the flying foxes.

In the hazy past, a sadhu had come out of the Terai jungles in the north; a strange being, like a shrivelled old dwarf-tree from the foothills that had uprooted itself and walked away, moving southwards with a purpose. He could have walked out of a book of witches and magicians. Long, silvery grey hair covered him like a cloak and a beard like wispy snow flowed over his front almost to the knees. Even his body, stark naked in the bitter cold of December, was smeared silvery with ash. He strode along, carrying a staff far taller than himself, and the village people followed in his wake, drawn like dark, wingless insects to an oil lamp. He had still a considerable distance to cover, in this his final journey to the Ganges; for the Hindu mystic knows when his 'time' is near and his spirit draws him to the great sacred river.

It was midday when he reached our khariyan, and stopped with the rigid discipline of ascetics, to rest and revive himself with water fresh from the well and a portion of the roasted besan he carried. Only then did he become aware of his surroundings; and looking around, his eyes came to rest on the row of shisham trees with the flying foxes hanging asleep in them. His gaze locked on the scene, trance-like; and when he spoke, the many who squatted around him like a restrained cordon of flies, heard him clearly: 'See those trees,' he said in a husky voice, raising one of his twig-like arms to point, 'now heavy laden with scores of flying foxes, like the wealth of this kothi. But when they leave these trees and go, so will the prosperity.' He sighed, casting his eyes wearily around. 'And everything fair as we see it this day!'

What could we have done to hold back the flying foxes, even if we had believed?

It was a serenely wooded place, with the cool, aromatic fragrance of wild flowers. Undisturbed. In fact, close by our ancestors lay resting in peace. Keen rays of the sun, dodging through the leafy density above, played on the marble statues and slabs in the little family graveyard, covering it with shadow lace. Few people passed this way, and those who did simply joined

Sylvia Dyer

the palms of their hands and, bowing their heads in reverence to the marble angels, moved on.

Sometimes in the summer, when daylight lingered awhile after sunset, we watched the flying foxes wake and leave their trees in low, erratic flight. Our dogs ran after them, taking wild leaps in the air, landing on one another or having head-on collisions that sparked off skirmishes among themselves, leaving the flying foxes chuckling. Or, once in a while, the boys took out their air rifles and brought down a couple for the locals to prepare as an asthma remedy they swore by. The fallen lay in a pool of their own blood, staring up, not in accusation, but just sadly, till their eyes closed. The flying foxes accepted this occasional sacrifice of their fellow creatures for a humanitarian cause. Nothing really disturbed them.

Yet in our days, they went. Imperceptibly, as though they had evaporated drop by drop. Like the minutes, hours and days of unwatched time, we didn't mark their going, till they were gone! And then, like a broken spell, it all vanished. Everything. Even those once invincible shisham trees were no more. It was obliteration that even the ruthless Baghmati decried, for it turned its face away and forsook the land.

All that remains, as I see it today, is the red brick bungalow built after the 1934 disaster. It stands knee-deep in weeds; its doors are jammed, its clouded skylights shut with finality, like dead eyes. Inside, it is almost bare. The high ceilings echo our dragging steps—Pig and Parrot, as we were once called—seeking a buried past. There is no fragrance left, except in memory. Nothing has been touched for years. Spiders hold sway, living out their generations without interference from the broom, spinning their webs to blot out the past, our past. Pale house-lizards with dark, wet eyes, stick to the walls, motionless and glum. No single tuk-tuk to greet us . . . A godforsaken place with nothing left to speak of its history but the few pictures nobody wanted, like this one in the spare bedroom where Alfred Augustus Tripe, Esq. peeks unvanquished from behind an almirah someone had pushed against him and the past. It reveals a powerful, uncompromising face with white hair, dense as the jungles of the Terai, and a walrus moustache. The challenge in the eyes has grown dim with the portrait's struggle for survival through the neglected dampness of many monsoons. Neglected and rejected.

And yet, this man was, for us, the beginning.

The Beginning

Alfred Augustus Tripe came to India in 1848. A young man from a prosperous family, he left forever his home in England for this distant, untamed land of Champaran. Was it only for the Blue Gold? If so, he succeeded beyond his dreams, becoming, in the course of time, the owner of seven indigo factories. This was the period of prosperity when 'gold came from the earth at his touch'. These so-called factories were actually plantations, each with its villages of tenants, labourers, processing yards, storage sheds and indigo vats. From some accounts, he was a fearsome being. Common folk dared not raise their eyes to his, but spoke looking humbly at his footwear.

And yet, our seniormost Brahmins like Sukhesar Ojha, custodians of history (in their heads), and spinners of rare yarns, spoke of Alfred Augustus Tripe with a mixture of awe and admiration, referring to him as the 'Sher'.

For years the indigo planters of Champaran prospered, living the lives of demigods, till the invention of a synthetic dye in Germany and political changes brought them crashing down to earth. It was a death blow for indigo and in the financial crunch that followed Alfred Augustus Tripe lost three of his seven indigo plantations. It hit him hard, this turn of the tide in the fading years of his life.

'There was a time,' he said, 'when I touched this dust and it turned to gold! But now, when I touch gold, it turns to dust!'

But his indomitable spirit never turned to dust, neither by the untimely deaths of his wife and his eldest son, nor by the harrowing presence of a brother called Tom, the black sheep of the family, who had followed him to India. His spirit remained unbroken, and he lived to see his seventy-fourth birthday, a rare thing for those days, when the span of a man's life could be counted on the fingers of seven hands.

His only surviving son, Joseph Rowland Tripe, had returned home to his father in 1890, a stranger to this land of his birth. It was a startling contrast to his life in London, though not without its sweet compensations. Despite the losses, this rich and beautiful land, as far as his eyes could see, would be his. And then, there was Sarah.

Here in the dining room is a portrait of him. A clean, young face with candid grey eyes, handsome in a gentle way, like a poet, with long sideburns and a well-disciplined moustache unlike his father's soup strainers. From his first sight of Sarah, he was in love. Sarah with her pale, square face and misty grey eyes; and a heart that seemed dead and buried in his brother's grave.

From her he learned about this land of his birth. They shared so many interests, books, painting, music and a love for the wilderness. They rode out together as the first light of dawn tinged the east with pink and woke this sleeping paradise to a brand-new day of euphoric bird calls, lingering to see the dewdrops come to life and sparkle on the leaves, to touch and watch them flee from their resting hollows; and she was laughing again. They laughed and looked at each other. And in his eyes she saw, for the first time, a love that had waited long.

'Sarah . . .' he said gently, taking her face in his hands, 'awake again? . . . Back at last from the past? . . . To me?'

Yes. For all the tears in this world would never bring back the dead.

A hundred miles away in east Champaran, Sarah's sister Mary knew little of love, trapped in a miserable marriage to an indigo planter. It had been this way for ten years with 'this lecherous and vile-tempered beast', we heard, wondering what was 'lecherous' and 'vile' while the elders sat talking in the drawing room after dinner. One night, 'Things had simply gone too far!' Just how far, was conveyed in whispers, because children with long ears were playing on the carpet; though it was by the zeal of these stretchable ears that we picked up valuable scraps of family history and dark secrets. The morning after 'things had gone too far' and he had ridden off in silence, Mary packed up all her belongings without a tear. The last one had been shed long ago, when he shot her cocker spaniel in a drunken rage, because he had tripped over it and flown headlong into a thorn bush. Her mind was made up for better or for worse. She gathered up her two children, Harry and Rosie, and called for the carriage.

'Quick!' she cried, as the luggage was hurriedly loaded (there wasn't much of it). 'To the railway station! We must not miss this train!'

'Baap re baap, memsahib!' The carriage driver's mouth dropped open. 'The earth will turn upside down and the sky will fall upon our heads! What will become of us when you are gone?' His voice came out in a croak. His hands shook and his hurriedly tied turban would be gone with the wind, when they moved off.

'Bus, bus—enough!' she snapped. 'It is finished at last! No time now for useless talk!' Her thin, pale face wore a determined look, and she held the bewildered children tightly against her. 'Stop fumbling, and move! Drive like the devil was on your back!'

'Ayyy Bhagwan!'

And the heavens did fall upon them when her husband returned late that night, staggering drunk, to find his family gone. Like a raging beast he roared and choked as he smashed the furniture and ripped pictures off the walls to crush under his boots. He kicked the dogs that appeared in startled inquiry, and threw the mynah, cage and all, out of the window into the black night, because all this time the bird had kept screaming 'London Bridge is falling down—Ack! Ack! Ack!' Then he turned on the gaping servants with his horsewhip and drew blood to get the truth out of them. But not one humble mouth opened to tell him what they knew. And all his efforts to trace her, the inquiries, the repeated appeals in the *Statesman*, ever got his family back again.

She had settled in a humble quarter of Calcutta, living on a pittance earned from days and nights of tireless needlework. Nor did Sarah in all those years know what had become of her only sister. And then one day in the middle of New Market, known as Hogg Market, where you could come face to face with people you hadn't met for years—'Mary? Oh, could it be Mary!'

'Sarah!' Laughing as tears rolled down their faces they held each other, words tumbling out, filling in the blanks left by the long years of separation, while an audience of shopkeepers collected silently about them to witness this real-life drama.

'Dear sister! Not a word from you in all these years! How could you, Mary, and when you had to live like this!' Her eyes moved sadly over Mary's tired clothes.

The shopkeepers' eyes too followed sadly over the tired clothes.

'I didn't want to burden my little sister.'

'Eh hay hay hay!' This drew a chorus of compassion and admiration from those familiar with English, who turned aside to share with the others in rapid Bengali.

'Burden? Oh, how could you think that?'

'Ahh haahaa!'

By now the audience was all in tears, drying their cheeks on their sleeves.

'But look, what's this I see? A baby on the way?'

'Mary dearest, it's why we're here!'

A suitable apartment was found for Mary and her children. Blissful days followed, with Gladys, my mother, born safely to crown it all.

And then suddenly this mountain of joy came crumbling down, hit by a declaration of doom. An examination at the Medical College Hospital revealed that Joseph had contracted phthisis, the same wasting disease that had claimed his elder brother's life!

'Nelly'—it was his pet name for Sarah—'I've suspected it for some time . . . this confounded cough! And now they've confirmed I have this accursed disease. Still, it's something I can face. But our child! Think of the exposure to my illness, damnably contagious thing, as you know only too well, my Nelly! And not just this, consider all the raging epidemics this little mite will be exposed to in the godforsaken wilds of Champaran—miles and miles from any kind of medical assistance—that's what scares the daylights out of me!'

But Mary had a solution. 'Sarah . . . if you can bring yourself to do it, leave her here with us. She'll be safe, loved and cared for like my own child, I promise you. Return with your husband. He's going to need you there, more than ever!' A bitter potion. They had to take it and drink it—bitter as it was.

They were trying years that followed—lonely, harsh and unsparing, coping with the estate and its multiple problems (Alfred Augustus Tripe was dead and gone by this time) while Joseph's health failed steadily. Sarah was often away to Calcutta, sometimes on protracted visits. During these separations he had written her letters, which we found when the old wooden chests in the back veranda were opened up half a century later to trace our roots. Slumped in their own dismal dust were the remains of letters and documents that had been the staple fare of silverfish and such during all those years. And the boys sat piecing them together on the veranda steps, with the dogs nosing around and getting in the way, till finally we had something . . .

Sylvia Dyer

My Nelly . . . writing this in the Hava Ghar . . . having my tiffin . . . . chair opposite me stands empty still! . . . Lonelier each day . . . I ride alone, eat alone, sleep alone . . . precious days and nights wasting away with me . . . empty . . . waiting for you . . . thinking to myself, when the paddy turns gold in the sun, when the breeze from the west blows cold and the wild geese return to the river, she'll come back to me!

And swiftly those precious days ran out, and he was dead; and his Nelly was widowed for the second time at twenty-eight.

Six years had gone by. Harry was seventeen, Rosie fifteen and Gladys six when Sarah brought them all home to live with her permanently. She grew deeply attached to this little family, and dependent on them, for they were all that she had left now, though the years of separation had made a stranger of her only child, Gladys. But there would be no more separations now. They were home.

Harry couldn't believe it. He had seen years of privation during which he had learned to worship money. Now he was face to face with it! A voracious learner, he learned to ride and shoot, and became skilled at both. He was soon familiar with his new surroundings: the fields, the orchards, the jungles, even a little sliver of the Baghmati that made its way through the property. He studied the crops that grew in rotation as the seasons passed, the ways of harvesting, processing and trading. And as the years went by, he learned more. With a shrewdness that was rare in one so young, he analysed the psyche of the people, both simple and wily, and made them all, in time, his puppets. He could make them dance. Dance till they dropped.

He could be quite charming too, when it served his purpose; and he played his hand very cleverly with Sarah. Harry could do no wrong, as far as she was concerned. Before long he was the manager of the estate, which brought him an annual commission of nineteen thousand rupees, for sugar cane supplied by the estate to the Belsund sugar factory. It was a sizeable amount in those days, when paddy was sold at one rupee a maund!

He had started an exciting business of his own too, for ideas came to his head like metal shavings to a magnet. As he looked at the jungles on the estate, he had a vision of husky young elephants bulldozing through the lush greenery to grow bigger and fatter for the Sitamarhi mela. Why not a business in rearing elephants? It would cost him little or nothing and the profits would be considerable. In those days wild elephants were captured in the khedda in Assam and handed over to koonkies, trainer-elephants who whipped them into submission, putting the fear of Moses into them before they were fit to be sold to elephant traders. Harry bought a few, between the ages of three and ten years, just young enough to handle, for elephants take about as long as humans to grow up.

The elephants grew quickly in height and girth in time for the Sitamarhi mela, where every year they fetched a substantial profit for Harry. It was a good business, for elephants were then like cars are now, a worthy form of transport and a status symbol, in addition to their many other uses. Rajas kept several high-grade ones in their elephant stables while lesser zamindars had at least two. 'Heh heh! It is simply like this. When one is out of order, I still have the other!'

Elephants were a rich man's pride and joy. They were forever comparing elephants. Looking out with a collector's eye for bigger, better ones. And their conversations were loaded with elephant-talk.

But Harry's mother was an unhappy woman with failing health, and within a few years she had become an invalid confined to a huge four-poster bed with servants to care for her day and night. Slow-moving servants with gloomy faces, like snails whose very shells have become a painful burden to them. The stark joylessness of the situation struck Sarah as she sat one evening by Mary's bed.

'Mary, my poor, dear Mary! I see now the sacrifice you made, coming to live here in this godforsaken wilderness and you did it only for me! How heavily the thought of it weighs on my conscience!' She took one withered hand into her own strong ones. 'For some time now, I've been wondering how I could ever make it up to you—and I've decided that the least I can do in return is to gift the three hundred acres my husband gave me as a wedding present to Harry and Rosie.'

Mary looked up at her in surprise. 'What is this, Sarah?' she said, blinking back the sudden tears. 'You've done so much for us already, you owe us nothing!' But Sarah, patting her hand, continued, 'The bulk of the property will naturally go to Gladys. But even when I am no more, I'm sure she won't grudge them a place in this house.'

'When I am no more . . .' Sarah sat thinking about her own life. Gladys, of necessity, had been sent away to a boarding school. During those years she had seen little of her. This had only widened the space between them. Had she been happy? But then, who was? Who was allowed to be happy for long? She looked across the room at Rosie sitting by the window, bent over the pages of a novel, her rich, black hair falling softly across her face. Had she ever been happy?

'Always with that pretty nose buried in a book! Tell me, child, about this one. Does it end happily?'

'Why, yes!' Rosie looked up, laughing. 'They all die together!' Her eyes were quite extraordinary, an uncertain mixture of blue and green and grey. They were large, and fringed with heavy black lashes. In the amber light coming through the curtains, she looked too beautiful to be the undoubtedly terrestrial creature that she was, warm and loving, yet with a violent temper that flared up at her husband, John White, in Samastipur. He was an engineer on the Bengal & North Western Railway whom she had married at sixteen. By twenty she was the mother of two children and happier in the wilds of Dhang than in Samastipur with her spouse. 'I agree, Aunty . . . You make your bed and you lie on the damn thing. But take it from me, this marriage is a bed of nails and I'm no nail-proof sadhu!'

Their quarrels raged like close-quarter battle, with hardware, glassware and footwear flying through the house till the arrival of a peacekeeping force of neighbours. Each time Rosie was back with the scars of battle, and her children, Dorothy and Ernie.

'Tell me, Aunty, does karmic suffering run in families? I could swear it does! First my poor mother, now my turn! Same bloody thing. I can't take it any more! So bloody-minded—and the world's most jealous bastard!'

The big house in the wilderness stretched out its arms to the war victims. It craved for 'family', the patter of little feet and the ring of human voices in any tone at all. So it became their home as well, where Rosie's children grew up, apart from the nine months of every year spent at boarding schools in the Darjeeling hills.

Meanwhile, Mary lay dying slowly, just withering away like a tree planted on the wrong soil. A tree that no longer feels the sun and the wind, nor tastes the sweetness of rain on its face; and finally she was gone and laid to rest with our ancestors, in the family graveyard.

The walls of this ghost house have no more pictures. But here, over the mantelshelf, is the outline of one that had occupied this space for a very long time, that is, till the day when (after it had all ended) it was carried off by Abhinandan, the dacoit. For a long time he had stood there, straight and tall, silvery haired and grief-scarred, staring at it. Staring as his thoughts flashed back over the years and his hand passed over his face as if to wipe out something he could not countenance. Then reaching up with long, sinewy arms he unhooked the portrait from the wall, tucked it reverently under his arm and walked away, leaving an empty space.

An empty space? But I can still see her there—Gladys, my mother, as she looked in that photograph taken in 1935; the fine features so like her father's, the firm jawline and soft, dark eyes with a shadow of sadness in them. It was the year after the terrible earthquake, when we had gone to stay in my father's family home in Calcutta, gone without my father, because he was no more.

My father, Edmund Coutts, had come from a close-knit family, the youngest of eight children. When his mother died giving birth to him, his eldest sister, who was nineteen with a month-old baby, became his foster-mother, while the others pitched in with the tenderness and laughter-filled guidance that went into the making of a beautiful human being. He was well employed with Duncan Brothers, a firm of tea brokers, when he met and married Gladys. Those brief years with my father in Calcutta were the happiest in her life, Mother told us, but so short-lived.

During one of their rare trips to Dhang, Gladys had a visit from an old family-watcher, a venerable old man with a strong sense of fair play. The affairs of the kothi in those days were everybody's affair, carried from mouth to mouth, spreading faster and further than any newspaper. 'Missbaba,' he said, 'I feel compelled to speak to you on a certain matter—and I hope you will not take it as impertinence on my part! It is like this . . .' His voice fell to a whisper, 'You are too much away! We know you have a new home now, but what of this, your ancestral home and property? One day, it should all be yours. But the way things are going, who knows what will remain? . . . We hear bad talk about Harry sahib. Your mother signs documents that he puts before her, without even looking through them! This is the truth, known to many, but they do not speak, for fear. Believe me, Missbaba, in time, you will lose—God only knows how much of your father's lands! She has come to trust him implicitly. But Harry sahib?' He shook his head sadly. 'He is not a man to be trusted!'

She had suspected it, being artfully kept in the dark. 'Don't worry your pretty head with all these troublesome papers, Gladys. What am I here for?'

Yes. What *was* he here for!

There was only one answer to this. Edmund would have to surrender his job and all that he held dear in Calcutta, for a life in Dhang. And he did it.

It didn't suit Harry at all. And even the 'old lady' (as Gladys often referred to her mother) was displeased and openly critical of a man living in his wife's ancestral domain. Edmund, if he happened to be present, would silently get up and leave the room, while Gladys flew angrily to his defence. There was an exchange of bitter words, searing words that could not be erased, and then an icy silence. An ominous cloud gradually settled over the entire household, with even servants and pets getting infected by the pervasive chill.

Every night in the splendid drawing room—fragrant with roses, with the sparkle of crystal, the gleam of polished teak, and silverware that the dacoits had failed to carry away on their last visit—they sat couched in luxury, sipping the finest wines, with darkness in their hearts.

'Harry,' Sarah said, one of those evenings, 'things seem to be going from bad to worse between Gladys and us. I've been thinking . . . why don't we give part of the estate to Edmund to manage?'

A flush spread over Harry's swarthy face and his jaw set like cement. 'Edmund! What are you saying, Aunty? It would be a disaster! Quite impossible! What does he know about agriculture?'

'Nothing, I agree, but he can pick it up, Harry, like you did.'

'Like I did . . .' He looked up at the ceiling and smiled a grim smile. 'Well, maybe. But does he have the foggiest idea of how to handle these people? No! He can never learn that—he's too soft. A gentleman! Ha ha! It doesn't work to be a gentleman in this place. Ask me! There's only one thing that works here—twist their tails! You must know like a cart driver, how to twist their tails!'

Sarah sighed. She was growing old, a solitary ship that had tossed too long on a turbulent sea. Too worn out for this eternal wrangling, this continuous state of siege. She was tired of dissension, and strife. Life was chock-full of the beastly thing. If

Sylvia Dyer

you wanted to go one way, it invariably pulled you in the opposite direction. Maybe it was best to leave things as they were, to be settled by time. So the matter was left hanging in the air.

It must have been a trying situation for Edmund, a man both strong and gentle. A man who the people of Dhang came to admire and respect, but who was in actual fact a nobody in his wife's ancestral home. If he had any regrets he never spoke of them; the love they shared together was compensation enough, he told her. And so they lived as happily as they could in their own wing of the house, with a few servants and a meagre income, for ten bitter-sweet years, during which time Reggie, Lenny, Lancy and I were born; the last two of us coming too late to know the love of such a father or to have any memory of him. In 1931, when he was thirty-six, Edmund had an acute attack of appendicitis. In the blazing heat of June they made the journey to Calcutta. A long journey of agony that could only end in death.

'Your poor father . . . there couldn't have been a nobler, more lovable man on this earth—yet he lived to see only the lean and bitter days!' Mother once told us, when happier, more prosperous days had come. 'I remember when Christmas came around and all the others had expensive new clothes, he got the tailor to open up one of his old suits. The pieces were turned inside out and stitched back to create a transformation. "Just look at this, Gladys!" he said, laughing, dressed up in his "brand new" suit. "It would fool anybody!"' He laughed that way at everything that must have hurt. Only once did he put his real, deep-down feelings into words. He said, 'Bitter is the bread you eat at another's table!'

Home Sweet Home

Of all Alfred Augustus Tripe's possessions the best loved was 'Puchkurwa', a hundred-acre plot of translucent, green fields with two villages that came as dowry with his Indian wife. Almost as if it had come gift-wrapped, an offshoot of the Baghmati called the Mahari, wound around it like a silver ribbon, carving it in the shape of a perfect horseshoe fringed with tall, slender shisham trees. It was something to behold. When the sunset tinted it with fiery gold, when the full moon drenched it in silver, or even when nothing spectacular happened, it took your breath away.

Here he had built the house of his dreams and furnished it with all the beautiful things that money could buy, European period furniture, paintings, crystal and Chinese porcelain. It was a double-storeyed house with a wide veranda and portico on slender columns raised maybe three feet above ground level, much like this present house, as a safeguard against the Baghmati floods and inquisitive snakes. A short flight of steps went up to the veranda and the living rooms with two staircases going up to the bedrooms in the left and right wings, and a spacious terrace upstairs. At the rear of the building spiral stairways connected with the bathrooms upstairs for the sweepers to ascend and descend—swift and discreet in their disagreeable but imperative missions of disposal, for those were the days of the thunderbox! They carried dainty little baskets with lids and handles so much like Red Riding Hood's that you could easily have been deceived about the contents.

The immediate surroundings resembled an English park, in striking contrast to the tropical wilderness around. There were decorative trees and shrubs of an amazing variety cleverly arranged about beds of multicoloured annuals with little crushed-brick pathways sneaking through. A rose garden and well-kept lawns stretched away to wide borders of cannas. In the backyard there was a thriving vegetable patch and some favoured fruit trees that were not natives of north Bihar like the mango and litchi trees that grew in orchards. Conveniently close to the vegetables was the kitchen, a smoking little thing commanded by well-browned cooks, sweaty and watery-eyed from their battle with woodsmoke and fierce spices. This too was built on a platform like the house and had its own little veranda where these champions of local culinary art emerged with masala-stained banians and girded-up loins for a whiff of fresh air and a taste of betel nut, directing their spittle with power and accuracy between rows of vegetables.

A driveway from the front gates cut across the garden, running through the porch, past the stables and out the back gates to the khariyan, the hectic operation centre of agriculturists. It continued past the cattle sheds to Puckry village, the abode of our domestic staff and field hands.

It was a comfortable life in this kingdom in the wilds. There were scores of servants, and luxuries from the civilized world, but it remained a desert for social life and communication with the outer world. Even the nearest doctor was fifty miles away; miles of lush green desolation with its attendant perils. Nevertheless, life went on leisurely and luxuriously. A tiny railway station consisting of two rooms and a mini platform, perched high on an embankment for fear of the Baghmati floods, waited all day for a train (the 1 Dn) that came, and another (the 2 Up) that went once a day, moving between Samastipur and Narkatiagunj. It brought newspapers, letters, soda water, ice and bread, even exciting parcels from anywhere at all. It took time, but they came. There were exciting pursuits too, like riding and hunting, and when winter brought flocks of wild duck and geese to the river we went up and down the Baghmati in boats. It was risky those days, swimming in the Baghmati, since the more enterprising gharials often moved up from the Ganges for a look-see, and got a bit rough with swimmers!

There was a good library and a large Columbia gramophone that stood on its own squat legs producing an incredible sound. Villagers begged permission to come in and see this thing with their own eyes and hear the sounds pouring out from its middle. 'O Bhagwan,' they hissed, with popping eyes and a snake-head movement, 'It's an English God!'

This 'English God' had a wide selection of music and a devotee in a spotless white uniform to wind up its handle and switch the records rapidly, for non-stop music. He was Ghogra, Harry's personal attendant or 'bearer'. Apt word, for he was to bear Harry over rough and perilous terrain when the earthquake struck. And easily, for he had the build of a bull and the face of a bulldog, though, concealed under it all was the heart of a chicken! He had attached himself pompously to this machine because it was 'one of the world's wonders', and he was such a show-off. It also gave him an excuse to be in the drawing room where he could listen in on conversations. Over the years he had picked up a bit of English that baffled the English-speaking visitors who appeared on rare occasions and inquired, 'Well now, Ghogra, where is the sahib?'

Ghogra would puff up with his own brand of English: 'Huzoor, piccaninny gone!'

Harry had gone for a picnic.

There were regular picnics and there were dogs and birds, horses and cattle. Harry's elephant business had closed down with the advent of the motor car. But by then he had made enough money. He bought a brand-new Ford V8 that drew even bigger crowds of rural folk to touch it with nervous fingertips. Their short-cropped hair stood on end to see that, when a steel rod was inserted in its front and jerked around, it suddenly roared into life and drove away with us.

Most evenings we had the thrill of driving out in this marvellous machine, arms dangling loosely from the windows and a cool wind blowing through our hair. Mother laughed.

Maybe life was good. But never, never perfect, for even paradise had its serpent. Sometimes arguments raged downstairs in the drawing room well into the night and when voices rose higher they reached our straining ears upstairs. 'Harry-Harry-Harry!' It was Mother's voice. 'Harry is the beginning and end of everything! Ask no questions; you'll be told no lies!'

'Gladys!'

'Sorry Mother,' she answered, 'but I have to say this: you've become a puppet, Harry's puppet!'

And so, time moved on. Days strung tautly on a chain, like sweet-scented roses with hidden thorns. Until that fateful day in January 1934 when it went snap!

Lunch was just over, it could well have been two in the afternoon, for the servants had cleared the table and gone home to Puckry leaving the afternoon silent and still. Gladys had the strangest experience as she climbed the stairs that led up to our rooms. She heard a voice, an unrecognizable voice, say quite distinctly, 'Something's going to happen on the fifteenth!'

Disaster

The sun was at its highest point in the sky, though not directly overhead, for it had moved south and its slanting rays were honey-gold, and as sweet. No more the tyrant of summer but a blessed, sought-out thing, for the shade was cold and the breeze that blew from the Himalaya in the north, though so gentle it scarcely stirred the treetops, had the breath of ice. Teak leaves large as dinner plates, gone dry and brittle, fell to the earth where others lay dead, and were stirred together by the breeze—Crackle-crackle-crack! There was a sleepy silence, broken only by distant human voices calling, melodiously and long.

But from the birds, today, there was no sound at all.

On winter afternoons, Sarah walked in the garden after lunch, as she was walking now in a navy-blue woollen dress sprinkled over with white dots, like snow falling out of the night far away. It had a wide lace collar and must have come from Oxendales, like the rest of her clothes and household linen, ordered from the stout seasonal catalogues that arrived regularly by post. Her long, brown hair streaked with grey was parted down the centre and coiled smoothly over her ears. At sixty-one she didn't ride and shoot any more but she could walk seven miles with ease, or run up the stairs (two at a time) when the servants were not watching. She loved this garden with its birds that were silent today—so strangely silent. 'What ails them?' she must have wondered. But as she passed by the trailing bottlebrush tree a crow, for crows in India will never keep their beaks shut, and it is believed they are the messengers of the animal kingdom, strained forward at her, crying out in a hoarse voice, 'Care! Care!' as they sometimes do.

Sarah smiled. She returned to the house and went upstairs to the north wing where she had her bedroom adjoining those of Harry and Rosie. For some reason she was tired today, and looked it too in the big cheval mirror in the corner, bags under her eyes, the corners of her mouth turned down. Tired. Was she tired too of life?

She lay down on the big four-poster and fell asleep.

In the afternoons my little brother and I, the smallest people of all, were rounded up by the servants and marched upstairs to nap, when the action was downstairs with Reggie, Lenny and Ernie who were home for the winter holidays.

Rosie's daughter, Dorothy, was no longer with us. She had abandoned schooling some years earlier, for a railway doctor in Samastipur. She was sixteen at that time, and strikingly beautiful with a mind that was fully made up. Life between boarding school and the jungle had become an insufferable penance and she was getting the hell out of it—fight or no fight. She was going to marry—and that was that. That day down in the dining room after a silent and brooding meal, there had been a battle of iron wills when her shattering announcement hit them. It was Rosie, Harry and my grandmother versus the child. Voices were raised as never before in this house

'Can you believe this? The heartless girl!' my grandmother said with an ice-cold look. 'She must have lost her head!'

'Her head?' Rosie burst out, glaring at her child. 'I know that defiant look. Aunty, just step aside, a bloody tight slap will bring her back to her senses!'

'No! No, Rosie!' Harry intervened, launching himself between mother and daughter. 'Calm down, this is not the way! We must reason with her. Reason!'

'Think . . . think, child!' he coaxed the girl who was staring obstinately at the wall. 'Think, at least, of your education! Education!'

In response to this gentle reasoning the 'child' had used language that was frightfully shocking for those days. She shouted back, 'Balls to my education!'

This was met by a deafening silence followed by a weak 'O holy Mother of God!' and my grandmother was out for the count on a convenient chair, being fanned and revived frantically with smelling salts, while Dorothy, pursued by a force of retainers, was speeding away to the railway station for the 2 p.m. train. Not to embark on a journey of flight, but to be 'cut up by the engine'!

She won hands down. There was a stricken, exhausted, weepy reconciliation, with shots of brandy, and peeping servants who drenched the drapes with their tears, and, naturally, an acceptance of the inevitable—a grand wedding with the railway doctor in Samastipur!

That afternoon began like any other—quiet, with the servants gone back to their village, leaving only a few women on duty upstairs. I ran across the terrace, tiptoed into Rosie's room to clamber up the high bed and curled up in the soft curve of her body, like a small, sniffy animal. She smelt like a cool white flower, a magnolia. Her eyes would open gently, with that fabulous smile, 'soft pink lips and teeth like pearls'. 'You, buddi girl!' she'd say, and her hand would stroke my hair so tenderly. With eyes closed and thumb stuck in my mouth (the perfect tranquillizer) it took just a few smooth drags to put me out for the count. But not that afternoon.

'Off you go, old hag!' Rosie laughed, dismissing me with a pat on the rump. 'Go play with your dolls on the terrace.' I kissed her plonk on the nose and went skipping away.

It was a large terrace with smooth marble flooring, enclosed by a balustrade. Through it I could see far out into the garden. Rows of sweet peas like a flowery, multicoloured wall and a sweep of green lawn stretched away to the garage where a puncture was being fixed, with rude interruptions. Harry's driver, Rama, was on his haunches dipping the tube in and out of a bucket of water, peering at it with keen concentration while the boys were laughing and horsing around with the foot pump, stepping briskly on it while Lenny from behind directed the air up Rama's dhoti. I saw him jump up and bowl the bucket over. 'Wind up his sails!' they cried, rolling with laughter on the grass.

But up here it was a pitiless bore, ever changeless, with Mookhia, Nagiya and Kalri basking in the afternoon sun— wrapped in white cotton saris with just a narrow border of colour and weighed down with ancient silver jewellery and the blows of adversity.

They were gossiping in whispers about matters 'unfit for a child's ears'. I knew it well, for they kept glancing my way and shut up the moment I got near. They were always like this. And Kalri was the worst of the three.

Painfully dull. I picked up my favourite doll. It was a large, smooth ceramic thing, come all the way from England. Just like a bald European baby. A beautiful thing. 'My word!' people would exclaim. 'Such lifelike resemblance to a six-month-old!' Though, unlike any six-month-old, it was hard as rock. There was no way I could cuddle it close like my little brother's teddy bear. But it was far better-looking; with big, violet eyes that closed when it was laid down. Always. And I began to sing 'Rock a bye baby on the tree top/When the wind blows the cradle will rock/When the bough breaks the cradle will fall/Down will come baby, cradle and all . . .'

Painfully dull! I lay it down on its bed. If I couldn't sleep, this thing would have to!

But it refused. Its violet eyes stayed wide open, staring starkly at the sky.

'Ay Kalri, stop this chattering and look here!' I shouted. 'This stupid doll won't sleep!'

Her fleshy, brown face furrowed, as she looked it over with her one good and one bad eye. 'Ayinh? Maybe we should just give it a gentle shake?'

A gentle shake?

And that's when we heard a distant rumble. It was like the afternoon train on the Baghmati bridge. All three women looked up, perplexed. 'But the train came and left some time ago!'

They stared up at the sky for an answer, when it was in the earth below. And it came soon enough. Too soon. The rumbling grew louder. Birds shot from the trees with shrill cries. It was upon us! A monstrous fiend, long imprisoned in the fiery pits of hell, was breaking through to the surface. And as it emerged in all its power and pent-up fury, explosions ripped open the earth's crust and boiling water burst through in jets, spewing out sand and black sludge. It gripped our home in mighty tentacles, and shook. The house began to shudder to a strange eerie music, and then to rock—caught in the throes of a horrendous dance, the dance of death. Below us, animals and humans fled past in a stampede of sound that was straight out of hell. Mother burst through the bedroom door with my little brother in her arms, as Mookhia and Kalri, beating their chests, dragged me along with them to the head of the stairs. Through blinding dust they groped for the bolt of the exit door. It used to be locked every afternoon when we came up to rest. Now it had stuck fast. They threw themselves at the door, wrestling with the bolt, and all the time Mother was saying, 'O Jesus Master!' while the women cried in desperation, 'Ram-Ram-Sita-Ram!'

But the door stayed shut with a great determination.

And then, as the thought struck her, Mother turned away. 'Quick! Quick!' she shouted. 'The spiral stairs at the back—the sweepers' stairs!' We followed her through the bedroom and the bathroom, dragging ourselves along in a human chain—blind and deaf to reality—while our home fought for its life. Pictures flew from the walls and furniture slid around in time to that ghastly background music, and as we reached the head of the spiral stairs there was a thunderous boom and the south edge of the building was ripped away.

We were looking into nothing. Just a cloud of crimson dust, for gone was the landing and the staircase we had been denied access to by the determinedly jammed door.

The significance of this struck home as we stopped to gape. 'No! Don't stop now,' Mother screamed. 'Run for your lives! Run!' And we moved on legs of lead, stumbling down the sweepers' spiral stairs in a mindless flight, running for our lives from the smouldering wreckage that just a moment back had been our home. Home sweet home!

And Mother, in the voice of a stranger, was crying out, 'Reggie! Lenny! Where are my boys? Oh my God! Were they . . . ?'

'No! No! Mummy! Outside! Near the garage I saw . . . I promise you . . . I saw them making up the wheel with Rama!'

We had stopped. There was a dry place to sit, the nagol, a circular stone platform like a dais, where we sat out on warm, happy summer evenings. Now it raised us above the evil flood bubbling from the ground. I stared up at Mother's face, at my little brother in Mookhia's lap, rolled up in a self-protective ball, like a hedgehog with his eyes shut tight. 'Close your eyes and go to sleep, and when you wake—everything will be all right!' The comfort pill.

And it was! The boys were running towards us, relief shining on their faces, they came stumbling forward to hold, to feel, to know she was not an illusion. 'Mummy! Oh Mummy!' they cried. 'We saw the house fall. O God! We thought . . .'

But Ernie was rooted where he stood, a terrible fear spreading over his face as he looked around . . .

'But . . . my mother? Tell me, Gladys! Where . . . where is my mother?'

Yes. Where was Rosie? He read the answer in our faces and, turning swiftly, ran back to the building. And now we saw that the north wing was down too. The demon of demolition had accomplished its work.

Rescue operations were in progress. A group of servants were collected around us. Kalri sat rocking back and forth as she looked up at the sky, chanting, 'Ram-Ram-Sita-Ram!' A mournful dirge that became a deafening chorus as others took it up. Then, suddenly through the rusty-red haze, we could see the lumbering form of Ghogra. He was carrying Harry in his arms like a child, covered in dust. His head drooped and blood dripped slowly from his foot.

'Harry, thank God you're safe! But where is Mother? Where is Rosie?'

'I don't know, Gladys.' His face wore a ghastly colour. 'I thought she was in the garden? Rosie and I were coming down the stairs, when it crashed upon us!'

'Then what?'

'We can only wait and see, Gladys, they're working at it.'

Quickly she tore strips from a bedsheet and bound his foot. 'This will work for now, Harry, but you need a doctor!'

'A doctor? Yes, yes, Gladys, all in good time!'

Then Ernie was running towards us, face white as a sheet. His eyes had a wild look and his lips quivered as he tried to get the words out, for panic had hold of him and was shaking him like another earthquake. 'Oh Gladys! Gladys, my mother! I could see her leg sticking out! They dug her free, but she's gone! Oh you should have seen! No! No!' he screamed, tearing away, running blindly till he stumbled up against a tree and fell on his knees. His arms went around the trunk and he beat his head with a terrible fury against it till the boys pulled him away, holding him tight against them as his breath came out in great, choking sobs. I didn't want to see any more. I covered my face with my hands, and it was all blurred and sticky and wet.

They still hadn't found Sarah. Harry, after a good shot of brandy, and with his foot tightly bound up, was in command again. He had himself carried in a chair to the site, where in the midst of crashing debris, for mild, spasmodic tremors still persisted, he began directing operations.

And now we became aware of the water around us. Instead of subsiding, it was rising like an incoming tide. A crowd of people had been drawn to the scene of disaster. The kothi had fallen and they came running to see for themselves, this greatest drama of all. Taking it in. Holding the anguish. Breathing it out. 'Ram-Ram-Sita-Ram!' Eyes dripping tears. Then, slowly their eyes took in the water level and they realized their own predicament. A howl of terror went up like a siren: 'Finished, brothers, we are all drowned today! The end has come! Ram-Ram-Sita-Ram!' But then, the surge of man's will to survive. 'The station! The station!' they screamed together. 'Run for your lives to the station!'

Not to be borne away from the scene of disaster in a train that came once a day, but because the railway track and station, in anticipation of the Baghmati's greater floods, had been built on a twenty-foot-high embankment.

Harry was back, this time in his new Ford sedan. He had ordered Rama to drive to the station. Ernie sat motionless in the front seat, turned to stone. His fine features, so like his mother's, were bruised and swollen. 'Hurry now, Gladys, get in! As we feared, your mother has been killed. Yes. We recovered her body,

Rosie's too. Nothing more we can do now. It's senseless hanging on here. We could be in great danger!'

'Harry, are you out of your mind? You talk of danger and you're driving to the station when we can scarcely see anything of the road?'

The road was constructed on a three-foot-high embankment that snaked its way through field and forest to the station.

'We can, in most places. We'll manage if you don't delay, Gladys,' he said sharply.

'So then go, Harry, while you still have a chance! Go!'

'And you?' Now the irritation showed clearly on his face.

'We'll wade through. It won't be easy, but it'll be a lot worse in that car!'

'This is utter nonsense! You'll never make it, Gladys, think at least of your children,' he shouted. 'Can't you see the water's rising?' The car bumped forward cautiously as he spoke.

'God knows I'm thinking of my children!'

'All right then, stay,' he snapped. 'You bring it entirely upon yourself. I'll say no more!' The car moved slowly away and out of sight. We remained, sitting miserably on the nagol. Why? Could Mother have possibly known what was coming?

They were carrying out something. No, someone. It was Sarah, my grandmother, in the dark-blue spotted dress quite ruined with blood and slush. Her face was set in a pale blue mask, her eyes were closed, still and silent, quite unlike the others who had been carried out; her own ayah Nagiya, for instance, who now sat by us groaning ceaselessly, with her lip and forearm torn open. Mother's eyes filled with tears. She swallowed hard, crossing herself as the domestic servants who carried Sarah shuffled on to the khariyan where the land was higher and still dry.

And now someone else was being carried out. It was Rosie covered over with a bloodstained sheet. The upper part had fallen aside, laying bare her face, and I saw with horror what was left of that dear, lovely face—a dark gaping cavity, with her long hair hanging loose and matted—before Mother's hand closed my eyes.

And then, Narain Singh was racing towards us. He stopped before Mother, consternation filling his face. 'Bad happenings, Missbaba,' he gasped out. 'Harry sahib's sipahis are ransacking the building for documents and other valuables! When I challenged them they laughed in my face and said it was an order from Harry sahib! What could I . . . ' He broke off, turning aside to hide tears of frustration and rage. 'Ay Bhagwan! Three of us against so many!'

Narain Singh was the youngest of three sipahis who with a few domestic servants made up Mother's meagre following. 'Sipahi' translates into soldier, constable or guard, and they came mainly from the Hindu warrior caste known as Rajputs. Hers were fine, young men, their hands unsoiled by blood and intrigue, hence, quite unequal to a situation such as this. The domestic servants who had rallied round her were murmuring their shock and indignation, but it all boiled down to nothing. Domestic servants were too low to raise a hand, at least openly, against the upper strata of Hindus. It would, in those days, have amounted to sacrilege.

This stunning new development must have been for Mother the final blow. She stood, with a swollen ankle, binding Nagiya's arm with strips of torn clothing. Suddenly big teardrops began to drip on the bandages—and that was like the end of the world for us. Mother, our fortress of strength, cracking up!

'No! Mummy, Mummy.' We caught her hands. 'Don't cry.'

She pressed us close, smiling through her tears into our wet, devastated faces. 'Pray, children,' she said sadly, 'pray!' And we prayed in our hearts, as little children pray, while the servants went on with their tireless sing-song litany of 'Ram-Ram-Sita-Ram.'

Suddenly there was a hush, like the silence that falls upon a jungle when the king of beasts appears. But this was no king of beasts; he could have been a king in a kingdom of men, making his way through the crowd as it parted quickly before him. 'I come to speak with Missbaba!' he said, in a deep, velvety voice. She looked up in surprise as he raised his right hand to his forehead in the traditional greeting. 'Missbaba!' he said, bowing slightly and looking directly into her eyes. 'I know that to you I am a stranger. But you have heard of me . . . perhaps?'

Perhaps? Who had not heard of Abhinandan Jha!

The man who stood before us was no ordinary man. A span taller than all who surrounded him, he had the stamp of nobility, his head held proudly high with a lean, strong face, skilfully chiselled. A man who was, by birth, a Brahmin, but by an ironic twist of fate, a formidable dacoit.

His dark, penetrating eyes were studying her face. 'I see you have heard,' he said with something like a sigh. 'So then, you know what I am. Who doesn't know what I am?' he challenged, looking around him at eyes discreetly turned away. 'A dacoit, daku.' He spat the word out at them. 'Too true! Too true! But tell me, is Harry sahib any better?'

There was a shocked silence in the crowd.

'As I expected, you have lost your tongues!'

Then turning back to Mother, with an expression strangely gentle, he said, 'It is the truth, Missbaba. But yet I am a man, and I have a heart. For years I have known of bad happenings in this kothi. There are secrets that everybody knows, but few dare to speak of. And I will say this here, before all who have ears. I know of Harry sahib's greed for wealth. So now in this hour of disaster, with you totally helpless, what else could we expect from him but a well-practised tactic, to ruin you completely for his own gain! And he will succeed easily with these clowns who stand by doing nothing.' He whipped around to face Narain Singh. 'Sipahis? And you stand here like a clump of bamboos? Tell me, are you even men?' An angry flush spread over his face as he raised an arm plaited with muscle, to point. 'Look,' he spat out, 'look at Harry sahib's scavengers! Thieves of the most loathsome kind, for they've eaten the salt of this kothi. And what do *you* do?'

'Babaji,' one of them said, looking down shamefacedly, 'we were only three.'

'Only three!'

He turned back to Mother, impatience now in his voice. 'So much talk when it is time for action. Missbaba, trust me only this one time to act as your servant, and upon my life we will see who takes anything that belongs to you!'

He stood waiting for her answer, watching her with those deep, penetrating eyes. Reading her thoughts?

While she was thinking, 'O dear God, what's this? I prayed to you in my dire need, and you have sent me, for my deliverance, the devil?'

But wasn't she losing it all anyway? She had to do something, and quick. Not just stand there thinking of Harry's perfidy. He would contest her claim in court, not that he had any himself, but as a strategy to put her in a predicament that could be turned to his own advantage. 'Your property? But where are your documents? And where is your father's will?'

Litigation! O Lord! She had no ready money for it, like Harry who had it all in hard cash. And with the property sealed by the court, there would be no means of raising any, even for a livelihood for herself and her children. Then Harry would play his trump card.

And now, this strange answer to our prayers. 'I am a man and I have a heart!'

Maybe he had, and was sent here to prove it. She would see.

So she said to this apparition standing before us, 'In the name of the God who is above us all, I will trust you! But promise me one thing, there will be no bloodshed!' for she saw by now that he was accompanied by several men.

He smiled a slow, grim smile. 'Such is not my style, Missbaba. But it shall be as you say!'

And he was gone; plunging into the scene of action with a fierce delight, for this sort of thing was his favourite sport. Our unseasoned young sipahis followed, transformed by his leadership into ruthless warriors. The air rang with the cries of close-quarter battle and the crashes of hanging beams and rafters as these last remnants of the house came sliding down among them. Harry's sipahis, taken completely by surprise, scattered like leaves in a sudden storm. Those fleeing with arms full of spoil swiftly unburdened themselves when struck by a clout from behind. It was the turn of the tide.

Presently he was standing before us, ragged and sprinkled with crumbled masonry. A ripped sleeve hung limply down his arm, while spreading patches of crimson were wiped impatiently on his vest-front so his blood would not soil the precious documents he carried.

Mother could not believe her eyes! Saved! Not only the documents, but the family jewels that escaped the dacoity of 1905, and now spared by Abhinandan the dacoit of current times, were restored to her!

'Missbaba,' he said, breaking into a smile that softened his features, 'you didn't really believe I'd do it.'

'I will not forget this day,' she answered him. 'You owed me nothing, and yet you risked your life to recover all this for me.'

'No, Missbaba, those foolish owls of Harry sahib's risked their lives; I simply took it away from them. And now,' he said with urgency in his voice, 'precious time is running out. I can see to what needs to be done here, but you must all make for the station. The river has broken its banks and the water level rises by the minute.'

And so it was. There was water, water everywhere. It had submerged the road, pathways, field dividers and ditches. Wells had become invisible death traps. We had half a mile to wade through, though not much more than knee-deep, with a skilled guide. But the current flowed swift and strong and we proceeded cautiously in a slow, broken line. Deepan Singh, the most able of our sipahis, with Mother and the boys took the lead while my little brother and I rode behind on the shoulders of Narain Singh and Jagdhari Singh. All the Singhs in those days were somewhat like King Arthur's knights. Then came a string of lesser retainers, while domestic females like Kalri and Mookhia with their children made up a tremulous and lamenting rear.

'Now keep directly behind me.' Deepan Singh called back, 'Who can tell what dangers lie beneath?' He could, for he knew from the way the water gushed and rippled and behaved. 'Take care! One false step could be your last.'

Silence hung over the dismal party, except for Mookhia, in a heavily pregnant state. She was sobbing aloud. 'Langra, my poor Langra, never will I see his poor face again. Hey Ram! Hey Missbaba, he had no chance with that leg of his. Lame he was born, because I, the fool, sat with my legs crossed, during the eclipse, and him in my stomach. Huuoonh,' and she gave her stomach a feeble blow, lurching forward in remorse and suicidal intent. A treacherous pit, carved out by an uprooted tree that lay vanquished on its side with its roots pointing at the sky, was waiting just for this. She sank in. Gone for a moment but then up again and into the arms of her older children—a miserable wreck coated in wet mud.

'Mookhia! Come now, pull yourself together,' Mother said tiredly. 'Have faith. We will find him well.'

And so onward in single file, through the swiftly flowing warm, brown flood, dappled with sunlight that filtered through the bamboo grove we were moving through. Diverse things sped past, bobbing upside-down chattis—clay pots—logs of wood, vanquished heaps of hay, dung and animal carcasses.

And then we saw what looked like torn clothing stuck fast in a clump of bamboos. Mookhia screamed. 'My Langra's banian! I knew it! Langra! Langra! He's . . . ' Here she was cut short by a thin piping voice from above us, 'Father, oh Father! Save me, I am drowned.'

We all looked up. And there was her son Langra, high, dry and entire, gaping down at us from a good height. He let out a cry of ecstasy, like a deranged waterbird.

'Come down, you clown!' Deepan Singh exploded. 'Bring

your backside down fast. What were you doing in this place? Your mother here was drowning herself with despair over you.'

What was he doing? He had come stealthily in the still of the afternoon to cut bamboos in our grove when the earthquake had struck like judgement from below.

Mookhia pulled herself together, releasing her breath in a long nasal 'Haaiiinhh!' She was thoroughly wound up by now. 'And calling upon his father if you please, haan? Is that fat bastard ever around when we need him?' Her mud-plastered frame quivered angrily. 'You . . . just come down and I'll fix your other leg too.'

A perfect ending—for those who could laugh.

And then, we were at the station. It had collapsed, with the platform cracked across as though it had been dropped from a great height. But some furniture had been wrested from the ruins, and we were installed in the Bengal & North Western Railway armchairs, high, dry and famished. My little brother let out a howl of hunger. And Abhinandan the dacoit, flouting the strictures of his priestly status (for when it came down to brass tacks we were but 'lowly Christians'), brought us milk to drink in his 'hallowed' brass lota.

The train service had come to an abrupt halt since the railway track had been breached in several places, severing us sharply from the rest of the world. Harry's car had stuck with finality in the slush, a little short of the station. His heel had been crushed, a calamity beyond the limited skills of the Dhang MBBS (failed). Just one option remained for him. He had to be carried to Sitamarhi, the nearest town, in a palanquin for the skills of the civil surgeon there.

Meanwhile, the earth had survived. The floodwaters drained off, and the road, what was left of it, reappeared. The sun was sinking into a ragged, melancholy horizon when we squelched our way back home. But where was home?

The best cowshed used for milch cows had been selected as a temporary abode for us, with the cows relegated to a less worthy dwelling for the emergency. It had been scrubbed clean, and several layers of new hay made up a wall-to-wall field bed spread over with mattresses and bedsheets. Screens had been fashioned from curtains and tablecloths salvaged from the big ruin and a commode installed discreetly in a far, screened-off corner. Abhinandan seemed to have taken charge, as though we were now his responsibility, and had the sizeable domestic staff on their toes doing creative things. My little brother's teddy bear appeared, and was fit for service after Abhinandan had dusted it with care, looking it over curiously as he did so, amazed at its likeness to the real thing. But there was no trace of the doll with the 'stuck eyes'. My beautiful, bald-headed baby!

'Crushed to powder,' Kalri said grimly, with eyes closed and a defeated hand on her head. 'Ay Bhagwan! It knew! It knew!'

Night fell glumly, and it grew bitterly cold. Strange gases escaped from the earth's torn crust, got ignited and went leaping about the sodden fields like great balls of fire. Packs of howling jackals and wild animals were driven by blind panic into villages, seeking refuge among humans who were defending themselves against these same balls of fire by beating on cooking vessels and screaming hysterically, 'Hai Bhagwan, save us! Evil spirits have come out of the earth to set our homes on fire!'

Inside our sanctuary there was solace of a kind. The lamps were lit. The women servants sat huddled in the shadows wailing ceaselessly over the covered bodies of the dead. From next door, our neighbours the cows lowed in bewildered inquiry, now a solo, and then a loud, melancholy chorus. It was the only music we had for the wake.

Mother sat up alone, saying the rosary on her fingers.

'Sleep, my darlings,' she said softly. 'Tomorrow can only be a better day!'

And we closed our eyes, shutting out our ruined world in the comforting embrace of old familiar quilts, a teddy bear, a tranquillizing thumb and pillows damp with tears.

The morning of 16 January broke bleak and bitterly cold with devastation all around. Curious patches of sand and black ooze had surfaced here and there, from long, jagged cracks. No birds sang on that day. Only common crows made clear, harsh statements from stricken trees. The Puckry village carpenters had worked through the night by lantern light, sawing and planing planks of shisham wood for big, oblong boxes. For Sarah and Rosie.

No flowers could be found to make wreaths for our dead. No priest from the Mission to perform the last rites. But there was a multitude of spectators for the funeral.

Reggie, Lenny and Ernie with some domestic servants carried the coffins cautiously through the slush, while we walked behind clinging to Mother's hands. Then, in correct order, came sipahis, servants, labourers, tenants and members of the local gentry. Tears coursed down faces, some genuine and some of the crocodile kind. The rest just hung around, dry-eyed and curious, falling over one another in their curiosity to see how the Angrezes ended up. All smelt muddy.

There was a haunting air of death and desolation.

Sarah and Rosie were set down, side by side in the family graveyard.

One large, watery grave dug for two.

Everybody took up positions around it. Ernie in a navy-blue serge suit, hair brushed with Vaseline, flat and shiny against his head, and his face set in a mask, pale as a magnolia, read the burial service in a stranger's voice. And as he read, 'Remember Man, that thou art dust, and unto dust shalt thou return . . .' his voice broke; the mask cracked and tears slid down his cheeks to make big blisters on the page.

The Aftermath

An interim house grew up slowly around us. Scores of male coolies cut and split bamboos and thatching grass while the women worked on a mixture of clay, cow dung, chopped straw and water, trampling it with tireless feet into a viscous plaster for the walls, a six-inch thickness of thatching grass, ribbed with bamboo strips. When the plaster had dried it was whitewashed with lime. A thatched roof was already on, so all it needed was a facing of unbleached cotton over the unsightly beams and rafters with loose particles of thatch that showered like confetti on us at the least disturbance. Salvaged furniture and furnishings appeared, and it suddenly became a home.

Warmer and cosier in winter, we children welcomed its proximity to living things, unlike the isolated splendour of the old house. Here, it bristled with activity in the midst of sipahis, coolies, ploughboys and cattle, the threshing, winnowing, storing and the distribution of grain in wages to scores of daily workers, accompanied by raucous voices, animal noises and laughter.

Every evening the khariyan was swept clean. A score of bamboo brooms went to work, sweeping briskly at sunset, a symphony of 'sweep-sweep', with the twittering of birds hurriedly winding up their affairs for the day. The sun disappeared behind a dense screen of trees.

A bonfire was lit as it began to grow dark, for the nights were still cold. Servants gathered around to gossip and warm their chilled parts, chewing tobacco and spitting into the night. Now there was only my little brother Lancy and myself, since Ernie and the boys had returned to school. Our 'keepers' sat by cross-legged, and we collapsed comfortably into their laps, listening to the chatter till we were called in for dinner.

Harry had returned from Samastipur, where he had bought two houses, to live in this makeshift home with us. There was no other. His foot had healed, but in a manner that gave little credit to the skill of the civil surgeon. He had a limp to live with now, and an ivory-handled walking stick to lean upon. Otherwise, there was no change in him.

'Gladys,' he said one day, with a mysterious air, 'the servants say there's a dog that howls every night on the spot where your mother was killed. It's causing panic. It's an ill omen, as of course you know!'

'Really, Harry. And does that frighten you too? Or is it supposed to frighten me—like the Hound of the Baskervilles?' She laughed a brittle un-Motherly laugh. 'Has it drawn blood yet?'

Harry winced. 'It is not entirely a laughing matter, Gladys. You've lived here long enough to know these people—superstitious to the core. Not a mother's son will venture there at night.'

'I see, Harry. And have *you* heard it?'

'I must admit that I have,' he said lighting up a cigarette and looking steadily at her through the smoke.

And that night we heard it too, an eerie sound cutting through the still, rural night, for the unlit country retires early to its bed of straw. It must have been about nine-thirty. With dinner over, the house servants had cleared the table, said their salaams and vanished.

Harry sat smoking at the dinner table. A Petromax lamp stood nearby, flooding the room with light and hissing gently while insects flew frantically at the glass chimney.

'A dog, but what dog can this be, Harry? Blucher and Timmy were both killed in the earthquake. Weren't you told? They were found chained . . . such a pity.'

Harry was staring at the ceiling, round, heavy-lidded eyes, a small beak-like nose in a strong square face. He blew out a stream of smoke. 'It's eerie, Gladys. Do you believe in spirits?'

'Spirits now! Dear Lord! After what we've been through!'

'Exactly, Gladys.' He added, 'Can you see yourself living here in this godforsaken place, earthquakes, dacoits, evil spirits, black magic and all that kind of thing, and with small children, cut off completely from society and civilization?' His eyes went to the ceiling. 'Edmund is gone, and now, your mother and Rosie. No place for . . .' He was cut short by another howl. It began on a low, melancholy note rising steeply to a quivering falsetto and slowly died down.

Harry stood up and called loudly to one of his nightwatchmen. 'Dhandhari Singh. Take a lantern, get moving, see what this is.'

Mother was drumming her fingers on the tabletop.

Harry was watching her like a patient bird of prey. 'No place for a woman with small children,' he persisted, frowning thoughtfully. 'See,' his voice grew gentle, persuasive, 'see, Gladys, I'll give you a good price for your property. You could live in comfort in Calcutta, a beautiful city. You have to face facts. I'm thinking only of what is best for you and the children!'

Mother stared coldly at him. He was thinking, rather, of what was best for himself. A good price from Harry! He must think her a complete fool.

The nightwatchmen, for Dhandhari Singh had not gone alone, returned noisily, their lathis clanking dully on the hard plastered earth, clearing their throats and spitting unspeakable thoughts out of their systems as they approached. Soon they were standing in the arc of light that spilled from the doorway of our new drawing room.

'Well, tell us now, what did you see?'

'Huzoor we searched everywhere. There was no dog! There was nothing at all.' The powerful hands gripping the lathis quivered, and it was not from the exertion of the search, for the staunchest people here lived in dread of evil spirits.

In the dark, still nights that followed we heard it often, and my little brother and I were more terrified than the servants.

'What is it, Kalri? What is it, Fauzdar?' we cried to our 'keepers'.

'It's a bhooth, a spirit calling out its pain,' Kalri said cryptically, with her mouth puckered up.

'Ayyy!' We leapt at them, clinging like two tree-frogs.

Fauzdar had replaced Mookhia when she left soon after the earthquake. We were told that it was 'to have her baby', but she never, ever came back. We liked him at once and, as a special familiarity, changed his name to Foster.

'Have no fear, children,' Foster smiled, gently disengaging himself. 'It cannot harm you!'

'No?'

'Oh no! Never ever! Because . . .' thinking fast, 'because you're Christians.'

And then, providentially, Terence came. He was tall and well built, with blue-grey eyes and a nose that turned up at the tip. In fact, he was called Tip. If we had liked him, we might have considered him very good-looking. But as things stood, we accepted him with mixed feelings. His visits to Dhang had become quite frequent, and we could see that they made Mother happy. Her face lit up in a new way and she laughed easily. So we looked forward to these visits, particularly now with the frightening things going on at night.

Every evening, as we sat in our interim-period living room, the big Columbia gramophone was wound up to perform. It had escaped with mere scratches from the earthquake's terrible assault. There was classical instrumental music to charm our savage breasts and sometimes operas with loud outbursts of song followed by sudden silences and unexpected shrieks; I wonder how that went down with our neighbours, the cows or the wildlife out in the still night.

That evening Harry retired to his room soon after dinner, though it was still early and we had not been packed off to bed. Mother and Tip were talking together; the music was too loud for us to catch what they said, as he sat with a tin of Players No. 1, smoking cigarette after cigarette with the smoke curling up and the ash rolling down his brown tweed jacket.

The record ended and Ghogra, who still retained his position as gramophone player, turned it over. He was winding up the handle, when suddenly the howl cut through the silence. Tip jumped up. He dropped the cigarette from his mouth.

'Quick, Glad, give me the .12 bore.' He loaded it with a few quick clicks.

'Careful, Terence.' She was really worried now, and he was striding off with long strides, the beam of his torch cutting a long, narrow swathe through the night, still and hazy with dew and woodsmoke.

'Jagdhari Singh! Narain Singh!' Mother called to our night-watchmen. 'Quick! Quick! Go along with sahib.'

They took a lantern and vanished into the darkness. The clearing of throats and the thuk-thuk of lathis faded out. Silence remained, except for the querulous barking of village dogs in the distance.

'Mummy, is he going to shoot the spirit?'

'Wait darlings, and see.' We ran to her, crowding into her lap from where it would be safer to 'see'.

Then suddenly we heard a shot, and then another.

'Kathi how ray hay? What is it, chaps?' Our watchmen cried from here. 'It's done,' came the reply. 'Coming, coming.'

Soon we saw the swinging beam of the torch, and the lantern. They were back. Tip stamped the damp earth clinging to his shoes.

'Huh,' he snorted, and his mouth curled up to one side. In the years to come, we knew this as his great sarcastic smile.

'Phantom Dog?' he spat out. 'Me eye 'n' Betty Martin!' There was a steely glint in his eyes. 'Just as I thought! Nothing but one of Harry's two-legged pariahs! I actually saw the blighter haring off into the bushes near the old well and let fly a couple of rounds in the air! Would rather have put them in his arse—sorry—just to scare the crap out of the bastard! A spirit! I could die laughing!'

But he didn't laugh. He broke the gun, removed the empties and blew noisily through the barrels while we jumped off

Mother's lap in relief. Harry's two-legged pariahs (whatever they were) would be better by far than spirits!

'A good price for your property, huh?'

'Shh . . . Terence.' Then turning around to us, 'Now children, you better be off to bed.'

From their first meeting, the animus between Terence and Harry was glaringly evident.

'Marriage,' Harry droned, when Tip had gone, 'is an irrevocable act. Think, Gladys, Tip is so much younger than you. I thought you would have more sense.'

And once, quite loudly for a man who never raised his voice: 'It's your money he's after. Take it from me, Gladys, he's marrying you for your money.'

'I don't have to take any more from you, Harry,' she flared up now in an unrecognizable voice. 'I'm not the simpleton you take me for, swallowing all your stories and glib explanations. Like when your servants tried to wipe me out after the earthquake. Oh yes, for sure, it was not by *your* orders! And so they were sacked. But do you think I don't know that every single one of them was re-employed by you later?'

'You don't understand me, Gladys.'

'Only the devil would understand you, Harry.'

That May we left for Darjeeling, Mother, Lancy and I, with Kalri and Foster in tow. Terence arrived soon after, and they were married in the chapel of Loreto Convent. Well timed, before the incessant drip-drip of the Himalayan monsoon. It was a perfectly clear day with not a cloud to blur the magnificence of Kanchenjunga, dazzling white and near enough, it seemed, to touch! There was soft green grass with flowers everywhere, sprinkled even on Mother's dress. She looked so very beautiful.

It was the first time I heard the angels sing. But it turned out to be only the nuns in the choir loft. The morning sun streamed through the stained-glass windows and spattered the congregation with radiant, rainbow colours.

'She looks so happy,' I was thinking, 'and a little sad, too?'

The priest was reading aloud, 'And forsaking all others, will you keep only unto him, for as long as you both shall live.'

Forsaking all others!

I turned in dismay to look at my little brother—soft, brown curls that ladies on the Mall stopped to rumple, and clear shining eyes, every bit like a cherub that has played too long in the Indian sun. And with an angel's mouth that spoke no word of support. He just stared, rapt, at the stained-glass windows, while Mother promised to forsake us for Terence who was called Tip.

The rains had come when we returned to Dhang. We stayed on in the reconstructed barn while money was being raised to build us a new home. The economic situation was bleak. The earthquake had given it a severe jolt, and so did Harry, who disclosed that there was very little money in my grandmother's bank account. There was even less cash in hand. Harry, who had it all, went off to Calcutta for another operation on his heel. The grain in the granaries, ten thousand maunds, could not be sold entirely. There had to be enough in reserve for the coming year, to pay our servants and labourers, who only took it in kind. So Mother was forced to sell some outlying lands. Moneyed buyers, knowing we were in trouble, offered very little, with feigned tears and the plea 'We are only poor people'.

Big plots were subdivided and sold to these 'poor'. Cattle in excess of our immediate needs went for just five rupees each, and reappeared later on Harry's property.

But money, more and more of it, simply had to be raised to build us a new home. We had our own masons, carpenters and labourers, male and female, in Puckry village. Tip was the architect and builder. He gave it the standard design of a railway official's bungalow with some fancy touches of his own.

'Never again a double-storeyed house,' Mother swore.

It took a lot of bricks and cement and lime. The beams, rafters, doors and window frames were made from the well-seasoned wood of our shisham trees. For months it was a hive of activity.

The sipahis with their big, bad dandas made sure of that, or the workers, lazy and easy-going by nature, would have fallen asleep with their mouths open, and it might have taken a hundred years to build this house. Glass, paint and furnishing fabrics were ordered from Calcutta, and arrived in due course on the afternoon train. Long strings of coolies carried back the crates and packages on their heads. They were happy. There was work for everybody, and money for fun. Things began to take shape. Only Mother—and Terence, who was now 'Dad'—knew what it cost.

Soon a tube well was installed, with a hand-operated pump and a lean, agile operator. It gave us the purest, sweetest water, refreshing in summer and comforting in winter.

Harry waited for everything to take shape; then all he had to do was make an improved copy of the house, for his own! Harry was smart and cool. He always had the last laugh. He had decided to build on an eight-acre plot of land he owned inside our Puchkurwa.

'Could you be serious, Harry?' Mother flared up, when he declared his intention. 'Bang in the middle of my property! Have you thought of the situation it would create between your servants and mine? Civil war! We won't know a day's peace. But then, I suppose this is your idea of living happily ever after.'

'Come, come, Gladys, you're making such a mountain out of this.'

'A mountain?' she said with a long, determined stare. 'Build here, Harry, and it'll be the mistake of your life. You'll have no access to your place. I'll see to that.'

'No access?' Harry laughed, though there was no amusement in his eyes. He knew he was defeated, for once.

Mother sighed wearily. 'That laugh always means trouble. Still, let him laugh in his house on the other side of the Mahari, while we get on with our own lives.'

PART 2

The Sugar-coated Days
(Of Parrot and Pig)

A new life began for us, with a new home, a new father, and brand-new names of Pig and Parrot, for my little brother and me. It was a glorious life, this.

We awoke to the crowing of a score of cocks, some drunkenly, while another score of geese released from the night's incarceration came streaming out to freedom, their necks stretched high, their wings spread wide, and honking loud enough to bring the dead to life. All creatures here greeted the day like it was a feast to be devoured.

Kalri came shuffling into our bedroom and frowned at the large, mysterious lumps under our quilts. She gave one of them a sudden poke. Instantly the quilt rose up, and 'forbidden' dogs shot out, one after the other. She stepped back, making sucking noises of disapproval with her tongue, while the dogs slunk away, belly to floor, their eyes roving fearfully around for parents, till they could make a clear break, bounding off the veranda edge to frolic in the sun. Free!

'Dogs in the bed! Chhee! Chhee!' she wailed, looking severely at us with her one good eye and one bad eye. 'Mummy will not like this.'

'Ay Kalri! Coming here to pester us. Go away—GO!'

'Come, come, now, I'll press your bodies,' she said with her usual cunning, to calm us down. She had a marvellous way of pressing bodies, even swathed in quilts. Her gentle hands went press . . . release, press . . . release, from shoulders down to toes and up again, extremely soothing and restful when you were a bundle of nerves.

'Press our bodies *now*? Have you gone mad?' we cried sharply. 'Can't you see, Kalri, morning time has come.' And we shot out of bed and into our clothes, bounding after the dogs, while she lamented, 'Gone! Gone! What about face and hands? Teeth and tongue? Ay hay! I'm going to tell Missbaba!'

'Tell, tell then,' we answered recklessly.

The sun was just soaking up the mists of the previous night, and taking its time over the matter. The grass, still asleep under a gossamer film of silvery dew, wet our shoes as we ran across, leaving flat, green footprints. Arms spread wide, we sucked in the heady air, exhaling it in little puffs of vapour. 'Look, Pig, I'm smoking!'

'See my mouth, Parrot, phoooo!' And we jumped skywards, briefly airborne like gas balloons—intensely alive and delirious with happiness.

We could touch God's toes if we jumped a little higher . . .

Touch them and wish for a miracle?

But this was a miracle!

The mist rose to a world of gold and green with ripening paddy, vast stretches of sugar cane and a thriving variety of oilseeds, pulses and other crops. There were mango and litchi orchards, bamboo groves and patches of jungle with gigantic old trees, so old that it seemed only God could have planted them in his young days. He planted trees for every purpose, and plants for every need. There were ancient peepul trees, at the feet of which Hindus performed their religious rites with tiny earthen mounds representing various deities. Smaller thorny patches harboured little creatures like civets that clung to thin branches and stared down at us with curious eyes. Red ants built leafy nests in trees, and honeybees massive hives that provided generously for our needs. The dense thorny interiors were sanctuaries for porcupines—and iguanas that shot out hissing defiantly and showing us their forked tongues.

Larger tracts of jungle, comprising a few good acres of timber and thatching grass, were the haunts of wild pig, barking deer and blue bull. Streams, turbulent and clotted with mud in the monsoon and languidly clear in the winter, meandered through, banked with tawny thatching grass or twisted trees trailing leafy arms in the water. Here and there, long strips of soft silt were pitted with the spoor of creatures that came to drink. Kingfishers, blue jays and hornbills glided over the water's surface, and green pigeons filled the peepul trees, stuffing their crops with berries, while thieving parrots from Nepal, visitors for every harvest, shrieked with insane exuberance, flashing about like showers of green arrows.

Barely twenty-five miles away the Himalaya rose up in a magnificent range.

'Come, take a look at this,' Dad said, 'and you'll learn something interesting.' He whipped out a map of India from an old, defunct Electrolux in the back veranda, in which he had taken to storing such papers. Smoothing it out on the dining table, he took a pencil and ruler and drew a straight line from Patna to Kathmandu. It ran right through us! It seems, in those days, pilots used our house as a landmark when they flew over in their cheelgaris (eagle machines), as the locals called them.

The Himalaya remained to delight our eyes, though often obscured by the misty haze of parched and dusty summer days, or the smokescreen from scores of village fires which hung on the evening horizon in an opaque blue belt, or the silvery mists of winter mornings. But there were days, after rain and wind had washed and dried our world squeaky clean, when they stood out in such startling clarity, that it took one's breath away. An ascending sequence of exquisitely painted ranges that ended up with, 'Well I'll be jiggered! There she is—sure as God made apples!' Dad pointed, flushed and beaming with the thrill known only to great discoverers. 'There's Everest!'

And maybe he was right.

On such days, we observed sunrise and sunset on 'Everest' from our terrace, at no greater cost than shinning up a ladder and directing our eyes north-eastwards.

Our front veranda overlooked a heart-shaped rose garden with a white sundial in the centre, where people liked to pose for photographs. The grounds had been restored to most of their original appearance, with lawns, hedges, beds of annuals, flowering shrubs and trees; and narrow pathways of crushed brick meandering through. From the front gates with their massive pillars curiously crowned by what looked like sailors' caps (the inspired artwork of a village mason who had worked in Calcutta), a broad driveway ran up to the house, circling the heart-shaped rose garden and on to the back gates.

Near the entrance gates was a rockery filled with palms, ferns and twittering birds and a raised pool set in rock, where goldfish lived safely sheltered by wire netting, in water ever refreshed by the garden well nearby. It was shaded by an intermingling mass of tall, leafy trees that formed a canopy over it. Inside, the light was a pale lime green from being strained through so many layers of leaves, and it was delightfully cool even on the stillest summer days. Taking advantage of its day-long shade, Dad had set up an akhara, a wrestling ring, at the far end of this hallowed place, which became the scene of rowdy, robust activity.

Wrestling in those times was like cricket in England, a gentleman's game reserved for caste Hindus, mainly Rajputs and the 'odd' Brahmin. Others could have the privilege of looking on. Our sipahis were wrestlers, every one of them, though none of repute. Aside from physiques that ranged in proportion from Mr India to King Kong, a wrestler could be distinguished by his 'cauliflower' ears, acquired from decades of having them mauled in the akhara. Reggie and Lenny were pushed rather nervously into this great Indian sport, spared of course from cauliflower ears. It was their bodies that had to be developed.

'You'll take to it all right,' Dad told them with his one-sided smile, 'sure as God made apples, it'll make MEN out of you!'

Pig and Parrot settled down at a safe distance to witness this transformation. It went something like this. Each of them was grabbed firmly by the neck in a python-like hold and swung around till his colour changed, and his eyes bulged from his head. Then came the slow and cunning movements. With hands locked behind necks, heads touching, sweat dripping, and gasps

Sylvia Dyer

of aaagh, haagh! two bodies, one brawny, one scrawny, formed a triangle with the earth till, swiftly and suddenly, a foot shot out hooking one of the boy's legs. And a cry of chith! rang out from the watchers, as down he went on his back, flattened out and looking foolish like an overturned turkey chick.

Reggie could take this public flattening-out. He laughed when he was down, but Lenny always walked away in a huff, to the discomfiture of all present.

This daily matinee show was accompanied by push-ups, sit-ups and a vigorous mustard oil massage. Every champion of the akhara smelt of mustard oil. We watched it all, smelt it all, through the ferns, the lithe, brassy brown bodies of a martial race, travelling muscles and smooth gleaming skins, a veritable feast for the eyes—even little eyes.

Our days were filled with wondrous things to devour with all our senses. The lilting voices of workers in the fields, the rhythm of drums in still, blue velvet nights spangled with stars. And scents! Our noses were everywhere, inhaling the fragrance of nature in the raw, of wood, damp from the night's dew, sun-dried herbs, exotic flowers, sugar cane juice, fresh cut hay and smoke that rose gently from cow dung fires, the sweet, warm smell of a cow! 'Cripes! Stop smelling that bloody thing. You'll catch one hell of a butting!' Dad yelled at me. And he was right!

We wandered everywhere, reckless, smelly and mud-spattered, missing nothing, ravenous for the flavours and treasures of this land. Seeking out strange plants and insects, fossils, shells and even minerals delivered up from the earth's bowels that had moved so awesomely during the 1934 earthquake.

In the years of financial disaster that followed, when land was sold for a song along with gold and silver, and it appeared to us that Mother had only two dresses to wear, we had dreamed of discovering great wealth. And one day, as we played on a patch of dazzling white sand near the old garden well, we knew the ecstasy of bumbling prospectors, when grains of gold dust winked at us in the sunlight. It was no optical illusion.

But it all amounted to nothing. Mother swept us into her arms, smiling through tears at the droll intensity of our economic foraging. They had had it checked out earlier, she told us. It was gold all right, but in too small a proportion to render its recovery worthwhile.

Earthquake! One of Pig's followers became highly agitated at the mention of the word. 'Oh baba, that earthquake! It threw out so many things,' he croaked. 'My grandfather was standing on the bund, watching the kothi fall, when all of a sudden the earth opened and baap re baap the old man went right in!' His tongue shot out from a dark, dry mouth. 'But it spat him out fast—as if it didn't like the taste of him!'

Secrets came to light when you dug deep or suddenly lobbed a stone into slumbering jungle patches, or sat on the riverbank with the paddy birds, watching the fishermen spill out their catch.

We had no friends, for there were no people of our kind, not for miles. But we had many 'followers'. The little boys wore nothing but G-strings called bhagwas. Lenny dubbed them the 'Bhagwa Brigade'. We had tried to put them into shorts, but they backed away, covering the grins on their faces with bony little fingers. 'Oh no, no, babalog,' they reasoned with us, 'we'll look like clowns and the whole village will die laughing.'

The little girls were inseparable from their ragged, wrap-around skirts that came from the ruins of old cotton saris. They were all children of our domestic servants, who fawned on us in an infantile way and shared our spirit, if timidly, for adventure and the 'forbidden thing'. They smelt of earth and goats and cow dung cakes. And they were priceless.

A family of sweepers that comprised our sanitary system lived beyond the henhouse, just a shout away and available round the clock. The minute their names were bellowed out, a sweeper came charging to the bathroom with the 'discreet basket' and what had to disappear from the thunderbox disappeared through the rear door like magic.

Our water supply, like our sanitary system, also ran on human legs to keep the jugs and bathtubs topped up with water, hot or cold, from the water-heating unit that worked alongside the kitchen, or the hand-operated water pump in our backyard.

Some of Parrot and Pig's earliest education came from Foster and Kalri, under the laburnum tree that grew in our backyard. It was a sturdy old thing whose densely covered branches made, through most of the year, a nice, green canopy for gossips, dogs and crows. Since it stood between the back veranda and kitchen, servants of all classes congregated in its vast shade to chew tobacco and gossip. Grass had grown there once, but got scuffed out by years of fidgeting feet and loitering bottoms. Its beauty emerged in April, when masses of silky, golden blossoms with trailing buds, made it a dazzling feast for all eyes till early June. Then pre-monsoon winds sought it out and the gold showered down on the earth making a gorgeous carpet for all who dared to sit, for it stained many a bottom with a yellow patch that drew suspicious frowns.

Kalri was dark, wrinkled, and full of foreboding. One look at her and your fire went out like a candle in the wind. As a child, smallpox had deprived her of an eye. Only a blue-grey blur remained where it had once been. The scars of the disease had worn off her face with the peeling of time, but the scars of life had branded her with the contours of a confirmed pessimist.

'It's a terrible, terrible world,' she said with a sigh, holding her head, 'full, full of bad, bad men—worse than the beasts of the jungle—and dangers that you children cannot see even in your nightmares.'

She had a way of dragging it out, pulling the end of her sari over her head and clucking at set intervals to send the wind up us. 'You think this is paradise? Hai, hai! Poor innocent things! You know nothing, tucked away like chickens under a hen. But believe me there's evil. Evil is everywhere, even evil gods! One of them created the manushmara. It means—do you know what? People-killer, a stream that flows with murderous water. Baap re, all but killed me! Ay Bhagwan! What, oh, what is written for us?'

Foster hissed, and his tongue shot out through the space left by missing front teeth. He raised his hand in disapproval. 'Come, Kalri, you don't have to tell the children all this stuff.'

'No, no,' we shouted, for little scared us in the hours of daylight. 'Tell. Let her tell.'

And she would tell, because once Kalri was wound up, nothing could stop her mouth.

Dhang was a spirits' paradise according to Kalri.

Bhooths were common, everyday spirits, *ghosts vulgaris* you might say, that came in two types. Type 1 were the souls of departed Hindus who had not departed, and hung about cremation grounds by the banks of streams and rivers, known as burning ghats. Type 2 were bhooths that lurked in Muslim burial grounds, but innocuous or otherwise, she could not say.

'Let them talk about their ghosts, we have enough of our own to bear with, like prachuths.' These were very special, fitted with teeth like pinking shears that left lasting impressions.

The syrcutta was a skeletal figure that rattled around on the darkest nights, thuk-tharak! searching for its head; and if you bumped into one, you had to watch out for your own!

Pundoobas thrived in minor lakes and pools. They had a large, curved claw for hooking swimmers by the heel, and dragging them down, down, down to their foul dining chambers, to store in bite-sized pieces.

Churails (water-side) sported on the edges of lonely pools at night. These were the spirits of women that lingered woefully on, since a cruel death in childbirth had left their newborn to the fitful mercies of this world. But their ire, for unexplained reasons, was directed at adult males whom they lured with sexy glances and gestures to the water's edge and pushed them in, in a kind of home-delivery arrangement with the Pundoobas.

Churails (tree-type) sat up in trees crying out to solitary males, in a comb-and-tissue-paper voice, for tobacco! Badri, Lenny's childhood keeper, was an authority on these, with some personal experience.

Sylvia Dyer

'But he must be in the mood to talk,' Kalri said. 'Falls asleep. Baap re! Too much ganja in his veins.' She moved her head regretfully while rocking unsteadily on her haunches. Kalri was not an opium addict but she chewed tobacco and some of her systems had got derailed.

'The Lakharsumha,' she continued, 'is not an evil spirit but an evil man, which is worse, with a magic stick. Just one smell of his stick—and he can take you to any corner of the earth.' The earth had four corners according to Kalri. 'The Lakharsumha can be anywhere,' she wound up, turning her one good eye to look squarely at us.

The last and least of these terrors were real, live witches, called dynes.

'What Kalri, witches now?'

'Baap re, yes.' She sucked in her lips and waved a dark, wrinkled hand. 'We even have one in Puckry village.'

Foster chuckled, seeing our faces. 'Most of this is nonsense.'

Just looking at him the gloom was dispelled. 'Come, Foster, let's hold hands and jump for joy! Jump, jump, sugar lump.'

'Yes, yes, why not.' He let out a wheezy laugh that he had picked up from too many beedis, and we jumped ourselves breathless.

Foster was not a great talker like the other servants. He had to be in the mood, or stirred up by something stunning, like an earthquake. But he was unshakeably dependable and good humoured.

Nothing ever rattled our nerves in this earthly paradise, except Dad. His roar could come out of a perfectly placid day like a thunderbolt. It felt like being struck dead. But only momentarily, for with the uncanny intuition of children, we knew there was a lot of roaring with scant threat to flesh and bones. Even so, the roar struck terror for as long as it reverberated. It could be heard far and wide in the tranquil surroundings, and everybody knew the king of the jungle had a flea in the ear. It was his strongest weapon, and he used it often and to great effect with us! When we recovered, Foster was staring at us with a supportive stare.

He caught our hands. '*Zum zum sooga lum,*' he suggested with a grin. We jumped. And the dogs jumped on us.

Moving On

Harry set up his domain on the other side of the Mahari, which became rather like the border between India and Pakistan, where angry words were exchanged like gunfire from both sides of the 'border' when the pot began to boil. Nothing worse happened, thanks to the cooling influence of the Mahari. It proved to be a great dividing line.

There had been a great division of staff, too, after the earthquake. Those who chose to stay stayed and those who chose to go over to Harry without any hard feelings, none at least that were obvious to us.

Harry lived alone in a snow-white house with a porch and an avenue of bottle palms that Dad sneered at—because it really looked stately. The house was quite splendidly laid out with furniture and things he had ordered from Calcutta, even a large Columbia gramophone and piano, like ours. There was nobody to play the piano, but he bought it just to be in tune. Harry had good taste and he was rolling in hard cash. This rolling in hard cash riled Dad, often to the point of urticaria. 'Rolling! Too bloody true! It sure was smooth sailing for the blighter, making hay while your mother looked the other way.' The outburst ended with a scornful 'Huh!'

'Shh Terence, the children.'

So he lived in style, with his own legion of domestic servants, bossed over by Ghogra, his 'gentleman's-not-so-gentle-man'. Ghogra was from the caste of milkmen. His business was the care of cows, but here he was, caring for Harry. Pompous, hulky and bulldog faced, he could if necessary carry Harry like a child, as he had done after the earthquake. But Harry with the square, clean-shaven baby face and serious bird-eyes could render Ghogra with all his bravado a quivering wreck when he was displeased. They seemed inseparable, in a slave and master relationship, sealed by the bonds of mutual dependence. But periodically in their lives together the bond snapped, and Ghogra would come flying to Mother in a spate of rhetoric and salt water. He had actually been turned out after all his years with Harry-the-heartless! And what now would become of a servant faithful until death? Where would he go? Fresh tears would spout, rolling down the bulldog cheeks to collect like crystals in his bristly moustache.

Mother sighed heavily. 'I know how you feel about it, Terence, but he's been with us since I was a child. Where else could he go now?'

But once Ghogra was installed, he became his old obnoxious self, needling the other servants, bragging and growing progressively puffed up till he clashed with Dad. One instant he was rolling his eyes at Dad and the next he had burst into tears, for he was looking into the flaring nostrils of the 'firing squad'! This way he migrated between Harry and us, in a dynamic 'hired-and-fired-on-the-spot' career pattern.

During his tenures with us, he fussed about the house, keeping it spotless; and while he was about it, he listened in on private conversations from behind the drapes. You could catch him out by saying that another servant could do a particular job better than he did. Instantly he would burst through the curtains to protest 'Ayiiinnh' in a cry of punctured ego: 'That fool? What can he make? And for whom? Let him step forward and say. Can he make gulab jamuns? Does HE know that when I worked in "Assehole" for the British, I made gulab jamuns for the governor.' He sniffed, and gave his chest a thump of triumph.

Ghogra's unforgettable 'Assehole' was actually a town in West Bengal called Asansol, and the scene of his glorious days serving members of the Indian Civil Service that were cut short by a freaky disaster. In a moment of distraction at a tea party for the governor (the same one who had eaten his gulab jamuns), Ghogra had poured boiling hot tea in the governor's lap—an act perhaps mistaken as his special little contribution to the Quit India movement! This careless act had incurred severe displeasure, and he had been banished from 'Assehole' and the favour of the Indian Civil Service, forever.

But Ghogra was no freedom fighter. He openly worshipped the British, and for the rest of his days all living creatures and establishments were compared unfavourably with them, and what he termed, with a supercilious sniff, as 'civilian houses'.

Harry's managerial staff consisted of two trusted lieutenants whom Dad called his right-hand and left-hand men, like his good and bad angels. Naturally they were Brahmins. On the right hand he had Mahanth Jha, handsome and well built, with a nobility of spirit, and charm that made him immensely popular. Kethar Ojha, Harry's left-hand man (for all things sinister), was the brain that savoured and nourished Harry's acquisitive tendencies, a lean, yellow-tinted man, with the beak of a predatory bird and a mouth thin as a razor blade. Very few words slipped from it except to slash—and a rare, sour smile, when somebody got caught in one of his traps.

One day a letter arrived on the one o'clock train. Mother and Dad had one of those private discussions in their bedroom, when we were told to 'run along and play, children'. A suitcase was hurriedly packed for Dad and he left in a cyclonic burst of action and swear words, to catch the two o'clock train. His departures were always like this, and had servants running like the house was on fire, colliding with furniture and dogs.

'Mum, where's Dad off to now?'

'Well, darling, he's going to Calcutta to bring his father back, to stay with us.'

'He has a father?'

'Of course!' She smiled.

The father arrived one afternoon with a black tin trunk like the boys' school ones. He was thin and bent and looked sad and worn out like his clothes. Pig and I stood sizing him up from very close quarters, as he slumped in an old armchair on the front veranda, going over him inch by inch: the pale blue eyes and long nose that turned up at the end; crinkled skin with fine red veins that ran about like rivers on a map of northern India; the droopy khaki moustache; and peculiar hair like khaki silk that sat limply on an egg-shaped head.

He was called Dada. And he spoke. 'Don't you know, children, it's rude to stare?'

'Yes Dada, but we're not staring—only looking.'

'Only looking!' His eyes lit up with a quick spark of humour. 'Oh I see.'

'We like you.'

'Well, that's nice. How nice!' Dada smiled at us. A warm, like-you-too smile.

And then, without any warning at all: 'Why do they call you Parrot?'

'Parrot? Oh-o.' It was an uncomfortable question. And when a question didn't have a comfortable answer, girls simply wriggled. Wriggled and disappeared.

The mystery of Dada unfolded slowly over the years, from persistent hows, whos, whys, whats and whens added to snatches of conversation picked up by our notoriously long ears. These we collected carefully and stuck together like the fragments of a priceless, broken ornament, to make up a whole, broken life. Some pieces, however, were lost forever and left little unfillable holes in our reconstruction work.

Dada had been an Irish Christian Brother, and a professor

of physics and chemistry. Vows to the church had been broken for vows to a woman, a beautiful woman, in a silver-framed photograph, with two children. A boy in a navy-blue suit, with a turned-up nose and fine khaki hair parted in the middle and plastered down, and a little girl in a sailor dress. She had wide-open blue eyes, and the happiest smile. This little girl whom he loved 'too well' (because she was loved more than God) died suddenly of meningitis. He said it was God's curse. He sought refuge in drink. The once-happy marriage began to wither and die in a lost battle against bitter remorse and alcohol. She took the boy with the turned-up nose and left. Within a year, she too was dead, tragically. No amount of whys and hows would fill the big hole left here. It was a dark secret that led to more and more drink. More and more jobs lost. He was falling slowly into a pit of nothingness. Nothing left to live for, nothing left to live on. No place to go. Only a bench in the park for this professor of physics and chemistry. And then the letter arrived in Dhang. A letter some angel must have written, and posted, for there are angels in this world.

Twenty years had passed since he had last seen his son, the boy with the turned-up nose. Years that had swept away all the ties that had bound them. Dada was sixty when Dad brought him back to live with us like a man recalled from the dead. He looked far older than his sixty years, and nowhere as tall as Dad, for he had grown bent, with one leg shorter than the other.

Dada, 'recalled to life', settled down nicely with us. He took charge of the estate accounts, with an overall responsibility for that hive of activity, productivity and rascality, called the khariyan. He picked up quickly, and soon became an invaluable asset in that quarter.

He was a genius at mathematics. He could work out some of the stickiest problems (where our tutor Bhagwat Singh, 'BA *plugged*', got hopelessly stuck) sitting up all night by lantern light, wrestling with the thing, till he could shout 'Eureka!'

We started with simple sums, Pig and I. But as we grew older,

Sylvia Dyer

he initiated us into the mysteries of algebra and geometry in a conscientious effort to implant some of his mathematical genius on the fertile soil of Pig's intellect or wither on the impervious rock of Parrot's head. But he was patient and restrained, never swiping out at slack pupils, like most Christian Brothers of his time. With his day done, he collapsed with a wheeze of pleasure into his favourite chair (it was a planter's chair) on the front veranda, with crime fiction. One leg was flung comfortably over the side, while his free hand hung down to pet the dog underneath.

Every unattached person needs a dog underneath. So Dada got Jackson who was the result of a flash love affair. His mother was a thoroughbred dachshund, but nobody could guess what manner of sneaky, cheating hound his father had been. Jackie arrived with an elongated body, short muzzle, and legs neither long nor short enough to please. Since his breeders could not improve on his proportions, they diminished them by lopping off his tail.

Dada adored Jackie. He was his dog. Whether reclining in bed or slumped in this favourite chair, his arm hung over the side so he could pat the dog underneath, whispering fondly, 'Jackie boy, you notty little doggy, nottylittledoggy!' And Jackie, if he was still underneath, would reciprocate the doting sentiments with a single lick.

They became as inseparable as man and wife. Except the age difference sometimes put an angry gulf between them. Jackie, driven by the lust for life, was often absent from his post under Dada. He wanted to be where the action was, throwing out dusty challenges with his hind legs. He homed in on cyclists and brazen trespassers taking a short cut through our compound. And when the floods came in July and August he joined in chases with the bigger dogs, after nilgai and wild boar when they broke cover in search of higher ground, often getting lost in the tall grass, or stuck up to his middle in the slush. He had to swim where the others had a walk over. This dog was not cast in the right

mould for the life he craved. Moreover, his periodic pursuits of
the opposite sex (an urge far beyond the control of dog) entailed
worrisome disappearances from home. A nottylittledoggy for
sure.

Evenings at Home

Our drawing room had been done up with things
retrieved from the ruins of the old house. They
were not many, since most of the beautiful vases, ornaments
and paintings had been crushed to powder. But some pieces of
furniture had escaped miraculously. Among these survivors was
a Kriebel piano that, like the big Columbia gramophone, had
escaped with mere scratches.

Roses were everywhere in this room. On the tapestry-covered
chairs, on curtains and cushions, in gleaming silver bowls. No
getting away from roses. Mother was madly in love with them.

In the mornings, it was quiet and undisturbed, with Ghogra
guarding it from unruly behaviour that undid his earnest labours
in this room. But it was a Sisyphean business for him.

In the evenings, when the Petromax lamps were lit, the
room that had sat quiet all day came to life and began to fill
up slowly. Sipahis filled the wide doorway. They were warriors
and wrestlers, some heavyweight champions with cauliflower
ears, oiled clean-shaven heads and well-rooted teekies, standing
restrained, silent and respectful. Blinking and tuned in. Their
names all ended with Singh (their caste name) which translates
into 'lion'. These lions were Narain Singh, Jagdhari Singh,
Khelowan Singh—in fact, a whole string of Singhs ending up
with Bum Singh, whom Mother simply referred to as 'that man'.

Sylvia Dyer

They had come to report on the day's events, but as they stood there, Pig and Parrot ran at them, seizing their hands and pulling them downwards on to the carpet.

'Sit, sit now. Tell us a story.'

They settled down crossed-legged in the doorway, like a flock of giant birds, to tell us long-drawn-out folk tales of rajas and ranis that always ended happily, or never at all, because the ballads (sung with one hand clapped over the ear like a cellphone) were so long!

The dogs were supposed to be out in the veranda but slunk slyly in, and growing gradually confident began to sprawl about on the carpet, till Mother, on her way to the piano, tripped over a sprawled dog with a little cry. Dad, with a face the colour of raspberry syrup, roared, 'Out!' In a well-practised drill the sipahis parted instantly down the middle, like the Red Sea for Moses, and half a dozen dogs flew through, followed by a large tortoise-shell cat. In ten seconds flat, the scene was cleared of animals, except for Pixie the blue-roan cocker spaniel, peeping fearfully from under Mother's chair, but holding her ground. Pixie was a 'delicate darling' who followed Mother everywhere with droopy eyes and long, curly ears that swept the floor.

Mother sat down at the piano. She had learned to play the piano at school, and played quite charmingly, but had to be coaxed, always.

'Dear me, children, whatever can I play for you?'

'"Rendezvous", Mummy. Play it, play it!'

It was her favourite, and when she played it, there was no horsing around on the carpet; we were captives under her spell.

But soon she had had enough. Or more likely, wanted to give somebody else a chance. 'Enough. Enough now, children. Come, Terence,' she turned and looked at that somebody sitting in his favourite chair by the fireplace, with the newspaper held at an angle, so he could watch what was going on at the same time. It was just what he was waiting for.

With the community songbook propped up before him, he could play anything any time, and loved every moment of it. He couldn't read a note of the music set before him, but could play it all by ear; and the words of less familiar songs were there for him to see. His right hand got the air perfectly; catching up a good handful of notes, but the left hand just rose and struck wherever it fell! It was all left to luck, he knew, and was shrewd enough to keep it soft. Pianissimo. But when he sang, the powerful richness of his tenor poured over the accompaniment, drowning out every imperfection. Songs like 'Irish eyes are smiling' and 'Rose of Tralee' rang gloriously through the house and the dark reaches of the countryside. It even touched us small barbarians on the carpet, making us look up from our play. His eyes shone, and his face lit up with the joy of angels, holding such a kindly expression as we never saw otherwise.

Meanwhile, the Petromax lamps burned with a steady sibilance. It was like a multitude of people breathing out together, an exhausting business. So it was necessary for them to be taken down and pumped with vigour from time to time.

Dada was in his favourite chair, alongside the gramophone, sunk into its soft depths and folded up like a concertina. He could remain like that for hours, motionless and almost invisible the way he merged with the tapestry. A visitor might have lowered himself into the same chair and risen in alarm from Dada's knees. His eyes were closed, and his mouth set in a tight circle from which came the muted sounds of his continuous whistling. He was a chain whistler, whistling outwards and inwards with no need to pause for breath. There were old-time favourites like 'There's a long, long trail a-winding into the land of my dreams'—his very own favourite—but there were also fast numbers, 'Ma, he's making eyes at me!'

The whisky in his glass was drained in one gulp. It was show-time! He was having his own non-stop show in an entertainment world of his own. He was the star. He was the audience. His was the applause: 'Nice, how nice! How nice!'

Dad's show was running concurrently at the piano . . .

Ra-*mo-nah*—I hear the mission bells above—
Ra-*mo-nah*—they're ringing out our song of love [rich and loud]
I *press* you, *caress* you—and bless the *day* you taught me to care.
To *always* remember—[soft and sugary] the rambling rose you wore in your ha . . .

At this point the two shows collided and 'Nice—how nice! How nice!' burst like a tidal wave over Ramona. Dad spun around to face Dada, his mouth still open on 'ha'. A range of emotions passed over his face, like sudden clouds across a clear, blue sky. Black clouds, grey clouds, smudgy white ones. There was the glint of tears in his eyes. He stood up.

'Christ Almighty! Dad,' snatching away the glass. 'Enough is enough! Will you never bloody ever learn when to stop?'

Silence in the room. People looked down and played nervously with their fingers or toes.

But people recover fast enough, and the gramophone was quickly wound up to play. It was a brilliant cover-up for ugly situations.

The dogs, meanwhile, had crept back to sleep fitfully while we waited for dinner.

It was always dogs slinking in and dogs flying out. There were never less than six at a time, ranging in breed from Alsatians, Airedales, hounds, retrievers and Labradors to inevitable cocktails of the group as the years passed. Foremost among them were Chumra and Horsy.

Chumra was an Airedale and a gentleman, a powerful, hairy, noble creature with a soul, who lived and died like a hero. Horsy was half Alsatian and half Labrador. A jet-black charmer with a ginger muzzle and eyebrows, and the shape of a dray horse! He was, perhaps, more intelligent than Chumra, but his courage was reserved for more personal issues. When wild animals were sighted in the compound, he had his own special strategy for attack. He'd lead the charge with all his might, but just fifteen feet short of the quarry he'd stop dead, while the other dogs, and even the tortoise-shell cat, went charging on into the jaws and claws of the enemy!

He was also the dog that undressed men, his devilish form of persecution for trespassers breezing through our wide-open gates. It was never a frontal attack, but a sneaky one from behind. He knew just where to pull on the dhoti, and how, without inflicting any physical injury but something far worse for these daring young men—a grievous loss of face, since there were no underpants those days! And they never passed this way again.

The cat had grown up with the dogs in a chummy and even familiar relationship. To its eternal regret it had been born a cat; for its every action seemed to cry out: 'Give me a dog's life!'

It set out for long walks with us, just like the dogs, but was soon tired, or pretended to be, and prevailed upon Chumra to carry it home. And he carried it home by the scruff of its neck, like a puppy. This cat took part in every charge of the dog's brigade when a prowler was sighted, springing along with a grrrrr and its tail stiffly raised like a standard.

They were all remarkable creatures, disciplined, fearless, and madly devoted to us. They ate the seasonal crops, just as the other farm animals did—rice, maize, oats, barley, wheat, sweet potatoes, cabbage, cauliflower, pumpkin, and almost anything else that grew out of the good earth, cooked up and served with a seer of cow's milk. In the cane season they lay on their backs and crunched sugar cane, skilfully holding the sticks between their forelegs and catching the juice with relish.

They were in marvellous fettle, with glossy coats, bright eyes and bursting with energy. Splendid vegetarians, but with a craving for meat, not often satisfied, alas, for beef was forbidden flesh here in Hindu land.

Sylvia Dyer

Our own daily fare was country fowl brought by Muslim traders, whose profiles bore a striking likeness to the birds they brought in string-covered baskets with long necks poking out—to be sold in lots of eight, four and two for a rupee, according to size. These birds were thrown into the henhouse, to lodge under the same roof with the geese that took strong exception to their nerve-shattering shrieks and objectionable smell, for they themselves were clean and white as driven snow, with enviable blue eyes and a natural grace in all their movements. They gave themselves airs, these geese, and would have killed the poor country fowls if it hadn't been for the bamboo partition in between. 'You see,' Foster whispered to us, 'it's because they're Brahmins!'

Bringing in the New

Winter mornings were the best. 'Kok-kok' came the crow's soft call, probing the mist with gentle inquiry. Soft, silver mist filled our green world. And suddenly the sun emerged, a ball of molten gold with vermilion dregs, growing clearer and brighter. It came through our window and the lace curtains, casting floral shadows on the wall.

And now, the soft silence was broken by the dove's call 'Cook-coo-coo! Cook-coo-coo,' its throat hoarse from the frosty night. Shimmering dew covered the garden and the webs that spiders had spun yesterday. And as the mist lifted and slowly vanished, another perfect day unfurled. Perfect?

Harry's car appeared in the distance, churning up a trail of grey dust between the litchi trees. It drove in through the wide-open gates, with his driver Rama's head no higher than the steering wheel, and stopped by the front steps with a jolt.

Harry stepped out gloomy faced. 'I have some important news for you, Gladys,' he droned. He had this way of droning—a bee going about its business and about to sting.

They went mysteriously into the drawing room.

But soon there were raised voices that we could hear. Mother was shouting 'What are you saying, Harry! This is preposterous! Can you expect me to believe . . .' Dad was standing in the doorway, with a cigarette drooping from his mouth and the smoke curling up into his eyes, to make them watery. He drew sharply on it and puffed two jets of smoke from his nostrils, like a dragon. More and more smoke came out. Then he looked down through the smokescreen and saw Parrot and Pig staring at him.

'Now, you two, just run along and play.'

The door shut in our faces.

But the meeting didn't last long. Dad came out, his mouth screwed up to one side. Mother's face was turned to stone. Then suddenly a handkerchief appeared from nowhere and she was dabbing briskly at her eyes, 'Oh dash it all—damn it!'

Then she saw our troubled, upturned faces and smiled gently. 'It's nothing, my darlings, they're only tears of anger.'

Tears of anger. Yes! Land revenues on the estate had not been paid for years, during the time when Harry was managing the estate and for no acceptable reason. And now he had come to drop a bombshell on Mother. She had only a short time to pay up twenty thousand rupees, which was no paltry sum in 1936.

So the Christmas of 1936 was spent quietly in Dhang, stripped of any feasting and merriment. But there had to be a way, Dad felt, to bring in the New Year with a bang. At exactly twelve o'clock, after an evening of low-key drinking and thumping on the piano, he went out with his rifle, pointed it at the mocking stars and fired at them. Bang! Bang!

It had an unexpected and almost immediate effect.

In the distance we heard a rumble rather like the train on the Baghmati Bridge, but coming from the opposite side, that

Sylvia Dyer

is, the direction of Harpur (the village of warriors) and as it grew nearer and clearer, could be identified as the roar of many human voices. And before we could make any guesses, the place was filled with Rajput warriors carrying pikestaffs and axes, big men with barrel chests and heavy limbs, smelling of tobacco and mustard oil. They stood before us looking cross-eyed, and for a moment speechless.

'Christopher Columbus!' Dad gaped at the new arrivals. 'What the dickens?'

'Huzoor,' Narain Singh spoke up from among them, 'they heard your shots, and thought we were defending ourselves against dacoits.'

'Ji haan,' they joined in, breathing heavily, for these men were built for power and not for speed. 'And how we ran. Baap re! Our legs moved so fast that fire came out of our arses.'

Narain Singh didn't rush them to the water pump. He merely said, 'Mind your language here, brothers,' while passing a hand over his quivering face. 'Two shots,' he explained, 'were fired into the sky—simply to bring in the New Year.'

'Gunshots to bring in the New Year?' Their mouths fell open and remained that way.

'Yes. It is the custom of the British.'

'A custom of the British? Well! Well!' That explained just about anything unfathomable, and they retreated into the night, wagging their heads and emitting sounds natural to baffled warriors.

All these chivalrous men were from the Rajput village of Harpur, like our own sipahis. Though this village belonged to the Raja of Sheohar, we always enjoyed the loyalty of its Rajputs. I can't say why. But Sukhesar Ojha, keeper of history (in his head), had a ready explanation, always.

He was a lover of women and epic tales, fluent in Sanskrit and Hindu lore. Tales of gods and goddesses just sparked him off, and he could go on for hours, standing straight as a ramrod, dressed like Julius Caesar in homespun cotton. A sheet of this fabric draped gracefully about his shoulders, concealed the mysterious stump of his left arm. We found out that in his childhood it had been amputated at the elbow, after a fall from a mango tree. He had climbed up the tree to sample another man's mangoes. In later years, his tastes were for other men's wives.

'You ask why?' He sucked in his breath. 'Courage, I say! What is there in this world like courage!' He swallowed hard and Pig and Parrot were distracted for a moment by the way his prominent Adam's apple moved up and down. 'Your ancestors had it. They had the courage to take on two hundred of the Raja's men.'

'Two hundred? Never! You're fooling us, Sukhesar.'

'Fooling? No! No! Well . . . maybe one hundred and fifty! My father told me this. I remember well what he said: "There they stood, the two brothers," that is, your great-grandfather and his brother Tom sahib who was not a good man, in fact he was big trouble. But never mind that, he had the heart of a tiger! Side by side they stood on the embankment in front of the kothi, watching them advance across the paddy fields.' His face glowed with a transcendental flame. 'And when the men came within range, they fired, though well above their heads. But still, the men came onward and in a move to encircle them! It was then that the sahibs changed their positions standing back to back, and fired their guns into the crowd, dhoom! dhoom! Some fell like ducks in the paddy field. Some dropped their weapons and ran, while others continued to advance. And the sahibs?' He sucked in his breath again. 'They held their ground. Oh yes! And they fired once again into the crowd, dhoom dhoom. And what do you think happened then?' He paused to look at us and his eyebrows went up. 'They all turned tail and bolted.' Sukhesar finished with a smile of restrained triumph. 'It resulted in a lasting friendship with the Raja of Sheohar.'

'Oh, but Sukhesar, what were they fighting about?'

'Oh that? Err . . . err . . . something to do with your honourable great-grandmother.' Sukhesar cleared his throat, holding our gaze as he retreated steadily into the sepia shades of the khariyan landscape and vanished right before our eyes.

It was yet another remarkable trait of the people of Dhang. The vanishing trick.

And another mystery.

Harry's Soft Spots

Harry's life, on the other side of the Mahari, was very different from ours. He was not enjoying his considerable wealth as we could see it. He lived well of course, but there were no luxuries for himself, like a great wardrobe, wild parties with city friends and holidays abroad. His pleasure came from watching money grow, and grow and grow.

It was 'that Dorothy' who knew how to diminish that money, going off to the world's hot spots to 'burn her candle at both ends'. Harry's eyes blazed, he almost frothed at the mouth. 'London is better than New York. Paris is better than London. Bombay is better than Calcutta. Any place is better than the one she is in! And this, Gladys, is the worst place on earth! She likes it wherever it's more expensive—turning day into night and night into day! Ah! And the driving?' He drew out a handkerchief and smeared the perspiration round his face. 'She took a policeman for a ride on the bonnet of her car—stupid girl—he was the police inspector.'

Mother could have burst out laughing, but she took a deep breath and just said, 'Oh dear!'

'And the divorce case!' staring glassy eyed at her. 'Money flows like water. And whose money?' pointing at his chest, 'My money.'

But when they were 'face to face' Harry softened up completely.

He had a permanent soft spot for these children of his dead sister, Rosie. Perhaps he welcomed the financial embarrassments that brought the beloved spendthrift speedily back to him. She had to come and get it, of course. That was the only rule.

Dorothy hated coming to get it. She had no time for nature in the raw, and endured it for the sake of the money-to-come. This life was not for her. Murderously dull, unless she brought along her friends and lovers. Harry suffered the friends for her sake. He found them frivolous and shallow.

As for lovers. 'I ask you, Gladys, what is this new thing? Into bed with anyone? Divorce upon divorce will follow! I tell you it's all these trips to Europe. This is what you get.'

He was not for a liberal love life. At least, not for 'the children'.

Dorothy had become more gorgeous than ever, with devastating South China Sea eyes, and features that were quite perfect. To complete the portrait of Dorothy was a stunning figure dressed in designer clothes and expensive perfume. Wherever she went, they stopped to stare at her. Not only in Dhang where people were best at staring, but everywhere. She was a high-spirited creature, warm and generous, bubbling with mirth and a wild sense of humour. But her love life was made up of high highs, and low lows. She was either in heaven, or in hell. For she got the wrong husbands and it wasn't easy shaking them off each time she found the right man. The *Right* Man!

'Glad!' she'd cry, flying up the veranda steps to seize Mother in strong, swimming-champ arms, beaming all over. 'Oh Glad, you should see him! Six foot three and oh so so handsome! Ask me, Glad, *huge blue eyes*!'

'Huge blue eyes? But, Dorothy, is that what really matters?'

But she only laughed, flushed and happy, at the concern on Mother's face.

And then, before two moons had waxed and waned, the Right Man became the Beast.

'Glad!' she burst out. 'You can't imagine what a jealous swine he is! The beast! I swear I can't take it any more!' She marched about the bedroom, where people usually opened up their hearts, heaving a sigh of rage and despair. 'And dammit nobody warned me! Nobody! Even you, Gladys!'

'Even me, Dorothy? What did I tell . . .' Mother stopped short and bit her lip, looking sorely distressed. 'Maybe, you should have stayed with Louis,' she said gently. 'He was a good man.'

'Louis! Louis! There you go again! Let's change the subject,' she snapped out irritably, resuming her march on six-inch heels. And then, slowing down, 'Don't look at me that way, Glad,' now brokenly, with those famously devastating eyes all swollen and watery red, 'Men! Uh, it's a stinking, bloody world! Take it from me, Glad, nothing good ever lasts. Nothing!'

Then there was Ernie, growing up to land in messes of his own creation, with his great Italian looks. His smooth, brown hair was parted down the centre and slicked back with Brilliantine for that patent-leather finish, and his dark eyes had begun to flash in a way that would imperil womankind. And there was more. He was acquiring the swift, supple grace of the hunting leopard that is never caught! Panther White, he had been called in school! He was utterly charming.

'Gladys, I fear he will turn out like Dorothy. God help us all!' Harry's mouth turned down like a man with a murderous toothache, so unlike the soft-spoken Terror who made men dance till they dropped. But then, these were his soft spots.

During his days in Dhang, Ernie spent most of his time with us. He was young and always keen to join in our games, coming up with brilliant innovations. And of course, he was the most fleet-footed of all—this panther with the mesmerizing eyes! By holding his hand I could fly. Besides, he had an endless stock of stories and funny jokes. You didn't have to be tickled under the armpits, to laugh heartily. Disputes between Pig and Parrot, over who should sit nearest him were decided promptly in my favour.

'Parrot will sit on my lap—because she's a girl!' he added with a wink at Pig, taking him aside to whisper, 'See Sonny—these girls are different from us. They're softies! They were made that way by God. It was his idea. The gentle sex, they're called! Not like us *men*!' He pulled up his shirtsleeve and pumped up his biceps. 'Hey! We men need to protect and favour them or the tears will spout from their weak eyes. Oh yes! It's always girls first, girls this, and girls that, make way for the girls! Sorry, girls, it was my fault! Eh?'

Pig was silenced, staring hard at the biceps, and I stuck out a victorious tongue at him. 'Airrr—Piggy Wiggy!'

'Parrot and Pig,' Mother said with a laugh. 'Who gave my darlings such names?' Reggie grinned. 'Who but Lenny?' (Lenny came up with nicknames for anybody at all.) 'He calls her Parrot. Maybe, err . . . her mania for green clothes. Or um . . . because she's stuck on parrots.'

'What crap!' Lenny revved up. 'Don't cover up for Parrot! She's a parrot because she repeats anything. Tell her a secret—and even the dacoits will know about it.'

'Shout at her,' Pig pitched in, 'and tears will spout. Her head's full of water—only water. And she still sucks her thumb behind the doors, baby Parrot, boo hoo,' and 'Airrrr' he added with a screwed-up mouth.

My thumb was a pacifier, no more shameful than a cigarette in grown-up mouths! But there it was—out, like a mortal sin in the harsh light of day!

'Enough, enough.' Mother closed the matter mercifully. 'But why Pig?'

Yes. Why Pig? But my mouth was sealed against further argument. Dangerous currents were building up inside, or I would have answered that one. He had a toothbrush. The end of the handle had the figure of a pig with the inscription 'Pewter Pig'. It was cute, in a yellow shirt and blue shorts—but why such a mad attachment for the thing? I simply had to find out what was so special about this toothbrush with the pig and I had barely put a blob of MacLean's toothpaste on it, looking at myself in the mirror, when my hair was seized from behind by its rightful owner, and there was a murderous look in his caramel eyes. 'Pewter Pig!' I screamed. And the 'Pig' part of it stuck for life. Some stupid things can never be explained.

Pig and Parrot clashes broke out frequently. There were changeless situations that triggered them off. I gobbled up my chocolate while he savoured his, lick by lick, looking my way from the corner of his eye as he peeled back the silver paper. This subtle form of torture stretched wickedly on till, snap, I pounced on his chocolate like a beast. It fell in the dust. At times like this, Pig, the man-child with a cherub's face, wanted to kill the beast. Slay it, knifeless, with his bare hands.

But Ernie was always there to prevent the killing. Holding Pig very gently but firmly by the shoulders, he'd say, 'Kill her tomorrow.' It worked every time like a mantra! And Pig went off instead with his followers, to kill hapless birds and smelly little fish.

During our cold wars, Horsy's loyalties were torn between us, but he usually settled for the manly outdoor pursuits of Pig. But Chumra followed me to the cassia tree. He walked like a strong, supportive man, asking no questions—and being told no lies. He simply accepted me with all the ugly features of my nature.

A cassia tree grew in the garden. It had tried to grow upwards: but year after year its top was ripped away by savage monsoon winds. Broken and bowed yet undefeated it lived, and grew in the best way it knew—till ultimately it became a wondrous creation. What it had lost in upward reach it gained in circumferential spread to become a living green canopy of dense feathery leaves that swept down on its outer edges almost to the ground, while its roots stretched out like powerful tentacles to grip the sweet earth that gave it sustenance. When you sat under this tree you were inside it, enclosed and secret, like a hallowed green womb. When the March winds blew it lost nearly all its foliage, rendered in the space of days into a petrified domelike structure of wooden fretwork. Just a beautiful piece of art. But when summer came and covered it over with cascades of gorgeous pink blossoms, it was a sight that could transport you to paradise—where it belonged! Mother loved this tree. I often caught her gazing at it in rapture as she stood on the front veranda, though she had little time to sit in its shade, as I did. You could gaze into its depths till you were lost in it, became a part of it. It had this strange and wondrous enchantment.

Tea and Its Discoveries

In winter, a mere trickle of water remained in the Mahari, and our expeditions of research led us along the dry stream bed where Pig collected little fish in a jar of water carried by his followers. There were other important discoveries, like cowrie shells, coloured pebbles, lumpy copper coins, little creatures like tortoises and crabs, and other mysteries. These expeditions were very time-consuming, but always timed to end up at Harry's place—at teatime!

Ghogra was waiting on his side of the Mahari, all dressed up in his uniform. He loved dressing up: a long white coat, tight-fitting trousers and a snow-white turban crowning his bulldog head.

'Aaiye! Come, come, babalog, Uncle expects you to tea.'

True enough, for there was Harry limping slowly down his backyard to greet us, his walking stick making a grating sound as he moved up the brick pathway in a tweed jacket and grey flannels, smiling a tight-faced smile.

'So I see it's Parrot and Pig,' he droned. 'Wandering, wandering . . . and what have you found this time?' He frowned into the jar, while the follower who carried it stiffened and sniffed nervously. 'Hmmm, fish. Very, very rare! We'll keep them very carefully outside, on this ledge. Yes, yes, like that.'

'But Uncle, they might try to escape?'

'No doubt they will try—but they can't go very far.'

We settled down on his big couch, swinging our legs that were well above the floor and humming to ourselves as we looked around. Large grey eyes in a square face with soft features looked down at us with a troubled expression. It was Sarah, our grandmother, captured for Harry's pleasure in an ornate gilt frame, behind a convex glass—one of the many modern wonders at Harry's place. This drawing room was immaculately neat. Ghogra kept it so. And of course it was never, never overrun by children and dogs. Even servants kept smartly out of Harry's way.

Ghogra came in and stood studying us for a while; then he sniffed, and clucked at our hands, 'Ay hay hay! Come, come children, we'll wash them in Uncle's bathroom.'

That meant going through Uncle's bedroom. It was a sprawling room very unfussily masculine, in sepia tones with dull-looking, striped curtains. A huge four-poster stood austerely in the middle of the room, covered over with a heavy grey counterpane. Austere. But underneath—come guess!—what do you think we saw? A pair of pink slippers with pompoms!

I gave Pig a sharp dig in the ribs and pointed with my eyes.

'Mm . . . ' Pig said, digging me back, and left it at that. Here in Harry's house, we kept our whys and whats sealed up in our big mouths.

Harry was waiting for us at the tea table. He was short compared to Dad, but thickset, with a serious expression and a composed manner. We never saw him 'blow up'. But he rarely laughed.

'Laugh?' Dad snorted. 'He'll laugh when he's done some poor pilgarlic in the eye!'

They never liked each other, these two, right from the start. Snide remarks flew between them like little darts when they met, and the air grew uncomfortable for the children.

But we liked Harry. He impressed us with his best table linen and china. And chocolates if we fell down and bled. He was always very affable with us, and generous, we thought. There were regular invitations to meals at which we were treated like people of substance, though of little worth. There was an air of mutual respect and congeniality between us. He nodded agreement and smiled at our talk, while his cupboard of goodies was thrown open by Ghogra to reveal rare delights.

'Now children, what would you like?'

We saw only the pleasant side of Harry, the side that had charmed the wealth out of my grandmother. Maybe he had a soft spot for children. His must have been a lonely life. No children to brighten or darken his days; no high-spirited puppy to tear around, chewing his slippers and leaving little puddles here and there; or sober, elderly dog to sit under his chair and look up with eyes of love.

We talked about many things, while Ghogra stood by the table pouring tea and flailing out with his gamchha at invading flies. Harry listened attentively and without chipping in to contradict, like most people we knew. It felt good, talking and eating up his chocolate cake. He didn't even seem to notice that it was disappearing like magic. But this was too good to last ('Nothing good lasts,' Dorothy had said) and we knew what was coming up.

'School. When will you children be going to school?' he asked seriously.

'School?' The answer came out in two croaks of dismay.

Harry cleared his throat, frowning down at the tablecloth. 'Not yet? Well, it will be soon enough, I'm sure. You must know, children, that school is the most important part of a child's life!'

Now he was softly thumping his fists on the arms of his chair. 'Education!' he cried.

It had come. The sermon after the feast—that made the chocolate churn in our stomachs! Sermons that should have hit Dorothy and Ernie (though not about education) fell on us as heavily as earth upon coffins.

'Promise me, girlie, when you grow up, you'll be a barrister.

A lady barrister!' He leaned back in his chair, frowning up at the ceiling from where a house lizard cried, 'Tut-tut!'

'And you, sonny boy,' he said turning to little Pig, 'a doctor. Or maybe an engineer. There's money in it.'

He rubbed his hands together in a special way he had, as if there were crisp banknotes between his palms. He was on to his favourite subject—money! And he droned on and on till he saw the squirming and the glazed look in our eyes.

'Mm . . .' He began to wind up mercifully. 'But remember this, children, earning is only the first part of it. The other is saving.' This was his final shot at us every time—straight between the eyes. '*Save*! Save for your old age!'

We looked at each other with toothless grins, Pig and I, for how could we know then that the next time life rendered us toothless, the laugh would be on us?

Lenny was the first to spot us when we got back. 'Ho-ho, here come the chocolate eaters.' He let fly a kick at an empty flowerpot. It overturned. A drowsy frog fell out and sprang awkwardly away.

'But this time you know, we have a secret to tell!'

'Oh yes, I know, some more of your crap!'

'Never-never Lenny! This is *real*! Harry wears pink ladies' slippers! They were under his bed—with pompoms!'

'Pink slippers with pompoms. So that's it.' Reggie took it very coolly.

'That's what?'

'He's keeping a woman.'

'Keeping a woman?'

'Yes. Living with her like man and wife.'

'But why isn't she his wife?'

'Oho, Parrot! Why-why-why! He can't marry her because she isn't a lady.'

'Then why does he live with her?'

'Why? Because passion is stronger than a man's good sense.'

'Now what's this passion?'

'Hang it, Parrot—you wouldn't understand if I told you. So forget about passion.'

'But at least tell me—who is *she*?'

'Oh everybody knows, but they keep their traps shut.'

It was a crack at Parrot's big trap, and at once his neck was seized by sweaty hands. 'Tell, tell me. I'll keep my trap shut.'

He lurched back releasing my hold on his neck. A broad grin spread over his good-natured face. 'O-o-oh, you don't have to throttle me—it's Syrbathia.'

'Never!'

'Yes.'

Our ayah Mookhia's beautiful daughter who had vanished after the earthquake, as if one of the fissures had swallowed her up into the bowels of the earth! It also cleared up the mystery of Mookhia's desertion (when Pig was just a piglet-in-arms) crossing over to Harry's side in the great division, without a word to us.

Syrbathia was the last of Harry's soft spots, now mistress of his hearth and home, which explained the faithless flitting of Ghogra between Harry and us, for he couldn't stomach the thought of being bossed about by a 'low-caste entity'. It made no difference to him that Harry with one stroke had raised her to Christianity. The mission priest from Morpa had come very discreetly one day, and christened her Margaret.

Everyone was curious about Margaret.

'Have you seen her, Dorothy?' Mother asked. 'I hear she's quite a beauty.'

There was an unfavourable reaction. 'Seen her, Gladys? If she showed me her face, I'd kick her arse into the Mahari.'

'And naturally, you wouldn't ask. But what does Ghogra say?'

'Ghogra? Everyone Ghogra detests is ugly as sin!' She chuckled. 'You know him, Glad. She's jiggered up his princely lifestyle. Now she's Queen of the Castle. I can't blame him for hating her guts. He was complaining that Harry always takes her side against him. He's booted down the ladder. Her magic wand has turned him to a louse in the house.'

She burst out laughing. 'I can see his bulldog face puffed up like a paper bag waiting to be popped. Poor bastard! As for Uncle—he pretends she doesn't exist. He's such a bloody hypocrite! Preaching to us like Moses on the rocks, with the word of God in his mouth, while he acts like—yuk! What's that thing, Glad—half-ram–half-man?' she asked with a peal of laughter. 'Do you think it's the effect of rhinos'. . .?'

'Shh, Dorothy!' They both turned and looked at us.

Most of Dorothy's outbursts were cut short with 'shh' and then, 'Dear me! Run along, children, and play.'

Nobody got to see Margaret except the house servants. There was a timely warning when visitors were sighted on any approach road, and Margaret just vanished. At the far end of Harry's backyard, by the banks of the Mahari, was a tiny cottage artfully concealed in the fragrant shrubbery of jasmine, champak and guava trees where she spent her invisible days. In time this camouflage came to serve a dual purpose—invisibility from Harry's guests and a cover for her lover.

A Man and a River

Abhinandan's visits, owing to the unpredictable forces of his lifestyle, were uncertain and irregular; but if he happened to come on a Friday, remembering the dictates of our religion, he came bearing a fish. Not just an ordinary fish but a magnificent mahseer caught in the upper reaches of the Baghmati. He came appropriately dressed as became a Maithili Brahmin, with a white khadi waistcoat stitched in the traditional design and a snow-white muslin dhoti, wearing his facial make-up of chandan lines and with his sacred thread peeping out from somewhere or other. His head was almost always shaved, for the relentless family feuds escalated the mortality rate, laying bare scars and craters that gave his head the look of an ancient battlefield.

The kitchen servants seeing him approach stood up smartening themselves to pay their respects—'Pranam Babaji!' Mohan, the cook, took the fish almost reverently, for it was a superb specimen, and put it on a large tray so it could be presented correctly to Mother.

'Baap re baap, what a fish!' he cried, his eyes popping and the tray wobbling in his hands.

'Well, then,' Abhinandan said, 'make something worthy out of it, for Missbaba.'

Trailed by the dogs, he took a quiet turn around the garden, which had a particular attraction for him, his sharp eyes never missing any change, any single detail, no matter how trivial.

Then he turned and went thoughtfully up the veranda steps. Mother heard the footfalls and looked up from her reading. Abhinandan stood before her, bowing deep, while his hand lingered on his forehead in a long, reverent greeting. And when his eyes lifted to her face, there was this strange expression in them that made you think, 'This is perhaps the only being, mortal or supernatural, that he believes in.'

Abhinandan, if he found her free, would settle down, cross-legged, at a respectful distance where a mat was placed on the veranda floor for him. And when encouraged to speak, he would give her the news of happenings a good fifty miles around, without any flowery nonsense. It focused on politics and 'disturbances'. If he had had a hand in any of the latter, he skimmed artfully over those sections of his news bulletin. He made no confession, knowing well there would be no absolution.

There were two clear-cut sides to this man. One we saw. The other was always hidden from us, like the far, mysterious side of a forbidden mountain. It was none of our business, certainly not for the ears of Parrots and Pigs. All we knew was that Mother had tried to convert him from violence. Tried and failed, repeatedly. There were times when he was received with an icy air, and Mother had nothing to say to him. She scarcely looked up from her work. For there were things that even Mother didn't know . . . *Or did she?* . . .

The first time she had rebuked him with her icy silence, he sat staring stonily at the veranda floor before him, and as he stared a strange thing happened. It was not the diamond pattern etched in the dull crimson cement that he saw, but the colour of blood-soaked earth with his mother lying motionless in the stillness of death and his world turned suddenly upside down! All these years it had remained a dark secret, engraved far deeper in the cement of his heart. Something had turned the key that unlocked what he had buried with the ashes of his father, and awakened it on this stone floor as vividly as the events of yesterday . . .

They were sleeping out in the courtyard, under the clear starlit skies, where the river played its cool murmuring music, and the moist evening breeze slaked the stifling heat of summer. And the lapwings skimmed over the water's shirred surface, shrilling out, *'Did you do it? . . . Did-you-do-it? . . .'* His father's enemies had come while they slept. It was the brutal sound of men, the thuds and blood-curdling screams of a woman—his mother—that awakened him from the placid dreams of childhood, and by the fitful flares of a broken lantern that illumined the darkness in stark, brief flashes, he saw unspeakable things. His mother on the mud floor, lying unconscious in his father's blood, with her unborn child in her stomach.

'Wake up! Wake up!' he had cried, drenched in terror, pulling at her clothes. 'Oh my mother! Are you dead?'

And when at last she stirred, and sat up with the blood all over her, she wept. He had never seen his mother weep before. And she caught him in her arms, sobbing softly, repeating in the voice of a stranger: 'They chopped off his head!' And rocking in her agony held him tight and made him swear that he would avenge his father's death—'Oh my son, never, never forget this night,' she told him.

The ghastly reverie faded away like the passing of a dream, leaving only the colour of blood-soaked stone for reality. Yes, he had not forgotten.

For a while he sat there, rubbing his eyes. Then abruptly he stood up to leave, and as he bowed to Mother he became aware of the offerings placed by his side. His favourite things—Lipton's Green Label tea and Kiwi boot polish. It was all he ever wanted for his all-time great service to us. Silently he picked them up and left with strong resolute strides for his home by the river, his eyes on the ground and his jaw set rock-hard, as hard as his way of life. Nothing could change that any more than changing the course of the river. In fact, in many ways he was like the river.

The Baghmati was born in Kathmandu. A great temple had been erected near its source, and named Pashupatinath. It was dedicated to the god of fertility, popularly known as 'Bhola Baba'. There was frequent gossip concerning it by Kalri & Co. as they sat by Mother's and Dorothy's chairs in the veranda, pressing their legs in a gentle, lazy rhythm. It was usually with furtive glances over their shoulders, as it was about 'things unfit for children's ears'.

And what did we learn? Women who failed to have children—no matter how hard they tried—*tried what?*—made their persistent and perilous way up rugged mountain tracks and jungles fraught with unimaginable perils, carrying only pouches full of sattu and stomachs full of hope. And the high priests of fertility saw to it that they got what they craved!

'Or at least they gave it a pretty good shot!' Dorothy chuckled. 'India doesn't expect every sadhu to perform miracles!'

But the river never failed to perform its miracle for the breathlessly waiting plains—plunging down the mountains, down, down, down, swelled by torrents of melting snow, banked by the moist green fur of the Himalaya. In and out, faster and faster still, a leaping, gushing, single-minded force, never pausing, never wavering in its frenzied drive, till in all its mighty, foaming magnificence it exploded from the foothills into the sweet, nubile plains of Karmaya. To these plains it brought a rare fertility, an unstinting, never failing abundance. And in a show of glorious thanksgiving, fields of mustard in bloom, as far as the eye could see, spread out a cloth of gold at the feet of the Himalaya that gave them this river.

Onward it flowed through the Nepal Terai, sunless and dense with gigantic trees that towered over an impenetrable undergrowth of tangled vines and creepers, past elephant grass and tiger grass teeming with wild game, big and small. Animals came to the river's edge to drink and wonder at their faces in the glassy water, patting the surface with curious paws and moving along the silt-washed banks, leaving their spoor and even droppings, for the speculations of shikaris.

Fourteen miles of meandering brought it to our fields in Batheesi, where it cut a wide swath right through our land.

It was a peaceful river, most of the time. In a way, it was the river of our lives, wandering through in its seasonal moods— winter, summer and monsoon madness. Without it, our land would have sickened and died.

On the western banks of the Baghmati was Rasoolpur, known also as the Village of Blood. Here Abhinandan was born and lived all the days of his life that were not wasted in jail. It was his river too, in a different way. As a child he had tossed sticks and stones into the river, but later when he had grown to be a man, his sworn enemies—just as they had tossed away his father's headless body. Nobody had kept an account for posterity, of why the first Cain of this village had killed the first Abel. But ever since then, the die had been cast in a herringbone pattern of vengeance. There had been no forgiving and no forgetting. But this was none of the river's concern.

It moved impassively on at its own pace, on its own course, in its own moods. In winter, when the water level dropped, sandbars appeared and grew longer as the days moved into summer. Some, nearer land, sprouted grass dense and high enough to hide in. Brahmini duck were here all the year round in their inseparable pairs, not much sought after, thanks to their strong fishy flavour. But in winter, legions of wild geese from Siberia, with long necks and brown-barred wings, arrived for a brief vacation on the Baghmati, printing a telltale pattern of webbed feet on the sands.

Abhinandan was always the first to bring news of their coming, waking us before the crows or the doves when only the top of a glowing red sun could be seen through the mist. He was on the veranda steps, pointing urgently in the direction of the river.

'They're back! They're here,' he announced. 'We must leave soon—the boats are waiting and I have arranged everything.'

By the time we were ready, the sun was out and the mists slowly clearing away with a frosty bite not yet subdued by the struggling sunrays.

Kalri stuffed us into our heaviest woollies, muttering, 'Hai, hai! Going again to shoot those poor birds!'

Ernie was whistling softly and fidgeting with his shotgun. He pointed it at the sky, then broke it and peered through the barrels at our faces.

'Got you!' he shouted.

The dogs caught the mood, and went chasing each other through the nursery where Dad's new rose grafts were in a 'delicate state'.

Precisely then, Dad emerged from his bedroom whistling a cheery air and froze. 'What in the name of . . . !' brought the sweepers tearing round the house.

The dogs were captured and led away in chains, giving us sidelong looks of reproof. But they would have been chained up anyway; they were not trained gun-dogs and became a nuisance on these duck shoots, chasing goats, scaring away the birds and bringing wetness upon us all.

'You are late,' Abhinandan whispered. He tucked up his dhoti. 'Now we begin!' And he was gone.

But the geese were there, waiting. As we took up position on the bank, hidden in the tiger grass, we could hear their honk-honks. Even when they flew over, they had things to say to one another. You had to be dead still and with your trap shut, for at the slightest sound, they stretched up, running along the sands on tiptoe, wings flapping, and up they went like aircraft. They were very fast. You hoped then, they'd fly over you, low enough.

'Now, for Christ's sake, don't fire the bloody thing off like that! Wait. Wait till you see the whites of their eyes!' and with that, Dad sprang into a boat with Ernie and was gone, leaving us staring at the tiger grass.

'How can we see the whites of their eyes with all this blooming grass stuck in our faces?'

'Shut your beak and wait, Parrot!' Lenny hissed into my face. 'In any case *you* don't need to see the whites of their eyes!'

He crawled forward, flat against the earth like an iguana, dragging his gun as he went. And we crouched in the tiger grass with suspense churning our stomachs.

Suddenly he looked back at us and hissed a second time, 'No farting dammit—the birds will blooming well take off!'

'What lies! That was a blooming frog!'

'Well, then . . . keep your eyes open—and everything else shut tight!'

We could see Abhinandan on the far bank, a tall figure waving a white cloth wildly. And then there was a patter and whoosh of wings followed by bang-bang-bang!

Dad's voice was bellowing hoarsely at the sipahis, 'Christopher Columbus! Get those ruddy boats! Move, move those blithering arses!'

Sipahis scattered, dhotis hitched up high, sinewy, hairy, scrambling brown legs, splashing in and out of boats in their role as retrievers, moving their 'blithering arses'. Meanwhile, flashes of white came through the grass. Geese were falling out of the sky. The rest had circled up high, honking their alarm. Often, a goose returned to search for its mate, and ended up as the best roast goose ever.

All we understood then was the roast goose.

We walked home across the fallow fields with Abhinandan. He was looking highly pleased although he had never sampled a goose.

'Tell us, Abhinandan, do you think birds live such a happy life?'

He looked down, frowning at the grey furrowed earth. 'Not quite so happy nor quite as miserable as humans, I think they live in the moment. Their minds don't torment them like ours.'

'Abhinandan,' squinting up at him, 'why . . . why do you kill your enemies?'

He stopped to pin us in our tracks with one of his deep, penetrating looks.

'So! Why do we kill our enemies? That is a good question indeed! Why do you kill snakes, vermin, dangerous beasts? Why do you kill mad dogs? And can you tell me this: why do you shoot men in war? They are good men—most of them! Can you tell me why?' he asked softly.

We squirmed in uneasy silence. It was too much for the likes of us to tell. We had never considered these matters. We would have to ask Mother. Abhinandan laughed his soft cascade of ho-ho-hos and the matter was closed.

Sometimes, we just went for a casual boat ride down the river, with sandwiches and flasks of tea, watching batches of pelicans cruising downstream, or storks on the sandbars standing by on one leg like a penance for sins.

Sometimes, we stopped to watch as the fishermen cast their nets where the river ran deep, and offered us with pride the pick of their catch. For this little portion of the river was ours.

'Wait, wait!' Mother restrained the eager sipahis. 'Take no more than we can eat. They are but poor fishermen.'

It was a moody river, so bountiful, gentle and benevolent

through the year. But when the rains came it went raving mad, like a powerful giant filled up with narcotics.

The Khariyan

The khariyan was a hive of activity with a central square that was the processing yard for drying, threshing, winnowing, weighing and finally storing the various grains in the granaries intended for them. The regular trading made it a social centre too. It was all ruled over by Brahmins, men of figures and letters, who ruled over most things. Harry had Mahanth Jha and Kethar Ojha, while we had Sukhesar Ojha and Abdhi Missir, all Brahmins, though as different from one another as fish in the ocean. Priestly birth didn't come with any guarantee of a priestly disposition. As in the case of Abhinandan.

Abdhi Missir was the colour of rich, dark chocolate in the shape of a bowling pin. He was draped in a cheap cotton dhoti, its free end flung casually over his shoulder, or drawn modestly across the stout torso when Mother was in sight. His head, bald as a cannonball, sprouted amazingly to the religious demands of a teekie at the crown, with an outburst of hair, like a miraculous shrub! This divine thing was tied at the end in a granny's knot. He had a singular ability to frown and smile at the same time. It gave him a quaintly childlike appearance. And in fact he did have the heart of a child.

We walked about the khariyan with him, while he told us about each thing there and its particular purpose, till we came to the old khariyan shed that was now their duty room. It was all that remained of our temporary abode in the days following the earthquake. We flopped down on his worn, smooth, wooden charpoy wiping the dust with our hands.

'No! No!' he cried. 'Let me do that.'

And he wiped it clean with the free end of his dhoti. 'Now sit down nicely,' he said.

'So, tell us a story, Abdhi Missir—a true story.'

'A true story? Babalog, Sukhesar Ojha is the one for stories,' with a soft chuckle and again that peculiar frowning smile, 'they pour out of his mouth like water from our water pump! As for me, I have had no great experiences to tell about.'

'Then tell us things you know, Abdhi Missir! Tell us today about air.'

'Oh! Air!' he whispered, drawing in a deep breath; his eyes closed, and his face filled with an ethereal joy that made it strangely beautiful.

'I will tell you something. This air we breathe has such power!' he said. 'When you are angry, when you are sorely troubled, just take in a deep breath and you will grow calm. When you are sad, your tears will go away. And even when all is well, take in a deep breath and you will feel a little closer to heaven. Yes!' He peered down at us with his frowning smile. 'Because air is the breath of God!'

Every evening the dry straw, smooth and gleaming, was gathered up and carried away to be thrown on the haystack, which grew steadily larger. The coolies enveloped in their loosely collected heaps of straw looked like golden bears scurrying swiftly away on little black feet—an irresistible sight to Pig and Parrot. We took a short, quick run leaping high on to their backs and sinking jointly down in an avalanche of straw and human struggle.

At the other end of the khariyan square, employees, tenants and idlers, of whom there were many, sat in groups, gossiping, while Dosadin women stood in a row in the sunset, duggras in hand tilted against the wind. They were finishing the winnowing of grain while Sukhesar's son, whom Dada called Shorty, strutted about taking stock of them. Shorty had not inherited his father's good looks or stature. He was plainly stocky, and strove to overcome this meanness on nature's part by putting on a swagger and twirling the ends of a remarkable moustache he had cultivated, to bewitch.

Though they were poor, most of the Dosadin women were loaded with silver jewellery that they wore all the days of their lives. They had an unhurried, feline grace in all their movements that was so attractive. Some of the Dosadins of Puckry would have made great models in today's world. But there and then they were merely committed to the pursuit of romance, unable to say no to the tireless Rajput and Brahmin lovers of repute, for the rigid dictates of the caste system kept all eyes tightly shut to fleeting passion spent in forest or field or in any place where the matter could be discreetly expedited.

At the close of each workday they all hurried off with their wages to the evening bazaar, where they traded any grain in excess of their daily requirements, for these poor people were not concerned with tomorrows: it was here and now. Each of the seven villages became the site for a bazaar for every day of the week. The pattern was set, and everybody knew where. Since every village had a tank, the bazaar took shape around the tank where grain was traded for vegetables and fresh fruit, fish, spices, oil, sweets, bamboo handicrafts, crude farming implements and whatever else satisfied their simple needs. You could hear the haggling from a mile away. It sounded like a riot, though it was only their habitual style of communicating. Every word had to be yelled out. If a man didn't shout, you knew he was very ill, perhaps dying.

You could also tell from the direction of the shouting which day of the week it was!

A dirt track fringed with shisham trees and flanked by mango topes ran straight from our khariyan to Puckry village which consisted of fifty or sixty huts made up of bamboo and thatching grass neatly finished with a plaster of mud, chopped hay and cow dung. Their main supports were the trunks of lean, twisted khaira trees, a cheap hardwood, resistant to water and vermin. The thatched roofs of these huts were covered with clay tiles. Those who were better off had whitewashed their walls and engaged the village artist to illustrate birds, horses and stick figures with huge, slanted eyes, in scarlet paint. Ash gourd creepers covered most of the roofs and proliferated into charming little arbours, in which buffaloes slumped hypnotically chewing the cud, lashing out with their tails at swarms of persistent flies. A maze of narrow pathways snaked through the village, punctuated here and there by a stunted black cow or bleating goat tied against its will (its will was to feast in our adjoining fields) to a stake. It was all encompassed by dense, green fields enriched by their daily deposits. So the nearer you came to the village, the lusher and greener it got!

Puckry village was blessed with two wells that never ran dry (a dry well was unimaginable in this land of the Baghmati), one in the east for the Brahmins and upper castes and the other in the west for the lower castes. Priests, warriors, clerks, merchants, farmers, blacksmiths, masons, carpenters, oil men, milkmen and the whole long string of trades that existed at the time. You could gauge from his surname what caste a man came from. Puckry village had just about every caste with the exception of Rajput warriors, even a witch—though there was no particular caste for her.

Castes were set like rungs in the social ladder—the great, social ladder of 'look down'. At the top, well enthroned and smug, sat the Brahmins like the cardinals of the Church. Then, descending step by step, came the upper castes of Hindus who looked down at the middle strata, who in their turn looked down their noses at the scheduled castes. Even these scheduled castes had their rungs on the ladder, with the pleasure of looking down on somebody else, till you were completely off the ladder with the Dombs, who had nobody to look down on but the bodies of the unclaimed dead they were bound to dispose of.

The entire ladder looked down on the skinny, black pigs, an

abomination reared only by Dombs and tribals. They reared the pigs and, on special occasions, fell upon them like a rare treat from Buckingham Palace. These Dombs, who lived in groups slightly removed from the village, wore tattered black rags and resembled the bogeyman invoked to frighten children. Tribals like the Musahars were better off in the seclusion of their own villages, wearing even less, and preferred it that way.

Dosads, who formed the upper crust of the scheduled castes, made up our domestic staff of cooks, bearers, kitchen boys and ayahs, for no high-caste Hindu could work in a domestic capacity for non-Hindus like us, without being defiled.

It was easy as sin to be defiled in those days—simply a touch or a splash of unholy water. Even the shadow of an 'untouchable' on food was like a cloud of some virulent bacteria, which, if reported, drew on the unfortunate Hindu an unsavoury penance like eating cow dung and sand, or coughing up money earned from days of toil and sweat, to fatten the Brahmins, before they could be purified and restored to grace. The Brahmins, as in most institutions, enforced the rules and reaped the benefits.

Many men didn't hold with this kind of thing, but the system, as old as the hills, had them fast in its grip. Abhinandan was openly defiant of the system. He often stood by our dining table, as the servants did during meals, with his arms folded across his chest, watching us eat, watching intently, intrigued by the use of cutlery even for Indian food, a skill so perfected by our elders that even parathas were dispatched with knives and forks, quite untouched by hand. He was too well mannered to show any surprise at these wondrous achievements.

But when we had finished with eating and the servants began to lift away our plates, he would swoop down and pick up a plate or two starting with Mother's. 'Babaji,' they whispered, staring at him in horror.

But he only laughed his soft cascade of ho-ho-hos. 'Let the other Brahmins put me out of caste,' he said, softly. 'Let them try!' But they never, ever tried.

Reggie and Lenny were home from the hills for the winter holidays. Lenny had changed over the years; the angry fires burning at his core had been cooled by the Irish Christian Brothers, and his energies were now turned to creative pursuits. Together, they created wonders like caterpillar tanks from wooden cotton reels and strips of rubber to move up slopes and little boats that worked on candle power that were put into action in the long cattle trough. There were colourful, dome-shaped pataras, a low-cost air balloon fashioned from kite paper stuck over a delicate bamboo frame. An oil lamp fitted to the base lifted it, bright and glowing, high above the heads of a multitude of bug-eyed watchers, into the night sky and out of sight, or down in flames, when every man, woman and child moved like the fire brigade!

Then there was Ernie. He was a grown man by now, with just about everything a young woman could wish for. Harry's money had completed the picture of Most Desirable Bachelor of All. But: 'Hide your daughters away from him, my dear—he's a slippery customer!' Mothers of unmarried daughters exchanged waspish remarks in their printed silk dresses at the Samastipur Railway Institute dances. While smouldering fathers with smoke pouring from their nostrils (every man was a great smoker) were more vociferous: 'Slippery customer—my bloody foot! He's an out and out bloody rascal! . . . Tell me, Ernie, what is this we hear about you in Samastipur?' Mother taxed him. 'They call you a Woman Eater.'

'Glad . . . ' He came to flop down on the arm of her chair, speaking with a mock seriousness, 'true, true, I love women. But not as wives! Tell me, Gladys—how can I be wasted on a single female?' He tossed back his head, laughing at the look on her face. 'Look at it this way, Glad, as a bachelor I can make so many women happy. But as a married man? Only one woman miserable! Doesn't that make sense?'

'Conceited rascal!' she said, shoving him off her chair. 'One

Sylvia Dyer

day you might come up against a husband who can shoot straight!'

'Then, Gladys,' he said straightening up with a sigh, 'it'll be death in bed—though not a peaceful one!'

But despite all the hocus-pocus in Samastipur he still came back to us. Here it was rough games with the risk of physical injury. Foremost among these for swellings and dislocations was whip.

'Hurry now, we'll join hands to form a long human string, the longer the better! Heh, heh!' Ernie shouted out. 'Come on, we need more people! More people! Ay, you there Banthi, come on and join in the fun!'

Banthi, the barber, a lanky man with loose limbs and a clean-shaven head with just a tuft of teekie (for being pulled up to heaven), stood waiting in the back veranda to trim Dad's fine, khaki hair.

'Come on, Banthi, move it! You're wasting your time just gaping there!'

'Accha, accha,' he agreed, attaching himself with a sickly smile to the end of the line. 'Good, good.'

'Good? Well, here we go!' And Ernie, rooted where he stood, began to whip the human string around like the hand of a clock. Sensibly, this game should have been played on a large grassy patch, unbroken by flowerpots, bushes and trees. But who was sensible? So as the whip gathered speed, Banthi at the end ran faster and faster till finally he rose up like a glider, with a whine, and crashed into the bottlebrush tree.

'Aiinnh! Lag gaya!' the spectators cried out in chorus.

And 'Christ Almighty!' from Dad who had emerged for his haircut in time to witness the take-off and crash. His roar brought the still form of Banthi back to life. Banthi's eyes opened, and he sat up, hands moving slowly to his chest. A pale, liverish tongue slid out, with an ayyyyynnnh! like a rusty door hinge.

Ernie looked sheepishly at Dad. 'Oh hell, Tip, he struck it! I guess we'll have to forget about this game from now on.'

'Too bloody true!'

Banthi was rushed off to our local vaid, Rauthinand Jha, a priceless man in cheap cotton garments, and large in all respects. He was our physician, philosopher and friend. Never flustered, never, never defeated. He could cope with most ailments of the body or mind with a gentle hand and a loud nasal drone. His great frame bent low to examine the stricken, dark form of Banthi.

'*Accha hai. Haan, kuch nahin hai*,' he said, while a special poultice of herbs was prepared and stuck on to Banthi's chest. And in a couple of days he had bounced back to normal, cutting hair everywhere.

Allopathic doctors were not a feature of our world, and we got by without the merry-go-round of radiologist, pathologist and surgeon's ever-ready knife. Some lived to be a hundred if they had stepped carefully during the monsoons. A few stepped on poisonous snakes in the dark, because they had forgotten to clank their lathis (like car horns) for the snakes to get a timely warning of their approach. We fought to save their lives with Dr Lorbia's Terriyac, anti-venom from faraway Germany, introduced to us by an American Jesuit. He cycled six miles over rough terrain to celebrate Holy Mass in our dining room twice a month and stayed for breakfast and a refreshing exchange of news, views and patent medicines like this new wonder.

Dr Lorbia's Terriyac worked well in cases of slow-acting poison, but never, never for a cobra bite. It was always too late, and they squatted on the ground weeping into their rough, worn hands, saying, 'It is the will of God!' And Kalri drew us away saying, 'Little children should not look upon such grief.' Some succumbed to cholera and smallpox, and some to diseases then unknown and put down to the acts of evil spirits. There was no getting away from spirits: diphtheria, hysteria, epilepsy and insanity were all attributed to them.

'Baaboo ho baaboo!' they screeched, with popping eyes

and a snake-head movement. 'The Spirit has seized him! Run brother, run for the bakhta!' Very soon, a lean and wiry exorcist clad only in a G-string and carrying a bamboo stick arrived on the crest of a human wave. Special rites were performed with droning sounds and sudden leaps. The magic stick was waved in the air, and descended like a thing from Mars on the victim's frame. Sometimes it worked wonders, but at other times 'it was the will of God'.

The Merry Days of Winter

'Quick, quick!' Foster hurried in with a pot of tea, tripping over a sprawled dog. 'Finish your chhota hazri. See, Ernie baba is here already!'

We left eggs, parathas, vegetable bhujia, everything—and shot out to see Ernie cantering up the road that cut through Puchkurwa. Ernie swung down from his horse with an easy grace; a snatch of hair falling over his face was flicked back in the charming way he had. He was beaming. 'Uncle's cane at Bhokraha is being cut today, Glad. Why don't we all make a picnic of it, and who knows, there might be wild pig?' He tried ceaselessly to patch up the break between Harry and Mother—and what better way of melting the ice and restoring communication than a picnic. And it worked. For in spite of Harry's regular games of intrigue, there was a willingness to forgive and forget and hold together in the wilderness.

Yes, wild pig. That would be nice, especially a wild boar. The nilgai, then known as blue-bull, were seldom picked upon since the Hindus considered them first cousins to the 'sacred cow'. So they were left alone to multiply and grow fat on our crops. Sometimes they appeared in the lush green fields of Puchkurwa, presenting a curious sight: a heavily built, smoky-grey male, with his dun-coloured does and calves. The minute they were sighted, a cry went up, 'Ee-ho! Ee-ho!' and they jerked around, bounding off in a comically awkward gait, tails tucked in and heads held high, raising a cloud of dust.

The cry of the chase had an electrifying effect. Dogs and servants shot out from the house, cooks from the kitchen, gardeners, sweepers and loiterers from anywhere at all bounded after them with sticks, in a thrilling chase that merely drove them out of sight.

Picnics brought a feverish zeal to our kitchen, though our picnics were understood as little as the gunshots to bring in the New Year. 'Think of it, brothers—going into the jungles to eat and drink! This is considered a treat!'

Foster and Mohan laboured, red- and watery-eyed over pooahs and pakoras, while Bonzo on his haunches fanned the coals with a scorched bamboo fan. The kitchen filled up with smoke. Abhinandan's head appeared hazily at the window, like a monarch surveying the picnic fare of his subjects. He took a secret delight in our picnics, moving here, there and everywhere, like a tenacious guardian spirit.

Ghogra was busy in the dining room making sandwiches at a side table. Cold mutton, chicken, hard-boiled eggs, cucumber, tomato, and a heap of finely chopped lettuce leaves neatly arranged in front of him. He looked up occasionally to admire himself in the big gilt-framed mirror: spotless white uniform and turban with a suit-the-situation crest 'THP' it was now—in brass. He was thinking, 'Chhee, those backward louts in the kitchen, with their native preparations! *This* is what they took to picnics in the ICS!' Memories sweeter than honey washed over the bulldog face framed like a thoroughbred in the large, antique mirror. Then he looked up and saw Abhinandan framed inside this same priceless mirror, with him! The mirror could have cracked! His mood curdled, and bitter faced, he hurried away to pack the tiffin box, cursing under his breath, 'Huh! Abhinandan! Here, there and everywhere to ruin a beautiful day! Who asked him?'

Certainly not Ghogra. He was scared stiff of Abhinandan, while Abhinandan regarded him with an amused tolerance ever since the 'incident'.

The 'incident' had taken place just after the earthquake. A diamond necklace was missing from the jewel box, and Ghogra had declared that the person responsible could only be 'The Bad Man from the Village-of-Blood, who on that fateful day had forcibly snatched the jewel box from Harry sahib's sipahis! Who else? Aynh?' But when Abhinandan's fingers had closed round his neck in a grip of steel, there were bulging eyes, and the mouth opened up to confess that, being a responsible man, he had concealed the necklace very cleverly from the countless godless thieves that infested this place—so cleverly that he himself had forgotten where.

Forgotten? But caught in this deadly grip, 'Chhorr-chhorr!' he croaked out. 'Ay . . . ay Bhagwan!' And memory returned as if a magic wand had been waved over his face.

He remembered where! Abhinandan had released his hold on the tortured throat. 'Next time, black buffalo,' he said, with a sardonic laugh, 'do your thinking before you open your big lying mouth.' And the diamonds were back. But the incident remained to feed Ghogra's nightmares.

Now, Harry's black 1934 model Ford came sweeping in with Rama at the wheel. Rama was a small man whose oily head barely showed above the windscreen.

When he emerged from the car to open the door for Harry, you noticed that the car had a very high clearance and its driver had a very low one. 'The fork of his trousers,' Dad summed up, 'was just a foot and a fart off the ground!'

Harry was looking about with a sly smile. 'But Tip, where is your car?'

'My car? Yes. Oh yes,' spinning around, 'what the! Where in blazes?' And we could see his neck turning redder. Harry's subtle goading could turn Dad into a T. Rex that roared, 'Chamanlal!'

Chamanlal, the elderly driver, was starting up the car. He had been acquired with it. A dreary, dispirited-looking man in neglected garments. A sparse salt-and-pepper stubble covered his skeletal head and wandered uncertainly over his chin. His eyes from close range, as when he turned around to communicate with the back-seat passengers, had the hint of 'cataracts coming on'. He coughed, wheezed, and smelt strongly of beedis. But he knew the secrets of this car. And he knew how to move it. It had been pushed all the way to the back gate and clean out of sight. Now it was being pushed all the way back, and suddenly a formidable-looking car, painted a deceptive dove grey, came into view. A Willy's Knight!

According to Dad, who had bought it from an English planter named Dobson, it was something very special. It was also very powerful, 'thirty-six horse power', and quite unpredictable when its accelerator stuck to the floorboard and the brakes went into a hang, especially in towns and cities where it was at its terrifying best. It had crashed through the level-crossing gates in Samastipur carrying away half the gate on its bonnet, and with Chamanlal screaming inside, whizzed over the railway track in the face of an oncoming train.

It is a wonder how with all its recklessness this car still retained the splendid lines dreamed up by its makers. On cold days, cranking it was useless. Only Chamanlal knew how to tackle its mulishness. Dauntless at the wheel, while a dozen men pushed, dhotis hitched high, wiry brown legs and posteriors labouring to build up enough speed for Chamanlal to release the clutch and jam down the accelerator, and the thirty-six horses came violently to life! They kicked, farted and opened fire from the rear. Those in the line of fire fell away, while those on the flanks sprang on to the footboards and were borne swiftly out of sight. For once brought to life, nothing could stop this monster, at times not even the brakes, as we well knew.

But now this car was tearing towards us in a cloud of rosy dust, a long dove-grey thing, embellished with gleaming chromium.

The pushers had heard the familiar roar of the T. Rex, and galvanized it into life. People scattered. Chamanlal grinned, for only he knew that the accelerator was not stuck. And all thirty-six horses of it slowed down to a smooth stop, purring powerfully. Harry smirked. 'So Tip, this is your brilliant new acquisition?'

'Damn right you are, Harry, I'd back her against any tank.'

'Ha, ha! You're right, Tip. Must have served in the Great War!'

Mother looked at Tip, and he let the jibe pass.

We piled into the car. It could be stuffed with family, while sipahis stood on the footboards, gripping the window frames with lusty fingers.

And away we went . . . whizzz . . . leaving a trail of dust. There would have been no whiz and trail of dust without our Musahars who kept the roads in good repair. The Musahars of Musahari Tola, Mother's second village, were tribals and the poorest of all. Yet they were sturdy people, short and tough with stamina that matched the cart bullocks, self-assured, black and happy in a land of cruel, cruel prejudices, caste and colour. They smelt of a blend of earth and decaying shellfish. Musahars didn't believe in baths, except for fun, and the little girls' hair soon began to resemble bouquets of rats' tails. These people had the bubbling cheerfulness of little children, and the simplicity. You could say they belonged to us, which gave them certain rights. The right to our natural resources like wood, bamboo, straw and thatching grass to build or repair their huts; and the right to justice, protection and medical care. But it got stretched a little further, to the right to graze their goats and pigs on our crops, and the right even to steal.

Musahars ate, drank and were merry, unfettered by religion and its painful taboos. Field rats dug from their burrows, porcupines, iguanas, wild cats, the low-grade crustaceans found in shallow streams and ponds, unpopular birds like owls and honey hawks, in fact anything that moved went into the cooking pot of a Musahar.

And so, we come to Bhokraha. All the jungles had been

brought under cultivation and now only tiny patches survived here and there with the exception of Bhokraha which still covered close to a hundred acres, most of which belonged to Harry. It was a beautiful jungle with tall amber grass and massive trees turning copper and bronze. Dry leaves lay crisply around, or were trampled into smooth pathways like khaki carpets, where creatures had trod or lain on their backs, rolling over to look up at the sky, always blue, through branches thick with foliage or bare and skeletal with the winter sun falling through. A limpid stream went meandering past, in which the Musahars caught little fish to be fried with salt and chillies in a smear of mustard oil, or oysters with tiny pink, misshapen pearls to be sold for a song.

The cars parked in an open glade by the stream. The servants, who had come ahead, set the tea things out, in readiness. Ghogra bustled about serving eats from the tiffin box; pouring tea and watching people eat at ground level. He rather liked the idea, since 'it was popular among the distinguished members of the ICS'. Harry ignored him very pointedly because he had quit his service a month ago and moved to our camp. Abhinandan, much to Ghogra's relief, had stayed away from the picnic because Harry was there. It was rather dull. They talked politics. Not a thing about wild pigs. On the opposite bank a young blue-bull stood staring at us with big curious eyes, then suddenly jerked away and trotted off into the tall grass.

'These wile beas,' I said, with an overstuffed mouth, to Reggie, 'are they very wile?'

'Wild? What would you expect, Parrot? A wild beast is wild though not always as dangerous as leopards, tigers and bears.'

He picked up a stone and threw it into the stream. It fell with a loud splash and a flock of startled green pigeons flew up into the sky. Immediately Dad and Ernie who had come for wild boar dashed away with their guns in pursuit of green pigeons.

'There . . . there they go! And what if pigs come out now—a nice wild boar!'

Sylvia Dyer

'Don't say that, Parrot! A lone boar with long, sharp tusks can be a very nasty customer. In the Old Man's days'—our great-grandfather was always referred to as the 'Old Man'—'they used to go pig-sticking. Wild pigs were driven out of the tiger grass by the Musahars, beating like hell on drums, while the planters on their horses had to stick them through with lances as they shot past. Don't laugh, Parrot! It wasn't so funny! Imagine pigs flying out like arrows all over—and even under! Once, a bloody great boar got under the Old Man's horse, and ripped its stomach open from end to end like a butcher! Oh hell! It would have finished him off too, while he was down, if he hadn't stuck it through first! Do you wonder why they called him the "Sher"?'

Often during those cold, dry days, a flock of cranes from the north, Siberia, they said, circled and settled like a grey cloud over the paddy fields. They were long, lean creatures called krakuls: long legs, long necks and foolish faces, though they were no fools when it came to filling their stomachs. As soon as they were spotted, an alarm went up, and away they flew, higher and higher, till they were mere black specks peppering the sky and their sharp metallic cries of kraa-kul! had faded away. Any skinny man was dubbed a krakul, derisively, for in those days of plenty, nobody had an excuse for skinniness. Those who didn't have enough could always steal from us!

Winter was the time for fun, especially in the khariyan with everybody moving about, brisk, busy and fulfilled.

And winter evenings were the best. The sun retired early, slipping slowly into a deep green horizon. It vanished with a cheery goodbye. 'See you tomorrow!'

There were countless tomorrows, countless, as we saw them. There remained an apricot glow that deepened to a dark vermilion streak we called the 'winter lining'. In the north, the distant snow range took on a surreal beauty over the darkening sugar cane fields. Smoke curling up in spirals from a multitude of village bonfires hung in the air in a diffused grey-blue belt.

The sky was patterned with homecoming birds. The sound of faraway musical voices came echoing along. And into the cold, crisp air was stirred, so skilfully, the scent of sun-ripe paddy, the faintly acrid smell of burning wood, damp straw, sugar cane juice, dried cow dung and the sweet, earthy smell of cattle. A banquet of aromas served up on mountain-fresh air.

The day's work was done by nightfall, and the khariyan swept clean with many bamboo brooms. It grew colder. A ghoor was lit and people stood around warming themselves. When fronts were done they turned their backs, and as they warmed up, bottled memories rose to the surface to be uncorked. Tall tales spilled out while the kooch-koochwahs cackled, loud and cracked in the darkness, like the mocking voices of witches. But kooch-koochwahs were only little owls that listened in (like Ghogra) to private conversations.

A soft little laugh came from Badri, in a ringside seat. His eyes glittered in the firelight. 'Heh heh! They might be asking for tobacco like the tree churails!' Badri, who had been Lenny's childhood 'keeper', was an authority on the secret lives of tree churails. A lemur-like man with a serene face and eyes with pinpoint pupils, he lived in a world of dreams—even in those bygone days, when he was brought sharply back to reality by a kick on the shins from Lenny, an impatient child with an uncontrollable right leg.

'Baap re,' he confided, in a whisper, 'that Lenny baba, his right leg was like a ferocious dog!'

The ghoor had warmed Badri up into a talking mood. He had had several advances from these tree-type churails addicted to tobacco, he told us, but never was he afraid of them. A bony, claw-like finger wagged in frail defiance. He had had discussions with them, even arguments. 'But,' he added with a soft, secret laugh, 'I never gave them a single shred of tobacco!'

You could never give tobacco to a churail, and no argument about that. In any case, we had no tobacco to give, except Dad's Three Nuns locked up in his almirah.

'Poor wretch,' Foster whispered to us, 'caught by opium. Got him where the churails failed!'

But there was a remedy, Badri disclosed, for the scourge of these tree-type churails, who lived in tree hollows. 'A Rajput from Harpur village had got foolishly involved with one,' he said. 'It interrupted his sleep every night, to . . .' He broke off, looking strangely at Parrot and Pig settled alongside.

'To what?' we cried. His eyes closed and we thought he was going to sleep.

'Badri!' Parrot took hold of his head and shook it up like a cocktail.

And his eyes opened. He cleared his throat, 'Er . . . to err . . .'

'Well . . . never mind,' Foster cut in, 'just get on with the story.'

'Story? Oh yes, yes.' He continued, 'The tormented man went to a famous, old churail killer. And this is what he said.' Badri swallowed, and the Adam's apple in his thin chicken-neck went up and down. '"You must thread a needle with a long, long thread on a reel, and when she appears in the night, jab it into her . . . er . . . er . . . rear part . . . er! No missing!" This he did well, for he had eyes in his head and the steady hand of a spear thrower . . . hunh . . . er . . . So when she left, she knew not of the needle stuck in her that part. And ha ha! The reel simply went on unwinding after her!' Badri's eyes closed again.

'Badri, wake up and move your mouth, before we move it for you!' Parrot threatened.

'No! No! Baba! This warm firelight . . . it brings the sleep . . . Soooo . . . Next morning the village people followed the trail. It led to a secret hollow in a big, big tree, where they found—ha ha!—what do you think? A heap of sucked-up, dried-up bones! And the churail killer, he shouted, "Ho ho! Brothers! Now we have her! Quick, make haste with these bones! We hold evil in our hands!" And he was trembling like a fish. "Every single piece must be burnt to ashes!" So this was done. And the burning bones danced about, singing shrilly through the nose. A murderous dance! We kept well out of the way! Till there was nothing left to sing and dance about . . . Just ashes were there . . . like you see . . . in this ghoor here.' Badri let out a deep sigh, his eyes turned a half circle and closed.

'Gone to sleep,' Foster clucked. 'Just managed to finish his story!'

All the ghoor squatters laughed, dark faces and white teeth gleaming in the firelight, and the kooch-koochwahs cackled loudly in the background.

They chewed a lot of tobacco, and did a lot of spitting. Besides, in the old days, people couldn't swallow all the things we have to now. There were spittoons in homes. Even pure silver spittoons. Outside, men were free to spit everywhere; spitting out paan and tobacco, noxious odours inhaled, revulsion, indignation, guilt and perplexity—unpalatable things seen and heard, that they could not stomach, and sought to expel with spittle, 'Thooooo!'

It was a spitter's paradise.

Foster sighed. 'Late! Late, children! Come now, Missbaba will be asking for you!'

We ran home to wash our hands in the bathroom, in a big aluminium mug with '1 seer' stamped on it. The bathrooms those days were very spacious, with polished teak wood commodes, bathtubs and grand wash-hand stands, each with a large mirror, porcelain washbasin and jug. A lantern sat on our wash-hand stand. Inside its polished glass chimney, from out of a bubble of metal, it stuck forth its yellow tongue of flame, steadfast and reassuring. But the water in the mug was as dark as the khariyan well with its monster.

'Foster? You put your hand in first.'

'Why Baba?'

'Why? There might be a fish to bite off my fingers!'

Foster chuckled loudly and bounced from foot to foot, like he always did when he was tickled.

'Foster, do you want to hear a secret?'

'Secret? Aaa, why not?' He smiled at us, his pleasant, brown face washed gold by the lantern's light.

'Sit down then. We'll tell it in your ears. Keep them wide open. Now, cover your eyes with both hands and don't move them till you've heard the secret! Eyes shut, ears open. *Accha*? Wait now.'

'Very well.'

Quickly we filled our mouths with water and blew it straight into Foster's ears.

Foster doubled up laughing. 'O-ho! You really had me!' He stuffed his fingers in his ears, wiggling them and tilting his head this way and that to get the last drops out.

'That was a good joke. Next time, try it on Kalri.'

'What a waste, she never laughs. Foster, have you ever heard her laugh?'

No. He had not. Kalri was just a dry shell, with the insides drying up too.

'So tell us, Foster, what's there for dinner?'

'Fried fish. You know, it's a fish that Abhinandan Babaji brought while you were out roaming. There's grilled widgeons, and today Ghogra has made country captain like he used to make for the ICS sahibs! But first you must have your soup.'

'Soup? No! No!' we cried together, covering our mouths.

The soup was more often a failure known as 'jharan soup'— hot water with a delicate flavour of the dishcloth. It was one of their great culinary deceptions, and Dad exploded when it went into his mouth.

In winter, dinner was served on porcelain hot-water plates with a blue-and-white willow pattern. The hollow centres were filled with hot water, and closed up with a button-like stopper. The grilled widgeons went into them with a dash of Lea & Perrins Worcestershire Sauce and a lump of home-made butter that melted over it like snow. It was accompanied by a hotchpotch of vegetables from the garden. Often there was rahu or mahseer, fresh from the Baghmati, filleted and fried with spices, or seasoned blandly 'English style' in egg and crumbs. Or when Ghogra was with us, baked fish and other creations picked up from the Indian Civil Service in their 'civilian houses'.

Country captain was a popular Anglo-Indian dish, a semi-dry curried preparation of mutton or chicken garnished with crisp fried onions. It was arranged around a cake of mashed potato, and fried on both sides till it grew a crisp golden-brown skin.

When lunchtime came around, the Muslim cook Smallie Jim, four feet ten inches of speed and culinary skill, would shoot in with a korma or some other speciality cooked in glorious ghee (nobody in those days ever had a heart attack from eating it). The aroma stole through the house and people appeared quickly for lunch. We were soon arranged at the dining table in our usual places: Mother and Dad at the head, Dada at the opposite end, with children spread in between. Four servants took up their posts at the four corners with their jharans.

Mother looked up. 'Um . . . And who cooked this curry?'

But before any of the servants could speak, Ghogra would reply with a subdued grunt, 'It was Moolajim, huzoor. But what does he know? Tomorrow I'll make you a far better vindaloo!'

This fierce competition kept us delightfully fed, though courting communal trouble in the kitchen.

Sometimes the servants had forgotten to chain up the dogs, and they made a sly appearance under Parrot and Pig's part of the table. And while the elders were engrossed in political discussions and arguments, we devised new teasers for the dogs, like poking holes in the parathas—small ones for eyes, and a large one for the mouth—from which we stuck out our tongues and waggled them at the dogs. The big ones looked confused and suspicious while the small ones retreated, barking shrilly. Only Chumra drew nearer, gently pulled the paratha off my face, and gobbled it up gratefully. It was convenient too, to slip him little pieces of meat, while Dad was looking the other way.

These dogs were so many things to us. They were our border scouts, guardians and friends. Our insulation from things wild and sudden, like for instance, a hyena at the drawing-room door watching Dad sipping Scotch. They were even our footstools in summer, and our foot rugs in winter, which roles they submitted to with a gentle ooonph of protest. They kept our grounds clear of prowlers with a taste for poultry, and raised an alarm over more serious matters of the night, that set off a chain reaction. We got up and yelled at the watchmen, the chief of whom was a man called Dopey (the soundest sleeper of all.) Dad snatched up an appropriate gun from the group kept loaded in readiness alongside his dressing table and ran out shouting. It was a drill well practised. For, anything from a cobra to a musth elephant could show up at the most inconvenient times in Dhang.

Mother did her knitting during the evenings, or she wrote swift letters to people like Suttons or Pochas Seeds, or the handful of in-laws still going strong in Calcutta. Knitting and writing were both done with a minimum of fuss or attention to time-consuming details. There were times when the wrong letters went off in the wrong envelopes. Or when a letter to Messrs Hall & Andersons, Department Store, ended with 'Yours affectionately, Gladys'.

Her knitting, too, ran into trouble as in the case of Dad's pullover. She had selected a stylish pattern in 4ply wool. A 'handsome brute' in the pattern book was wearing it with a challenging smile.

But the 4ply wool was not immediately available. 'Uf! Fiddlesticks!' she said, and started the pullover in double-knit. It grew and grew over a few evenings. And when finally Dad tried it on, though he was a large-sized man, he was almost lost in the blooming thing.

We named it the 'Pull-all-over-and-under'.

'By jeepers!' He beamed, rubbing his hands briskly together. 'This'll keep me warm as a bug in a rug! Just capital for my shikar trips!'

Dead right. The animals would never figure out the armed and dangerous creature inside!

Spirits

Our garden wizard was a Musahar who we called 'Man'. Man was a work of art in ebony, and unlike most Musahars he was gentle and refined, even quietly philosophical. He spoke very little; he just worked. Through the biting cold of winter, the steady drip-drip of seemingly endless monsoon days, or in the blistering heat of the summer sun, his bare back glistening with sweat, he worked unsparingly. We were silent witnesses to his working life. From time to time, he'd round up the sweat beads from his forehead in the crook of his forefinger, and dash them into the flower beds with a quick, light flick. Then he'd look up at Parrot and Pig standing by with a grin. A happy grin! Truly, this garden grew by the sweat of his brow, and was the lovely gift of Man.

'Tell us, Man, what flowers are these, and these, and these?'

'These are lah kiss purr . . . these are jeep suppla . . . . Those are calfonia puppy.'

'Very good. But say, when are you coming to play with us?'

'Play? Oh not now, children, I have all this weeding to finish!'

'So, when? When? When?'

'In the evening when it's cool. Baap re! Standing out here without your hats! Now, run into the house, or your heads will ache.'

'Oh Man!'

In the evenings we were off together to the khariyan, where he played last-touch and heep-hoop with us. There was this status of kaccha roti that was rather like diplomatic immunity. If you were kaccha roti it exempted you from being 'caught'; so, all the thrill of running with the hares, yet knowing that the hounds were rendered toothless when at the crucial moment you yelled kaccha roti, was ours. And we were the shameless, ever-surviving hares, while our followers were eaten.

At harvest time, all the bundles of paddy were grouped in the khariyan. There were neat stacks of varying dimensions. Large ones from big plots of land and little stacks that belonged to sharecroppers, with uniform dividing spaces that created a maze of narrow passageways through which we ran hiding or seeking, or clambering up the stacks to vanish among the bundles at the top. You could also jump like a paratrooper from the top of a big stack on to smaller ones alongside. There were drops that ranged from six to sixteen feet, to suit our whims.

'Na-na-na! Baap re baap, not so high up!' Man rubbed his ears in distress. 'What will Missbaba say!'

'Nothing! Watch this, Man—wheeeeee!'

Man grinned continuously. He retrieved us when we got wedged between bundles, or disappeared with a cry, and honoured our kaccha roti status. He never laughed aloud or spoke unless we encouraged him. But then, words were not necessary between us. So deep was our understanding.

Then there was the pora ka taal, a haystack approximately sixty feet by forty feet at its base that just kept on getting as high as the straw produced in that year's harvest. It all depended on the monsoon, and the mood of the Baghmati. While it went up, it was good for diving. The hay was soft and springy, and we sailed through the air to plunge in, screaming in ecstasy and landing on well-seasoned bottoms. A fine powdery dust rose up in clouds from the hay, filling our eyes, ears and nostrils, but failed to dampen our drive. We just went on and on breathing hard, flushed and sweaty and with the glint of madness in our eyes.

Some of our happiest moments were spent together with Man. We sank back in the dusty, warm straw.

'Tell us, Man, are you afraid of the dark?'

He grinned. 'Why? We live half our lives in the dark.'

'But—spirits! Aren't you scared, like us?'

'I might be too. I've never seen spirits with my own eyes, but my father and many of his time did, once. He was afraid even to speak of it, as if speaking might bring them back!'

We shot bolt upright. 'But did he speak?'

'Well, yes. It was long ago, when Missbaba was only a little girl. About that time there was a rumour that scared the dirt out of everybody—about a headless ghost, a syrcutta. Not just one, but a number of syrcuttas!'

'Aaa! How many?' Pig's voice quivered. His face was grey with dust and ribbons of straw were caught in his curly hair.

'I don't know.'

'Oho Pig, shut up and let him talk.'

'These syrcuttas worked in a different way. The heads went about looking for their bodies! The Brahmins can explain this. They study these matters and always come up with a good story! The Brahmins of Puckry village say that long, long ago, maybe as far back as when Rama broke the bow in Janakpur, a king was defeated in battle. His head and the heads of his courtiers were chopped off and carried away, God only knows where. And so, they say, these heads had returned to this land, searching for their bodies!'

'Your father saw these heads, then?'

'Oh yes! One afternoon the sahibs had all gone to the Baghmati, for what you call peekneek. The sahibs rode on horses, and the memsahibs sat in the tamjaans carried by the Musahars. The sun was going down, when they saw a strange kind of glow in the sky—and suddenly a string of lights. A big one in the centre, with smaller ones on both sides.'

'And then—what happened?'

'Happened? Baap re! The Musahars almost died of fright! They were stuck to the ground like rocks, their black faces had turned grey and their teeth were rattling in their mouths, while the sahibs rode forward on their horses and fired their rifles! Then the lights rose up and were gone! "Quickly, quickly, let us be gone from here!" the memsahibs cried. But the Musahars' legs of stone could hardly move—till the sahibs came galloping up and shouted, "M-O-V-E!" They picked up the tamjaans, and their legs never stopped moving till they reached the kothi.'

'Ooooo, it's getting dark now. Was it about this time?'

We dragged our way home, feeling the earth like lead under our feet.

Lenny was in the veranda teasing the cat with a small rubber snake.

'Parrot and Pig, where on earth have you two been? You look like the Musahars dug you out of a rat hole!'

'We were on the pora ka taal, stuck in the straw,' Pig burst out. 'Man told us an offel story! Heads came here, looking for their bodies!'

'That was no story, children,' Mother told us. 'It actually took place and was known as the Bihar Torch Lights. It was seen by people in many different parts of Bihar!'

Some evenings, Man went to the Basbita bazaar on the Nepali border, where illicit liquor was brewed with impunity and sold at a price within a poor man's means. A poor man had just as much need of an occasional drink as anybody else—maybe more. He came back happy.

'Man, do you know what day it is *today*?'

'Arre baba, who doesn't! Fifteenth of January, the day of the big earthquake.'

'Then cut us nice, nice flowers, we're going to the graveyard.'

'Good. I'll bring them quickly. Missbaba went there early this morning.'

We made our way through the khariyan and past the shisham trees where the flying foxes hung. Most of them were asleep while a few quarrelled shrilly over property rights. Here the mogra bushes grew wild and fragrant, and the tangled undergrowth was laced with dreaded gokhul thorns that gave you a seven-year sore.

'And watch out,' Reggie said, 'for snakes. You never can tell.'

The decrepit old walls of the graveyard were encrusted with moss and lacy, grey lichen. The narrow, rickety gate creaked unwillingly open. Inside was a row of graves that had suffered the erosion of countless floods, leaving the inscriptions barely legible. Reggie bent over, his fingers scraping at the stone.

'Here, it says Thomas Tripe.'

'Who was Thomas Tripe?'

'Our great-granduncle Tom—he was the Old Man's brother.'

'The bad one that stood with him on the bund, and fought two hundred men?'

'Now, who told you that?' he asked quickly.

'Sukhesar—who else!'

'Well, it was something like that.' He straightened up and saw that a couple of dogs had sneaked in through the open gate and were sniffing around. 'Out dogs!' he shouted, and then breaking into a grin: 'Come to pee on our ancestors.'

'What are ancestors?'

'These,' he said, pointing down at the graves.

'Thirty-three is not very old. Why did he die so soon?'

'He was murdered.'

'Murder!' Pig backed away from the grave, groping about for a hand to hold.

Reggie took his hand. 'I'll tell you about it sometime. Not now, not here.'

Meanwhile, the dogs had slunk back and were nosing around among the graves in an ill-mannered way. But Reggie had not noticed. We moved on to where a large impressive grave rose three feet from the ground. A beautiful angel, glowing white in this forever-green shade, stood gazing down at it with folded hands and an enduring marble compassion. Silence too endured here. People rarely passed this way. But when they did, they stopped awhile to pay homage to the angel. With joined hands pressed to their foreheads, they whispered reverently, 'Gor laggai chii, we touch your feet.'

We placed our flowers, tiptoeing and squinting to see what was written on top.

Sylvia Dyer

SARAH INDIANA TRIPE. ROSALIND DOROTHY WHITE.
2.15 pm. 15th January 1934.
R.I.P.

'R.I.P. What's that?'

'Rest in peace.'

'But are they not in heaven?'

'Oh-ho, Parrot! Everybody doesn't go zoom to heaven, like the good thief! They're in a place of waiting, that's what we believe.'

'I'd *hate* to be resting in peace—how boring!'

'What are you saying, Parrot?'

'Yes. I'd like it to be like this, Reggie, *always*—the way we are.'

'The way we are, huh?' He stopped short, staring. From behind the angel there was a sudden flutter of white cloth like terrified wings, except Pig and Parrot were more terrified and fled crashing through the bushes heedless of snakes and seven-year sores, for these were nothing compared to—'Ghosts!' we screamed. 'We saw *ghosts*!'

Reggie caught up with our headlong flight, as we reached the khariyan. His cheeks were puffed up with locked-in laughter.

'Come on, kids,' he burst out, 'there were no ghosts! It was only Sukhesar's son, Shorty, and Foster's daughter. The dogs flushed them out and chased them over the wall. I saw it with my own eyes.'

Shorty and Foster's daughter in our graveyard! Behind my grandmother's grave!

We crashed out on a bundle of hay, relief flooding through us like a good shot of Dad's brandy, so sweetly that we never thought to ask, 'What were they doing together, behind the angel's back?'

Coming Events

It was the end of February and the days were growing warmer. We lay on the soft grass watching Man and his assistants at work in the rose beds. Masses of annuals in full bloom made it a fragrant, busy afternoon. Droning bumblebees in their football jerseys hovered about the sweet-pea fences and butterflies flitted drunkenly into our faces. A gentle breeze blew from across the river carrying with it the sounds of distant human voices, musical and rhythmical.

Then suddenly our own names were being blared out in a most unmusical way. 'Where in the blazes were you two loafing?' Dad barked at us.

We could hear the rumble of the train on the Baghmati bridge. The servants were bustling about, packing our clothes.

'What's this? Where are we going?'

'We're going away for a short time,' Mother said, frowning thoughtfully into her big white almirah.

'No! No Mummy! To where?'

'To Kurseong. Quick, children! Hurry and get dressed. We're dreadfully late. Oh dear me! Narain Singh has gone ahead to catch the train.'

Gone ahead! There was a travel procedure in those days, for when we were positively going to miss the train. A couple of sipahis tore away on cycles to detain it at the railway station, or if it had already left, at the level crossing, while we followed speedily, with our luggage on the heads of a string of trotting Musahars.

Dad was in a tearing hurry, locking away papers, moving about with long strides, and in a good mood, whistling 'It's a long way to Tipperary', while in the distance the train was whistling, kook . . . kook . . . kook . . . koooo!

The Musahars appeared, hurriedly carrying the tamjaan,

which we called Tom-and-John. It was a mode of transport we used mainly during the floods, and consisted of two facing chairs fixed on a wooden base. From behind each chair, a shaft extending about six feet was borne on the shoulders of carriers. They moved at a steady trot, arms bent at the elbows and going like pistons, their laboured breath coming out in a rhythmical hain, hain, hain, hain till it became necessary for them to stop and switch shoulders, or be replaced by reserves trotting behind. They had to be as sure-footed as mountain goats, for it took just one false step, during those squelchy days, to plunge the whole lot, carriers, riders and Tom-and-John into a mud bath! But in dry weather, like now, we always went by car, or if the road was washed away, in a tyre cart.

'The Tom-and-John? But we can all go in the tyre cart.'

'No,' Dad said shortly, 'Mummy can't travel in the tyre cart.'

'But she used to—always.'

'But *not now*! Christ Almighty! Buts and whys! Get cracking or we'll miss that blasted train.'

The wide tyre cart, with easy chairs set in it, was comfortable enough we thought, as we sprang in. The cart drivers, Bullfrog and Snouty, sitting side by side, at once caught up the bullocks tails, twisting them. 'Move, husbands of prostitutes!' they screamed at the animals. And we moved, bumping and lurching, clinging like leeches to the rails to keep from wingless flight. We reached the station, covered in dust, the big, powerful bullocks snorting and patched with sweat. And there was the train, hissing and spewing out black smoke. The cycling sipahis had dashed up the railway embankment, and leaped on to the engine as it was steaming out. This alarming intrusion was never cause for silver streaks in the engine driver's raven locks. He knew it was no attack by dacoits, but simply—'*Dhang ka sahib log accha accha!*'

We climbed hurriedly into the compartment, followed by our heavy baggage, which was really heavy since it comprised all manner of things for our sustenance and comfort in the event of an emergency. Sipahis were swinging in and out, arranging stuff, doing the dusting and switching on the fans. Followers stood looking up from the embankment, grinning and fidgeting. 'We'll miss you babalog!' With deep, deep sniffs and runny noses: 'The light will go out from our lives!'

Meanwhile, Chhota Babu the assistant stationmaster, was striding along the embankment with our tickets and a syrupy smile.

'So your honour is proceeding to hills and all,' he said, rubbing his plump little hands together. 'Er . . . err . . . madam, before you take departure, I would make the pray for one only thing.' His eyes closed in prayer. 'It is simply this—one female cow-calf!'

The prayer of Chhota Babu was granted on the spot. Next time it would be Bada Babu the stationmaster's turn, followed by the engine driver, guard and fireman. The 'pray' came in orderly rotation, like the seasons in this blessed land.

With everybody happy, the engine stepped up its hissing to a deafening pitch, spewing out clouds of coal dust. The sky turned charcoal-grey and soot came down like black rain upon the assembled crowd. It whistled a shrill farewell and puffed off with a sporadic clank-clank and a long-drawn-out kooo-eeeeee.

We spent all summer in Kurseong, in Granny Corbett's Boarding House, with Foster and Kalri in attendance. It was like Shangri-La wreathed in silver mist: its hill slopes covered with springy green parachutes that were tea bushes, or cryptomeria forests lush with orchids, hydrangeas, bracken and wild flowers, and with the snow crests of Kanchenjunga, majestic and dazzling white with the purity of the gods, presiding over it all. It was a small hill station in the heart of the tea country, where the Darjeeling Himalayan Railway toy train came wheezing and puffing up from the plains, spewing out clouds of smoke. Two hillmen sat on the buffers with bags of sand to drizzle on the railway lines, so the train wouldn't slip backwards as it zigzagged, like a sewing machine, threading its way through villages, crowded bazaars and sudden cars that shot out of the ever-present mist.

And as a final reward of its stupendous Himalayan assault came the tiny station of Ghoom, eight thousand feet above sea level, where it did an exultant loop-the-loop and, screaming madly, rattled down the mountainside to Darjeeling, the Queen of Hill Stations. This was the land of the Bhutias, those magnificent, incredibly strong people (who could singly carry a piano on their backs!) with rosy cheeks and broad, happy faces that laughed at everything, including themselves.

Reggie and Lenny who were schooling in Kurseong, at Goethal's Memorial School run by the Irish Christian Brothers, came home for the weekends, while we waited for July and our youngest brother's entry into this world. Mother was in her forties at the time, and his entry was thought of with such apprehension that she made a swift and dramatic last will and testament, in secrecy and tears, amid the gloomy drip-drip of the monsoon. But he was born quite straightforwardly into the hands of Dr Goenka, who laughed aloud and cried, 'Oh madam, you have brought forth yet another son!'

Foster brought the news to us with a beaming face: 'Jai Bhagwan! A small baby has arrived,' and his tongue shot with delight through the vacant space left by departed front teeth. 'Quick! Quick! Come and see!'

What we saw was a long, white cocoon in a bassinet. It had an egg-shaped head topped with fine silky hair, the colour of damp straw, and a red, grimacing face. It was sorely distressed and letting out hiccuping cries in a shrill soprano. Tiny red hands broke through the cocoon and quivered in the air. This was our baby brother! People were making cooing sounds and trying to calm him down with drops of Woodward's Gripe Water. Mother was lying in bed, with Dad sitting alongside, holding her hand. She looked so happy, but there were tears in her eyes! She saw the alarm written on our faces and laughed.

'Don't worry, my little darlings,' she said, 'they're only tears of joy!'

Could there be *tears of joy*?

In a few months he was a delightful thing, totally wrapped up in his toys; but as he grew older he grew weary of these simple pleasures and took to following us everywhere with sharp, curious eyes, and a big mouth that blurted out our secrets— 'They went alone to the Banswari,' 'They took your mosquito net to catch fish,' and so on. He just had to let it out. There were no secrets any more. Maybe the demands of his conscience were beyond his control, and he had to purge himself instantly of everything he saw, heard, thought and even imagined. We called him Chatter Cat.

People of any substance rolled in bearing gifts. These were invariably hard cash, an investment, since gifts were reciprocated with interest, or won back by wily ways!

Rajan Singh and Bhajan Singh arrived grimly together, on an elephant. It was Bhajan's, since Rajan's elephant had ended its life during the marriage season. And since he had no reserve elephant, being an overly thrifty man, he was reduced to taking this sour-faced lift with his brother.

These two were landlords from Harpur, the village of warriors: Rajan Singh, thin and tall as a telegraph pole with an ascetic air, and Bhajan Singh, short and square with a ruthless stamp. They were brothers and foes. Even the pleaders of Sitamarhi court, whose very livelihood depended on litigation, referred to them as 'notorious litigants'. They had cases against everybody of means, but mostly against each other, and spent their days going and coming from the Sitamarhi court, amid the pervading smoke and smell of beedis, like business people commuting to office, finding it a pleasurable, if not always a rewarding pursuit.

They even fought each other out of court. That is, their 'armies' did, with ripened paddy fields as their battlegrounds. This took place when disputed land was ready for harvesting. But before going into battle each brother warned his eager army. 'Look, you bloodthirsty scoundrels. Open your ears and hear clearly! You can kill each other—indulge yourselves. But God help the murderous brute that lays a hand on my brother!'

The court pleaders too were sometimes put in a similar predicament and found themselves and the magistrates tied up in peculiar knots.

They were on equally good terms with us, and Harry. In fact, they were on good terms with everybody, since good terms for them meant a jovial cordiality on the surface, while under the table, they were figuring out how they could take you to court.

Occasionally they paid a courtesy call on Mother, though never together as they came now. Bhajan Singh sat leaning forward in a planter's chair on the front veranda. He looked inquisitively around him, at curious objects like Dad's stag antlers ranged on the walls, a talking hill mynah in a cage, Parrot and Pig sprawled on the floor, feeding a mongoose with biscuits, and last but not least boxes of pansy faces grinning up at him, while he jigged his legs. We stared fascinated at the luxuriant hair sprouting from his ears.

'Missbaba,' he sucked in his breath sharply, 'you are being hoodwinked by some of your trusted sipahis. We all know that during your absence, some twenty cartloads of paddy harvested in Batheesi by the riverside, left from there, heh heh! But only twelve reached your khariyan! And why? The rest were diverted after nightfall—to Harpur village.'

'I suspected so, Bhajan Singh, but I had no proof. There are none who will come forward to give witness. It's very distressing. Every time we leave home . . .' She broke off with a sigh.

His square, bony face tilted up at her with its shrewd, close-set eyes. 'Heh heh, you must know how to deal with it! Missbaba, you are too soft when they come to you in tears. Never forgive. Look at Harry sahib, heh heh ha haynnnnh.' He broke into peals of laughter almost choking himself. Then, growing sober as he saw that she did not share his mirth: 'Look at us, Missbaba, we thrive on tricky situations. In this place you must be ruthless. Heh heh! There are ways . . . a little twist, a little turn—using the right tools and the right traps at the right time. Timing is of utmost importance—and you have turned loss into gain. Such a good game to play! We all play games. How dull this life would be otherwise! Heh heh!'

'I don't play games,' she answered him.

'Then,' he said, shaking his head in baffled regret, 'you will be the loser every time. Missbaba, you are too soft!'

Our Bovine Creatures

There was never a slack period or lack of employment. The innumerable crops came in regular rotation. Every January, the mustard bloomed, turning the fields to carpets of gold. Mustard was followed by linseed, which when in bloom looked like the sea on the calmest, clearest day.

Man chuckled softly. 'You know,' he told us, 'once a drunken Musahar was on his way home from the bazaar. It had grown late, and a full moon was up. He came to a linseed field and—baap re, he tried to swim across! He thought he was drowning and started shouting. In the end he gave up and fell asleep in the linseed!'

January brought the harvesting of sugar cane, and the fields came alive with the sound of merriment—hacking, cleaning and lopping off of the leafy tops. The cane was tied into bundles of uniform length to be loaded on to bullock carts that stood waiting by. Soon the carts were all loaded dangerously high, because of the stiff competition between carters to carry the heaviest load. With heavy loads on treacherous roads, the carts set off in a long line for the weighbridge at the railway station siding, lurching and swaying like drunken monsters. But skilfully steered and controlled by seasoned Musahar drivers like Bullfrog and Snouty they arrived intact, usually. But there were times when the axle snapped. The shaft flew upwards, the bullocks released from the yoke hightailed it to safety, and the cart driver sprang free like a frog from a log as the abandoned cart capsized, spilling its load. But no one was abandoned in his downfall. There was no dearth of helping hands—carpenters, blacksmiths and wayside spectators—to get things going again to the weighbridge. Here the cane was weighed and the sugar-mill representatives with their important books and looks took over the burden of its transportation to the Belsund Sugar Factory, in Riga.

This feverish activity continued for three months, till all the cane was cut, and the fields left bare and stumpy. Workers scattered the dry leaves evenly around, and set fire to the fields. They flared up with a crackling fury, spitting ashes all around while eliminating any lurking impurities, so that the crop could start again with a clean sheet the following year. And lo, after a light hoeing-up and a shower of seasonal rain, fresh green shoots began to sprout from the charred, old stumps.

The days of mechanized farming were still years away. Everything had to be done by manual labour. The Musahars and the lower castes of Puckry village were field hands and labourers. They did the hoeing, ploughing, levelling, sowing. Men and women did the planting and transplanting of paddy, the harvesting, threshing and winnowing. But very little could be done without bullocks, for tractors were an unimaginable wonder at the time. So, there was need for cattle. We had about a hundred head of the Montgomery strain, and a bull called Birju Dhaakar. He was a magnificent brute, the colour of a Rhode Island Red, who went slowly round the cowshed and granaries bellowing, bringing it up from the powerful depths of his abdomen which rose and fell in mighty spasms. This awe-inspiring performance by the king of the cowshed was for the benefit of the cows—plump, pretty and rusty red, with short, perfectly curved horns. But it was the bullocks that we valued most. Though not as magnificently impressive as Birju Dhaakar with the mountainous hump and one-track mind, they were brawny with the ready amenability, agility and stamina needed to draw carts, ploughs and levellers, all day, and in the busy seasons, day after day.

Their seniors did the threshing when the season came, going round and round the threshing pole till all the grain dropped off the stalks, a labour not without its compensations, for as they trudged hypnotically round, they caught up sly mouthfuls of forbidden grain and munched appreciatively. The cattle hand, walking behind with a stick, swore at them; and every time a bullock raised its tail, he was alert and ready to receive the soft, warm cow dung in both hands, like a gift from the gods! Precious cow dung with its endless uses: it was used as plaster in the construction of huts and granaries, and made hard floorings smooth; it was fuel for cooking; and it was the best fertilizer ever. Behind the cattle shed there were pits, waiting perennially, for the wealth contributed by a hundred cattle. At midday the merry-go-round ceased, for a break. The bullocks were untied and led to the cattle trough for a reviving drink of cool well water. They managed the lighter fieldwork too, in these, their declining years. But most of the year they had an easy time grazing in the parthi lands and gazing into space.

Parthi lands were just grassland, where uneven terrain or sandy patches thrown up by the earthquake rendered cultivation difficult and unprofitable, so it was left for the growth of thatching grass and weeds. Here, cattle and lawless goats grazed fearlessly. And the thatching grass, when full grown and golden brown, was cut and dried for use with the combination of bamboo strips in the construction of huts and enclosures.

It was such a hospitable land. Everything grew in abundance, and was freely available for the simple needs of the rural poor—twigs and dry branches for fuel, straw for bedding and cattle fodder—and any time a man's bedding was gobbled up by a ravenous cow or insatiable goat, it was the simplest matter to tear out a heap from our immense haystack.

The cattle owned a large, three-winged shed. A short one in the middle for cows and calves, a long wing on the right for cart bullocks and the other on the left for the elderly members of the herd. Birju Dhaakar could stay where he chose—a freelancer all the days of his life. There remained a clear, enclosed space in the centre, like a playground where calves frolicked madly and young bullocks rode each other in a boisterous game of make-believe that often brought the barricade down. Their keepers leaped about, like live exclamation marks, swearing at them. 'Husbands of prostitutes' they were called repeatedly, when they could never aspire to being the husbands of anything. The curtain had been brought down on their sex lives even before the show had begun. It was a dull, barren life of toil for these bovine sons of the soil, while Birju Dhaakar had all the fun.

But there were times when a white or a black calf appeared mysteriously in our herd of reds. 'Sukhesar,' Dad pointed it out, 'take a look at that thing—there. How do you account for that?'

And for a moment Sukhesar, who was responsible for the cattle, was speechless, with eye contact gone haywire. Then he recovered, cleared his throat and said, 'Huzoor, there are mysteries of nature that only God knows of.'

Dad knew too. A village calf, with or without Sukhesar's knowledge, had been substituted for one of ours, and we had become the owners of a bullock, black as coal. It was bony and stunted with forward-pointing horns and the strange intensity of madness in its eyes. The cowherds said it was possessed of a wicked spirit that slept through the dark nights. But when the moon was full, baap re baap, every man had to watch out for his fleshy parts! Luckily the scene of action was sprinkled with trees and haystacks. The pursued could even take cover under the granaries, peeping from between the stout wooden legs like caged rats, till a rescue force arrived.

Lenny had a name for it right away.

'I know what. It's Beelzebub.'

So Beelzebub it became; though the servants' tongues

twisted that into Bijlee-Bulb, which means electric bulb.

When the barricade came down each morning, it was always the first thing out, standing stock-still, switching its head from left to right, taking in the scene with smouldering eyes.

We stood watching it from Abdhi Missir's shed in the khariyan. 'Come on, Foster. Let's have some fun with it.'

'Fun?' His tongue shot through the gap in his teeth. 'Arre baba! What . . . ' But before he could finish, 'Hooooo!' we screamed at Beelzebub in a shrill togetherness, jumping up and down, flailing our thin, provocative arms in the air. It convulsed and charged!

Oh, when this animal moved, it was like a collection of loose bones in a black velvet bag, propelled by demonic force!

'Run, Parrot, the thing is coming.'

The flight home over rough country, for Parrot and Pig, was terrifying in the extreme. But we reached the nearest litchi tree and streaked up with Foster close behind as the hooves came pounding nearer and the head went crash! against the trunk, mere seconds after Foster's bottom had passed that way. The tree shook. Pig and Parrot screamed!

Bloodshot eyes were glaring up at us, while its body language proclaimed as plainly as words, 'Come down descendants of apes and see . . .'

There was shouting from all around, 'Daud-daud-re! Run run, Bijlee-Bulb is loose.'

And a wail from Kalri who appeared suddenly on the back veranda steps, holding her arms over her pounding chest.

'Hai hai Ram! These children will be the death of me!' Then with closed eyes, 'Oh what is written for us.'

A special strategy was used to have Beelzebub captured without further casualties. Our strongest pair of bullocks, known as the Chinamen pair, were rushed to the scene with their keeper Snouty taking cover behind them. We could see Snouty's spindly, brown and hairy legs moving light as feathers among the Chinamen's solid ones. As they came within arm's reach, Snouty made a sudden lunge for Beelzebub's nose-string. Swiftly the beast lunged at him, but as Snouty dodged swiftly away, it missed him and struck instead—a Chinaman! Oh! What followed was something to see! Quick as lightning both Chinamen turned upon the creature, pressing it with their massive heads to the earth. They didn't strike, they didn't trample, they simply subdued.

And Beelzebub was marched off, wedged tightly between the two, straight to the cowshed where it was given a cooling herbal drink and tied between two stakes that checked the limits of its fury.

And then came the final episode of Sukhesar. Sukhesar in the garden, just after lunch, holding a red, red rose to his nose. It's the red ones that smell the sweetest. He held it in his right hand while the account books were tucked securely under the stump of his left arm. Sniff, sniff, with his eyes closed. Too late he heard the dogs; and before he could turn his head to see what was coming up, he was on the horns of Beelzebub, moving forward at high velocity in a reclining posture, flanked by the attacking dogs, and launched into space. His dhoti flared and he landed on the sweet-pea fence, while Beelzebub and the dogs in a cloud of dust moved on to become mere sounds in the distance.

'Holy Mother of God!' Mother emerged from the house with that sure-fire remedy for blood sports—the bottle of tincture iodine.

'No! No! Missbaba!' Sukhesar backed away trembling. 'Let sahib apply it! Err . . . err, I am hurt . . . in a very bad place!'

Crime and punishment; but for his negligence in the affairs of the cattle shed, he would never have been hurt in a very bad place!

'I've had enough of this nonsense,' Mother declared. 'This animal will have to go.'

And when we pleaded with her, 'What sheer madness, children,' she exploded, pacing about angrily, drumming her fingers on her thumb. 'You call this fun? One of these days, somebody will be killed outright.'

Her mind was made up. 'Take this crazy animal anywhere,' she said to its keepers. 'I will have nothing more to do with it.'

They had a head for business. It was November, with the Sitamarhi mela in full swing. At the crack of dawn they gave Beelzebub a package beauty treatment. It consisted of a herbal sedative, followed by a bath and a brisk brush down with pads of straw. Two strings of turquoise-blue beads went around its velvety black neck, to complete the plan of deception, and it was hurried off to the Sitamarhi mela where it fetched them a tidy sum of fifty rupees.

'Not a bad bargain,' the buyer said, circling around it with a speculative, screwed-up mouth. 'Only one thing, brothers, you call it Bijlee-Bulb, but to me, it seems to lack power.'

'Power? Take it home, brother, and see how it moves!'

Which brings us to the Sitamarhi mela.

Twelve miles away from us was Sitamarhi, and six miles further down the line was Janakpur, two places of very special religious significance for Hindus. Janakpur, it was said, had been the heart of the kingdom of Raja Janak of the Ramayana, and Sitamarhi, the place where he had found the infant Sita, while on a hunting trip, like a miraculous answer to his prayers for a child. A little way north of Janakpur station, just across the Nepali border, were the remains of the bow Rama had broken to win Sita's hand in marriage. It became a place of pilgrimage for Hindus, while at the site where Sita was found in a small lake, a major fair was held every year in the month of November. It was the Sitamarhi mela. The most sensational event of the year.

Everybody turned out in their festive garb: home-dyed saris and dhotis saved for this best occasion of all. The women decked out in wavy, rainbow hues, hair washed, oiled and neatly coiled up. A smear of oil went over their faces, and a bright red tika on their foreheads, outlined in gold or silver. Heavy sets of earrings, chokers, bracelets and anklets in solid silver produced the final transformation. Though in the presence of males much of this splendour was hid by the free ends of their saris pulled modestly across their faces; while from behind cover came their famously coy, ayyiiiinnh with the serpentine wiggle so irresistible to men!

The men were not to be outdone, sporting dhotis in shades of pea green, lemon or shocking pink, with long kurtas and mulmul turbans to match. A ravishing change from their everyday dusty white garb topped by shaven heads and carelessly knotted teekies. In this glorious way, and with unbridled joy, they swept off to the mela. A multicoloured flood of humanity surging into the passenger trains to be conveyed back and forth free of charge—for who had the money to squander on tickets? When the compartments were filled to overflowing, the overflow surged upwards to the roof, settling there like a shower of festive confetti; and the train crawled away with its phenomenal load.

Frequently, someone pulled the communication cord. The labouring engine hissed and ground to a halt, screaming toot-toot, toot-toot, a signal for the guard at the rear end to release the vacuum. So the two extremities of the train were kept busy while from the middle rose a din worthy of the last day on earth. Upstairs, paan- and beediwallahs did brisk business, springing deftly from bogie to bogie, while those with bursting bladders slid down and relieved themselves on the grassy embankments. Any man trapped in the core of a compartment was set free by an urgent appeal, 'Move, brothers. Let him free—pisaab! The pee is coming!'

But finally the train reached its destination. Passengers poured out of the compartments through doors and windows, like the bursting of a dam. Rooftop travellers slid down the sides, groping about with rough, muddied toes for a foothold, often engaging a shoulder, neck or oily head below. Toes were large and splayed out, never having known the confines of boots or shoes, and muddy from the day they were born, and the men ran as though the mela was but another train to be caught.

But the mela was here to stay for fifteen rollicking days, with its bullocks, milch buffaloes, ponies, horses and camels. There were great big Jabnapari goats flipping the flies with foot-long ears, and elephants of every size that an elephant came in, some fresh from the khedda in Assam, all roped up, and little ones free for mischief with darting eyes and searching trunks. There were stalls with cauldrons of bubbling oil where halwais' assistants stripped to the waist, fried goodies, sweet and savoury, mopping up sweat and swatting at flies with their gamchas, an ever-present cloth that straddled their shoulders in readiness for any service at all. While yellow, ring-tailed pi-dogs watched, blinking—blinking away flies and hunger, hoping that time, patience and positive thinking would be finally rewarded.

Then there was the nautanki, a show for men only. Completely uncensored I would say, for we only heard whispers of what went on in there—the whispers of Kalri & Co., 'Chhee! Chhee! Dancing girls and bad, bad things!' It was completely curtained off to the curious world, while inside, they had a rip-roaring time. But when they came out, many of them had, in Dad's words, 'caught their packet'.

We had no idea what packet they had caught; and the boys simply said, 'Ask no questions, you'll be told no lies!'

At these melas, the women of Puckry sought to improve their modest fortunes. Wedging themselves into the throng, they set about their old tricks. Knowing that men kept their money tied in a knot, tucked into the waistlines of their dhotis, deft little hands aided by the general pushing and jostling, wrenched them free, snipping with penknives. Some picked up odds and ends from stalls while the keepers were busy haggling with customers. Others surrendered their virtue at mela rates, with a cool, economic reasoning: 'It does not diminish us. Other commodities we relinquish for money. But here, we get the cash, and hang on to the commodity!'

Anything could be traded in this mela. But there were painful consequences for some. Invariably after the carnival was over, we noticed a sipahi at the khariyan with his dhoti wrapped loosely around him, lungi style. And walking a wide-legged walk of groin injury.

Sylvia Dyer

'Ish!' The servants whispered with a shifty look, 'Pakad liya, garmi ka bimari! He's caught it! The disease-of-heat!'

Everybody had a cryptic comment.

Dad, looking up from his *Statesman* crossword, snorted, 'Christopher Columbus! Sure as God made little apples, he's caught his packet!'

Often, someone or the other had this 'bad disease', and was avoided like stinging nettle. No sitting on the living room carpet with the children in their laps. No games, no stories, no radio music, nothing. It was really a bad disease for them.

'You're getting too big to sit in their laps, anyway,' Reggie said, sternly.

Harry too began to be ill and went to Calcutta for expensive treatment. It was always an Austrian doctor.

'Austrians are the most isspensive,' Pig announced. 'They have spectikkles, pointy beards and ice-blue eyes.'

'Who told you that?'

'Ernie said.'

And Reggie said, 'Just remember this. When you kiss Harry, kiss him on the cheek. Not on the mouth. Do you understand me?'

'But why not?'

'Why not?' Lenny brought his face very close to mine. 'It will be the kiss of death!'

A Grave Tale

'Ghoogni?' Reggie grinned. 'But the peas! Where are the tenderest, greenest peas?'

'Come quickly, Man. Let's find the peas.' We raced him to the vegetable garden, where he showed us how to choose the tenderest green pods.

'See here,' he explained, 'they should look and feel like this. Listen, squeak squeak. Yes! Now, toss these in your mouths and see how tender and sweet they are! English! Missbaba ordered them from Sattan [Suttons].'

We picked out the green pods, rubbing them together to make them squeak, filling our pockets and the lower reaches of Man's dhoti, while Chumra walked among the upright rows, taking a nip here and there to be in tune with us. His upper lip curled in an arc as he delicately snapped open each pod to get at the tender, fat peas which he grew to like, for our sakes. As he looked up chummily at me, I caught his loose jowls, pulling the skin as far as it would stretch, and planted a loud smack on each hairy cheek: 'Chumra, you mad dog, I love you!'

He looked up at me, and his eyes said the same thing back. He had grown accustomed to my madness by now. Man stood grinning, with a dhoti-full of green peas. A choola was hurriedly constructed under the laburnum tree, with a few stray bricks, as we sat shelling them. It was all presided over by Reggie with just the right touch of winding up for us. He derived a secret delight from observing us in action. In fact he was studying us, like a pair of rare and freaky life forms under a microscope—a pleasure he hid behind a poker face.

'Oh the world's best peas! Quick quick, the mustard oil.'

The mustard oil was heated up, with a good bit of coughing and sneezing in its vicinity. And then, after its fierce pungency was spent in the air, dried red chillies were tossed in, followed by chopped onions and the succulent green peas, stirred vigorously while eyes and mouths watered and the peas popped in the pan and flew about.

'Can we stir too?'

'Here, take the spoon, but no stopping.'

We sat eating the ghoogni with bread that Foster brought, hot from the oven, while Horsey looked on with a frown that seemed to say, 'What is this green nonsense?' We gave him a spoonful to clear up his doubts. He thought it was OK even for dogs!

The sun was setting and the cacophony of the evening bazaar came pleasantly muffled, over the air.

It was time for the birds and animals to come home. And here was Ramgolam, the syce, walking the horses back to the stables, with Queenie, a beautiful snow-white mare, in the lead.

'Just look at her!' Reggie cried. 'Ay Ramgolam, did you ever see a whiter horse?'

He was an old man, and the eyes in his wrinkled face narrowed as his thoughts moved slowly back to the distant past.

'Oh yes.' He sighed. 'I remember it well, Suno Starram. Its whiteness was dazzling, like the snow peaks in the Himalaya when they catch the sun. And, oh baba, how it could run! Only Tom sahib could control that horse. It was his horse.'

'I've heard about this,' Reggie said. 'It was called Snow Storm.'

We stared at him. 'Ramgolam saw this horse?'

'You bet he did, though he was just a young boy then. He was there when Tom was murdered.'

'Oh my gosh—the murder! You promised to tell us! You . . .'

Reggie backed away, hands up, to ward off the physical assault that was coming.

'OK then, Parrot,' he said laughing. 'If you must hear that, then shut up, stop fidgeting and close your eyes so, maybe, you can see it all happening just like it did.'

Reggie was a born storyteller. The way his eyes grew wide, or narrowed into mere slits, his voice exploding in your face or pitched low and spooky, gruff or sweet as candyfloss, and the way he paused for effect—he could have you partying in Fairyland, or dangling from a precipice by a pyjama string.

There were sounds of a pig and a parrot merging into a knot with the dogs, as Reggie continued: 'That night, Tom had dinner with the Old Man, our great-grandfather, in the big old house. He didn't live here; he had his own place at Amooha Dine Kothi, about four miles away, at Majorgunj. Ghogra had grilled some cotton teal with . . .'

'But Ghogra was not there then!' we shouted together.

'Well . . . whoever was, had made grilled . . .'

'Maybe his father . . .'

'Now, if you kids want to hear this story, shut your traps and keep them shut. OK?'

'OK.'

'Well . . . dinner finished late, very late, for there were always matters to discuss, and arguments. They didn't hit it off together. But the Old Man had to put up with him. You see, he was the black sheep of the family and had left England under a cloud.'

Our great-granduncle had been a black sheep under a cloud!

'What cloud?'

'Now, that's another story. It seems he got into serious trouble in Harrow, where he was schooling. He lost his temper and biffed a master—knocked him out cold! It was a terrible thing that had a more terrible punishment—a public flogging and expulsion.'

'O my God! What's expulsion?'

'Parrot, it means being thrown out in disgrace, and that, after the public flogging. Think of it! So to save him, that night up in the dormitory, the boys tied their bedsheets together and made a long rope for him to slip down it and escape.'

'Poor thing! And he escaped straight to India?'

'Yes . . . well now, to continue with our first story. Tom got on to his horse and rode away. This same white-as-snow animal we were talking about. What was it called?'

'Snow Storm.' The answer was croaked out.

'Right. And so, they all went to sleep. It was a moonlit night, but nearly over, for it must have been about three o'clock in the morning. The moon was pale. Do you know why?

'The moon had spent its silver

In the hours of the night

And when it realized the fact

It just went pale with fright!'

He stopped to ask, 'How d'you like my poem?'

Horsey yawned loudly and Pig and Parrot said, 'Just tell the story, now! So . . . so then?'

Sylvia Dyer

'There were dark shadows everywhere, and trees were jet-black shapes against the sky,' Reggie continued, watching our faces, 'and then the sound of hooves—terrified hooves—coming nearer and nearer, and out of the blackness came a misty white horse.'

There was more snuffling in the audience and wriggling closer together. 'Ghosts are misty!'

'But this was no ghost! Ramgolam awoke with a start as it broke into the stables. "Baap re baap!" he cried out. "It is Tom sahib's horse, soaking wet, like it fell in the river! Something bad . . . something horrible has happened." He was shouting loud enough to burst people's eardrums. Everyone jumped up, running around in a flurry.

'"Quick!" the Old Man shouted, "saddle the horses. Bring as many men and lanterns as you can find. We'll go at once to search!"

'They all set out along the route Tom must have taken. Three miles away, a jheel skirted the road.

'"Here . . . this is where we must look," the Old Man said, and his face was as pale as the moon. They waded into the water with their lanterns held high, searching, searching everywhere, and just as dawn was breaking and the wild geese began to fly over, honking loudly, Tom's body was dragged from the weeds!'

'O Mother Mary!'

'Yes, Mother Mary! But it was worse than you think. He hadn't got drowned, but come to a violent end. Both his arms had been chopped off. They said it was an act of vengeance.'

'Now, what's vengeance?'

'Revenge. You see, Tom had many enemies. His body was brought back and buried here in the graveyard. The Old Man wept for him. "This won't go unpunished," he swore, for in spite of all their bitter differences, Tom was his own brother. But who was to be punished? The police came with their dandas, to beat out the truth, but not a man would open his mouth. And there was no way they could have got it from the horse's mouth! So it just grew older and older, and died with its terrible secret.' Reggie finished with a sigh. 'So, how do you like that?'

We had nothing to say, for once. The ghoogni had grown cold, and Chumra had polished off the bread.

Seasons with Reasons

The sugar cane fields produced well for two successive years after which the crop was exhausted. The ploughboys took the ploughs on their shoulders, driving their bullocks before them, and off they went to the dry, bare fields. Most times the bullocks went placidly, their heads swinging left and right, but there were days when something in the air made them buck and prance. The ploughboys needed to buck and prance too, to keep pace with them, but with the weight of the ploughs on their shoulders all they could do was swear at these 'husbands of prostitutes'.

The stumps of the previous crop were uprooted as the ploughs dug deep into the earth, going back and forth, churning up big clods. Little boys ran briskly about in the dust, picking up the knotty stumps. They beat out the clinging earth with gusto and collected them in heaps to be burnt. It was positively the end of one crop and time for a changeover.

The next step was the leveller: a heavy, wooden bar on which the ploughboys stood while bullocks pulled. They moved over the rough, ploughed fields having a wobbly joyride, as the clods were crushed beneath, and the field was finally levelled out, light, smooth and receptive for the broadcasting of seed, and the first showers.

Year after year showers came to bless this land, without fail. There were songs, poems and even jingles about weather patterns, so farmers wouldn't be caught on the wrong foot.

Summer was coming in.

It came into the khariyan, sweet and sensuous. The scent of lemon blossoms suffused the air and crept into the wide-open mouths of the empty behris. It was one of those rare evenings when the jackals and pi-dogs were giving their throats a well-deserved rest.

Abdhi Missir, guided by a cheap oil lamp, dragged out his wooden charpoy from the khariyan shed, and sat on it, looking up at the brilliant, uncountable stars. On a night like this he could have no doubts about the supernatural beings he believed in with the unclouded faith of a child. Tomorrow would bring the feast of the Devi and he would perform the puja with his peculiar frowning smile. He took a deep, deep breath of ethereal air and breathed out slowly, eyes softly closed, saying to all, 'I'm so happy! How good to be alive! To have all this—to be a part of all this! The imponderable wonder of it all!'

A frog sprang over his foot. He felt its gross and clumsy intrusion in a moment of spiritual bliss. Yet he didn't kick it away in sharp irritation, like the rest of the men would have done. He just gave it a smiling frown—with him it was either a smiling frown or a frowning smile, you couldn't have one without the other—and sipped some water from his shiny brass lota. 'Hawa-pani'—air and water—those two vital and priceless elements, that was all he was having for supper, free for every living thing.

Then, slipping off his wooden khadaun, he stretched out on the wood bed, covering himself with a coarse cotton sheet. He pulled it tautly over his frame, tucking it under head and feet. It was his insulation from the night's mosquitoes and other forms of indigenous mischief. The big stomach straining against the sheet was soon moving smoothly up and down like a slowly respiring hill. Alive, well, and sound asleep.

But not for long.

Soft wake-up fingers were drumming on the doors of his consciousness. He saw the glow, even through the sheet, and sat up quickly, rubbing his eyes and blinking at what they showed him. A woman carved out of the darkness by the glow of an oil lamp that she held in her hand. All that she wore was a silver hasli around her long, smooth neck, and massive silver earrings that dragged down the ear lobes with their weight. Her long, black hair hung free over the supple, gleaming, sensuous body. For a man like Abdhi Missir it was an overpowering sight.

What was this? A temple idol, come to life? Could such a thing happen? The conviction grew on him as she began to dance in the style of a goddess he recognized. And he threw himself on the ground at her feet.

'Devi Maharani!' his voice came out like the croak of a stricken frog. 'Your worship comes on the day of your feast! Why have you honoured me so? Is there anything that you wish of me? You have but to command.' And with head bowed low, his ears strained to hear the commands.

They came in a husky voice. 'There is a woman, Jokhni Paswan of Puckry village. You know of her?'

'Ji Maharani!' he gasped, never daring to raise his eyes. 'Ji haan.'

'It is written in your account book that she owes the kothi five maunds and thirty seers of grain. That is a very serious mistake! Totally wrong and you will cause her name to vanish from the list!'

He bowed even lower. 'I am your slave, Maharani ji. It shall be done as you desire.' His head struck the earth, and remained in that punishing posture, quivering from the shock of this hair-raising brush with the supernatural combined with the pressure on his abdomen.

For a minute the light danced wickedly on his polished head with its big beads of sweat, and then it was all darkness.

The discrepancy was noticed shortly after, when his accounts did not tally with Dada's. Then came bewilderment and a sense of betrayal for Abdhi Missir with this absence of any back-up divine intervention! With a smileless frown, he told Dada about his supernatural experience.

Dada's pale-blue eyes gave him a long, hard stare. 'Supernatural! Are you telling me, Abdhi Missir, that you didn't see in this "Devi" a resemblance to this same Jokhni Paswan whose name had to vanish from the list?'

'Sahib . . . ' Blinking back embarrassed tears: 'What can I say, but that I'm such a simple fool to be caught in this trap! I didn't dare to look at her face, or I would have seen the witch of Puckry village. Only now I . . . er . . . er . . .'

Dada smiled. 'Well, for this once we'll comply with her wishes, but next time—she'll have to dance for me!'

Summer moved forward, and warm March winds began to blow all day, with a bit of grit for the eyes. And the leaves danced. Every day they danced, their lacquered faces shining in the sunlight. And in batches they dropped, and died. It was like autumn after winter! But that is how our seasons were.

And now, Kalri the perennial gossip sat at Mother's feet pouring out ills she felt Mother should know about. This time, it was about Sukhesar's son and his notorious love affair with Foster's daughter. She was in acute distress over the matter.

'What can I tell you, Missbaba,' adjusting the sari over her dried-prune head, 'it has gone too far! Such a shameless affair! Ay hay! He struts into the village like a laat sahib, twirling his moustache. And right before everybody's eyes, he sweeps her up in his arms like a child! Chhee! Chhee! Little, little love bites on the neck and he runs into the hut with her! So brazen, Missbaba! They're not even afraid any more, toba, toba!'

She went outside to spit.

'And Mothi, her husband, what does he do?'

'What can he do, Missbaba, against Sukhesar's son, a Brahmin! He sits outside the village with his head buried in his arms. Maybe he weeps. Ay Bhagwan!' She looked up at the ceiling with her one good eye. 'A wicked, wicked world, Missbaba!' And then, with a woeful sigh she concluded,

'Oh how different it would be if all people were like me!'

And the days grew warmer. Gone was the glorious winter. Off and out of sight went winter woollies. Now, it was sandals and flowery, organdie dresses, 4711 Eau de Cologne and Yardley's Lavender to sprinkle liberally, fragrant bel sherbet and lemon juice, with ice going tinkle-tinkle in tall glasses.

And like spring, new leaves appeared, and flowering trees were covered over with blossoms. You couldn't see the trees for flowers—flowers in the passionate colours of Indian summer. It was sensational. Many birds went mad with passion and sang themselves into a stupor, what with the heat and the perfumed air. The coppersmith, crow pheasant and koel contributed hysterically to the performance, but the Grammy Awards every year would surely have gone to the brainfever bird.

'Sukhesar,' Mother said on one of these heady days, 'you must do something about your son. You know, of course, what I'm referring to. It could lead to a grave situation.'

Sukhesar went home in the heat of the afternoon, to confront his son.

He found him sprawled out on a charpoy, dreaming. The little courtyard was fragrant with jasmine bushes sprinkled over with starry white flowers. A goat stood on its hind legs tearing mercilessly at a pumpkin creeper on the bamboo fence, its black pills scattered carelessly about.

Shorty sat up abruptly, staring at his father. Suddenly he was in a black rage. His face twisted into an ugly thing with a quivering moustache.

'Who's talking now!' he screamed. 'My affair, a disgrace? And what about *you*. Hanh? What about the countless affairs *you* have had? You were not even choosy about your women!'

Sukhesar cleared his throat and spat out his anger at the goat.

'You should know everybody is talking. Your wife, poor woman, is neglected and humiliated. Today, even Missbaba spoke to me of this matter. Nothing but ill can come from this attachment I tell you. It is madness. Listen to me only this

Sylvia Dyer

once. End it. Oh my son, I have . . . ay Bhagwan, such a sense of foreboding!'

'Foreboding? Enough! I have heard enough.' Shorty jumped up, his finger stabbing the space between them, like a sword, and there was a black fire flashing in his eyes, 'Leave me alone—and mind your own affairs. This is my life and my affair!' But the shouting rang through Puckry village and became everybody's affair.

And the summer grew fiercer. Its fierce heat was a great purge of the stored-up fats of heavenly winter, and the smugness. Now all the impurities were drained out in a purgatory of sweat. But this purgatory had its sweet compensations. Fat green litchis appeared on the rows of squat litchi trees. Contractors arrived to make a bid for them, in time to foil the flying foxes and summer birds, for soon they would be cherry red and bursting ripe, so when you peeled off the crisp goose-pimpled skin and bit into the firm, sweet white flesh with the faintest scent of roses, the juice squirted out and ran down your chin and forearms. There were no litchis, those days, as in our district of Muzaffarpur.

But this fruit of the gods was, for us, the forbidden fruit in our Garden of Eden, ever since Lenny at the age of six had gorged himself sick on litchis, and began to turn green and vomit in a most terrifying way. With no medical facilities within reach, the experience had given Mother a severe shaking up, for the litchi season was also the dreaded cholera season.

During those days a vile-natured bird cried wickedly from the heavy, laden trees, with a catch in its throat: *chal ghat par*—come along to the burning ghats! That was enough to give anybody the jitters, and it was rated the most unpopular bird of all time.

So litchis were enjoyed only in secrecy after lunch, while the elders lay flat out in bed, under fitfully swishing punkhas. For the heat those afternoons was so stupefying that every self-respecting person removed himself completely from the public eye.

A punkha was a heavy cotton frill attached to a wooden bar suspended from the ceiling. A connected rope passing through a metal pipe in the wall went out to the punkha coolie in the veranda, who sat cross-legged, pulling the punkha back and forth, stirring up the slack air with a vigorous swish-swish. But often in the oppressive heat he slid into a horizontal position, while the rope was switched from lusty hands to listless big toes. The punkha movements grew erratic and gradually ceased. Then angry shouts cracked out from inside the room, '*Aaa! Kheencho, gadha!*' (Pull, donkey!) And when this had been repeated to no effect, a sharp tug on the fan rope jerked the big toe at the other end. It produced an immediate response of 'Aiieeenh!' and the fan began to swish again.

Dada lay stretched out in bed. His room was simply furnished with a few essential pieces of furniture. In one corner stood a revolving bookstand that once held Shakespeare and other classics that had survived the earthquake but succumbed later to Dada's preference for popular thrillers. During our absences from home, when he remained in charge, he had traded them with the travelling book man for masses of hair-raising stuff like *The Corpse That Screamed* and *The Un-nailed Coffin* that now filled the shelves conveniently at hand for Dada the bookworm, chain-whistler and chain-smoker.

It was quiet, but for the frenzied shrieks of the brainfever bird, an utterly tireless thing. Other things too, were tireless. In the veranda, a squadron of tireless flies swarmed down on the nodding punkha coolie. While inside, Jackie dozed fitfully under Dada's bed, with his tireless ticks.

Dada was propped up in bed, rolling cigarettes. He liked the do-it-yourself kind. Drawing out the papers one by one, he laid a portion of tobacco in each, rolled it carefully, licked the edges, sealed them up and laid them out in a row, ready for a nice, long chain-smoke. He lit one and dragged heavily on it, eyelids growing heavier and heavier. 'Ah! How a cigarette fills in the gaping mouth of time!'

His pillow was sticky with sweat. He realized the fan had stopped, and shouted, '*Dammit saala ulloo, kheencho!*' (Pull! you brother-in-law of an owl!) The fan began to stir fitfully.

A few more puffs, and he was asleep with the glowing cigarette butt in his fingers, while the brainfever bird shrieked, 'Brrrain feever! Brrrain feever!'

The punkha coolie too fell asleep, one pencil-thin leg in the air with the fan rope slack on his big toe. He woke with a yell as Jackie's teeth fastened on his ankle. At once he saw the smoke and began to howl, '*Baaboo ho baaboo! Buddha sahib ko aag lag gaya!*' (Father oh father! The old master has caught fire!) Clouds of smoke were billowing out of Dada's room.

Everyone was up and moving. The sweepers shot like arrows from their huts beyond the vegetable garden, while other punkha coolies converged on the scene, hurrying along with buckets of water, vanishing into the smoke, and out again, coughing, choking, and away to the water pump for more.

'Move, babalog, we beg you. Stand out of our way.'

Pig and Parrot jumped out of their way, the undigested litchis in our stomachs smouldering, as we pictured the final outcome. We had seen burning wood turn to charcoal when they threw water on it. Dada would look like one of those long, black logs—burnt through and through—and of course, he would be . . . No! Close your eyes . . . And when you open them again . . . everything will be all right!

Then all of a sudden the thuk-thuk of a walking stick broke through our communion with the upper world. A thuk-thuk wildly accelerated, and Dada shot out from the bathroom doorway—alive and flaming red, though untouched by flame.

'Dada, Dada!' we screamed together. 'You're alive!'

'Yes, yes, children, dammit all, I'm alive!' he called back, as he fled.

After this fiery episode, he switched from cigarettes to cigars. He enjoyed the rich, strong aroma, and puffing little clouds of smoke into Jackie's face. Jackie would jerk his head from side to side in distaste, drawing back his lips to reveal disapproving fangs, yet wagging his stumpy little tail in a placatory gesture as he disappeared under the chair.

Mother lived her own busy life. Every morning there was a curious gathering of people outside the front veranda. She sat in an armchair and they came forward singly with whatever business had brought them. It was, in a casual way, like holding court. There were complaints against one another and appeals for help in diverse matters.

A sipahi who stood by called out, 'Come forward and air your problems.'

The 'airing' went something like this:

'Doohai sarkar! Mercy Lord! We are two brothers living alone, together. Last night our hut burnt down by the displeasure of the Gods. But, by the grace of your footwear [aap ka jootha ka akwaal se] it will be raised again. Grant us only some wood, bamboos and thatching grass.'

Next, 'Huzoor, we have brought you this rare, speaking parrot from Nepal. And [putting his finger nervously into the cage] swear to God it will not bite your honour!'

Then there were people who had been injured by sharp instruments or bitten by creatures other than speaking parrots, on whom tincture iodine was applied unsparingly. 'Isss! Isss!' they hissed like iguanas, as the fiery stuff was dabbed on, but never did a single injury get septic.

A couple of heavyweight, cauliflower-eared men came lurching forward in a rather disturbing way. 'Huzoor, we are wandering wrestlers who have come to know that you patronize this great sport of ours! Let us show you . . . ' they broke off with a startled, 'Ayyyyn?'

For before they could show anything, shouts of alarm were ringing out from the direction of the rockery, 'Thakkara! Thakkara! Bhaag re hay!' And the whole assembly vanished into thin air, like ghosts who have finished their business. For even those who had come here with parrots, with bites, with the urgent need to build a hut or wrestle with each other, knew—and moved like forked lightning to save their skins.

It was the hit-bird.

The thakkara, a species of honey hawk, had its own rascally performance for keeping things lively in our world. This fierce and swift-winged bird swooped down at a beehive, and tearing off a chunk, fled with its loot and a trail of angry bees in pursuit, to wherever a group of humans was gathered in close communion, skimming low over their heads to divert the terrible purpose of the bees from thieving bird to blameless man! People knew all about this downright dirty trick, and a timely alarm of 'thakkara, thakkara!' shrilled out like an air-raid siren when it was sighted.

Our followers turned turtle with glee, spindly limbs moving in the air like egg whisks.

'The best way to save your skin from the bees is water!' they advised us. 'Just jump in, and stay down!'

And the best way to disperse a crowd in Dhang was to shout 'Thakkara!'

On summer evenings we sat out on a small cemented square in the garden. A couple of Musahars stood fanning us with large palm-leaf fans, handles resting on the ground as they were swung from left to right.

Harry had come over to visit us. His visits were quite regular.

Ghogra appeared all dressed up, with drinks on a silver tray. He loved dressing up when guests arrived, admiring himself in every mirror he passed, always in a fresh white uniform and turban with a crest—Harry's or ours! He engaged our family dhobi, and probably got better service out of him.

Harry looked him over with a crusty smile. 'So, Gladys, I see he is back with you . . . Big mouth . . . has his nose in everything. Let us see how long he lasts!'

Ghogra just gritted his teeth and looked down at the tray.

They sat chatting together. They sipped their drinks and discussed politics and domestic problems. Harry loved politics and other people's problems that could be turned to his financial or political advantage. There were always veiled allusions, as to 'who had to be watched', and, 'it will all come out one of these days' to give Mother the jitters. But if she wanted to give it back to him, she simply had to ask, 'By the way, Harry, what news of Dorothy?'

His expression changed.

'Oh don't ask me, Gladys! Divorce, divorce! Now there's going to be a divorce. This flame and that flame, here, there, everywhere! A count in Paris, she doesn't know where to stop. And Louis, poor husband. Such a fine-looking man! A gentleman to his fingertips. And tell me, whose idea was it? Sixteen years old and running away to marry him. Marriage or death on the railway track! Stupid girl! She made such fools of us at the railway station, dodging and dancing about like clowns, to stop her from getting near that train. Such a public spectacle. I tell you, Gladys! Sukhesar got a clout on the head with her handbag.'

Harry flushed darkly at the recollection. His eyes went glassy. 'She had her way. Education went up the spout. Always her own way, that girl!' He began to drone, 'And now, all we hear is divorce, divorce! And Frank Anthony's fees.' Then, pulling himself together, he looked at Dad who had been suppressing a smile all this time.

'By the way, Tip, she writes to say you were at the Samastipur club last month. We thought you had gone for a Bihar Light Horse meeting in Muzaffarpur?'

Dad turned flaming red in the face, shouted at the punkha coolie to 'step it up'. There was an awkward, heavy, loaded silence.

A week earlier the dhobi had pulled out a letter from Dad's trouser pocket and handed it to Mother. It was in a lady's handwriting. We were told to 'Run away and play', and a row began behind locked doors in the bedroom. *Run away and play?* At a time like this? We hung miserably about the house till there was silence. Then we crept back. The door connecting with the dining room was left ajar and we trickled in, our hearts in our mouths. Dad's brown suitcase was on the bed, and he was packing to go away. His face was flushed, and tears fell like drops of slow rain on the clothes. We were filled with horror. A shattered Parrot and Pig stood silently by the bed and our tears too began to fall like raindrops. Then Chatter Cat appeared out of nowhere; he clung tight to his father's trousers and set up a howl.

Mother came in and took in the scene. Her eyes were very red. They looked at each other—these two who had quarrelled—over our heads. Then Mother's eyes came down to us.

She smiled sadly. 'Run along, my darlings, it's going to be all right.'

The summers were full of mischief. Aside from snakes, there were tropical diseases, floods and fires, dacoits, evil spirits, wild beasts and mad dogs. Our dogs and house servants provided a buffer against the visits of mad dogs that came along, or else they could have burst in during meals, and bitten our legs under the table. As things stood, a timely alarm catapulted us to safety on chairs and tabletops, while Dad made a run for his .12 bore and emptied both barrels into the rabid creature, before it could conclude its business.

We slept out during those hottest nights of summer, heedless of dacoits who were now letting us rest in peace. It had not always been this way, and we surely owed this change of heart to Abhinandan. All we had to watch out for now, while emerging from the mosquito net to grope about with naked feet for slippers, was that they didn't come down on a poisonous snake. Some dogs curled up under our beds, while the more spirited ones padded about sniffing and giving a hind-leg salute to every passing bush.

The nightwatchmen formed a cordon around us, stretching out on the grass with their lathis alongside like bodies felled on a battlefield. Safe as babies in cradles, we lay gazing through the mosquito nets at the countless glittering stars, while the crickets chirred us to sleep.

But Dada felt differently, and had his bed placed on the veranda, sacrificing the benefits of the cool westerly breeze for the preferred advantages of peace and security.

Peace and security.

And then, in the middle of the night, sipahis were shouting, 'Pagal kutta! Pagal kutta! A mad dog!' Dad tore out of his mosquito net. 'The gun, damn it all, the gun!'

'Terence! Oh be careful!'

'Yes, yes! Cripes where's that bloody torch? Now, you kids, stay where you are. The torch, blast its guts!' followed by a crash and 'O Christ Almighty!'

And, where was the mad dog?

The night buzzed with people walking 'on pins', lanterns held high over their heads, scanning the pitch-black scene for a mad dog; while our own dogs streaking back and forth going kwee-kwee and pant-pant-pant directed the search past beds and bushes, to the veranda. And up there, as lanterns converged to form footlights, it assumed the appearance of a stage with Dada stretched out in bed, bare to the waist in purple striped pyjamas rolled up to the knees. He was muttering like an old pirate in a drunken stupor, and his right arm hung over the edge of the bed with fingers fluttering a few inches from the mad dog's ear: 'Notty li'le doggy . . . yew . . . noyee li'le doyee!'

The torch beam focused on Irish hand and rabid-canine head. Tricky with a .12 bore. Too bloody close. Could you hit one and yet miss the other?

Dad paused, gauging the spread of shot No. 1 for wild geese, and such large birds. Every winter he went to the Terai for a tiger shoot; and every winter (though he could shoot straighter than most people) he missed his target. 'Christopher Columbus, what rotten luck! In that split second it turned its blasted head! But I could swear I grazed the temple!'

Then he heard the voices of the sipahis, 'Shoot, sahib, shoot!' they yelled together.

And bang went the gun.

Dada shot upright in bed, wide awake and yelling, 'Dacoits, dammit all, dacoits!'

Sylvia Dyer

While below him, the mad dog lay in a pool of blood, released forever from the sorrows of this life.

And the saddest thing might have been that it wasn't really mad. Was it?

There was no telling in the circumstances.

Still, the matter was ended.

But the matter was not ended.

A series of rifle shots came cracking out from the direction of Harry's house, and at the same time a roar of voices from Harpur village, with the thump-thump of heavy feet coming to our aid, in the familiar pattern of a bygone New Year's Eve.

'Now, what in blazes . . . ?'

'Hold on! Hold on! I'm coming! Coming!' It was the voice of Ernie. And 'Bang! Bang!' the voice of his gun. We saw his figure set in a pool of light, tearing down the centre road with Ghogra (responsible for the pool of light) stumbling along at his heels with a Petromax lamp.

The dim night-scene filled up with a score of dark, hefty figures and the smell of tobacco and mustard oil invaded the air. Ernie in khaki shorts stood panting before us; the gun against his chest was pointed up at the sky. 'My God!' he gasped. 'We heard your shots! Where, where are they?'

'They . . . who? What the dickens are you talking about?'

The Petromax lamp sent out a hiss and a fiery signal. Ghogra quickly put it down and pumped it with vigour. The scene lit up brilliantly to expose us in 'airy-fairy' nightclothes.

'Who?' Ernie panted out. 'The dacoits of course! We heard your shots. I grabbed my gun and ran like the dev—' He stopped short, puzzled, seeing our strange looks.

'God's truth,' Dad's mouth curled in a crooked smile, 'it was only . . . a mad dog.'

Ernie flopped down on the veranda steps, holding his sides. He threw back his head and laughed till tears rolled down his cheeks. Then we were all doubled up and roaring with laughter, while the dogs barked and jumped at us, irritably, because they never understood the joke.

The last days of April were dry and oppressively warm, with the fields singed and stripped of crops. The cattle toiled all day pulling ploughs for the planting of new cane. Some days, a hot wind blew straight from the devil in the west, carrying sand from the river. The earth was irritable and looking for trouble. Waiting for a chance. Then came an outbreak of fire in one village or another, and grimly against the horizon you could see the angry scarlet glow, and hear the frenzied cries of a whole stricken village.

It was on one of these troubled evenings, while walking in the garden, that the six o'clock train was heard tooting persistently. It just went on and on. Dad, who was scowling at what the hot winds had done to his rose bushes, said, 'Sounds like the bloody whistle is stuck.'

'No, Terence, something is wrong.' For now the sound of voices from the direction of the level crossing had risen to the pitch of a full-fledged bazaar.

'You're dead right, girlie. Sure as God made little apples, something's happened.' People were running towards the station, more and more people, excited and chattering, while snatches of information were relayed back.

'An accident . . .'

'It's the train! The train!'

'A man, baap re, cut up by the six o'clock train!'

'Sukhesar!' Dad spotted him standing on the veranda steps, waiting for Dada with his account books. 'Hurry along and see what exactly has happened there.'

It was some time before Sukhesar returned; his eyes strangely dull. 'Sahib,' he cleared his throat, with effort, 'a man threw himself before the train. The body was in pieces but it has been identified as,' he swallowed hard and finished in a hoarse, unsteady voice, 'as Mothi.' (The husband of Foster's daughter.)

Mother waited for him to leave. 'So, it has happened! I fear now, there will be consequences.'

The next morning brought the sub-inspector of police, who was called the daroga.

'Hanh, plain and simple case it is of suicide,' he declared, collapsing into Mother's favourite chair in the living room. But though he had collapsed, his starched khaki shorts stayed obstinately up to form twin tunnels. Some who had switched from dhotis, in which private body parts were nicely concealed in folds, failed to see the need for underpants when wearing shorts, or that there was a guarded way of sitting. The daroga was one of these carefree people. And with a habit that shocked even the servants. When he cracked a joke (which he did, to switch the subject from dark to brighter) he roared with laughter, while his hand streaked up his shorts to stir the 'Lions Couchant' in the dim interior!

Mother stood up, looking like she'd been hit on the head by a tennis ball—and left the room. Dad remained to hear him out with a straight face, while Parrot and Pig were dispatched, with a gruff 'Now, run along you two, and play. Have you finished your sums?' And we ran.

Everyone was touched in different ways by the tragedy. The old women of the village spat and pursed their lips, saying that God's wrath would now come down on the shameless lovemakers. But the affair of Shorty and Foster's daughter just went brazenly on. No amount of cold shoulders or dirty looks could dampen its flame. In fact, the removal of Mothi's sullen face from their world was like the clearing of a long-overcast sky.

As summer moved on, mangoes grew bigger and fatter on the trees, hanging delightfully on long, green stems. Contractors returned to bid for the mango orchards but the best trees were reserved for us. A long pole with a hook at the end dislodged the mangoes while servants waiting below caught them up in a tautly spread-out sheet. More and more glorious mangoes thumped down to be carried home and arranged carefully in packing cases, to ripen in the pantry between layers of chaff. Soon, trays full of ripe langras with pale green skins and dimpled chins filled the house with the most tantalizing scent. They appeared on the dining table, to be eaten decently—or carried off to bathtubs where we fell upon them like cavemen, ripping off the skin and biting deep into the firm, sweet, golden flesh. The juice squirted down our throats and dripped on the red cement floor. And for the big, black ants that hung around, it was like the gold rush.

There were many varieties that kept up the feasting, from early May till the end of August.

Our local philosopher, friend and man-of-medicine, Rauthinand Jha, said you could indulge yourself freely—and any resulting riots in the stomach would be quelled with a few sips of milk!

The Monsoon

The days grew progressively hotter as they shifted into June. Masses of grey clouds began to move across the sky, with their message of deliverance. And all at once the monsoon arrived in a tearing hurry with a raging wind driving the dust before it. Cattle came charging home through the blinding dust, lowing and stamping and pounding at the bamboo fence. Cowherds worked frantically at the barrier, teekies and loincloths blowing erect. Trees bent back, their branches streaming like wild hair, dancing a desperate dance with the wind, a dance in which the weak and the frail fell never to rise again. Crack and crash they went, while the wind whistled wickedly, lashing the earth as it tore along. Crack and crash went the thunder, and flashes of lightning, for brief seconds, flooded the scene in an eerie yellow-grey light. Then, suddenly the rain fell in mighty drops, pinning the dust back to earth. Dust to dust. The wind dropped and the rain came down as if the sluice gates of heaven had burst open, and you could smell the parched earth's cool, fragrant bath.

For days it poured, and poured. The ice melted up in the mountains to swell the rivers and the floods came in leaping, rolling sheets, spreading out across the hungry land with glorious silt.

There followed monsoon days when the world was glassy green. Paddy seedlings in the waterlogged fields where they had been transplanted in even rows, six inches apart, stood in still water, no longer churned and muddy but calm and lucid, reflecting white puffs of cloud sailing across a silky blue sky. Clouds were always on the move. The wind meant business up there; whipping the clouds into diverse shapes, it drove them relentlessly across the sky from horizon to horizon till the sun went down. Then they seemed to stop transfixed, in a tableau of immense fairy-tale figures to wish the day goodbye.

It was the end of a grand performance and a perfect day.

The night fell glumly. Thick grey clouds spread across the sky, and it began to rain without stop. The orchestra of monsoon creatures struck up in the paddy fields. Miles and miles of bullfrogs with their voices raised to the rain gods in a great rasping symphony of 'ghonnnh-ghaaahn'. Nearer home, a mixed insect band strained to compete with the bullfrogs. There were insect violins, flutes and sitars, and a choral group that swelled out in harmony if not melody, with sudden impromptu solos by more spirited members, talent being no criterion for the airing of voices. Mosquitoes had their clear, nasal sopranos and sang lustily if anything did, for it was bloodlust. Every mite had a voice to air in the night, some sentiment to express, undampened by dampness like everything else those days.

But a different kind of performance had been played out that day, at Harry's place.

Harry was at his writing desk leafing through a formidable file. He drew out a small slip of paper: 'Abdhi Missir, do you recognize this thing?'

Abdhi Missir adjusted the spectacles on his big, brown nose and peered at the document.

'It is a thumb impression, sahib.'

'Exactly. And it is yours.' Harry put his finger on a figure: 'Five maunds of paddy.'

'But huzoor, this was years before the earthquake! In the time of the senior memsahib.'

Harry laughed softly. 'Your memory is poor. Who do you think was in charge those days? You took it from me. Me! You see before you the note, which now with the interest compounded comes to a considerable sum.'

As Harry spoke, big beads of sweat sprang up on Abdhi Missir's forehead and his dark face turned a sickly grey. 'Sahib,' he said, 'I am a poor man.' His voice broke and he began to breathe heavily. Harry had been studying him closely. 'Well, we can remedy that, you know . . . if you are sensible.'

'Sensible?'

'Yes, sensible.' Harry stared up at the ceiling. 'You have access to Missbaba's documents. There's a certain document I require, very useful to me—worthless to her. It won't be missed for some time. In any case she'll never suspect you.'

Abdhi Missir's great paunch heaved. 'What are you asking me to do, sahib—betray Missbaba? Never! Never could I do such a thing!'

'Yes, of course . . . Never could you do such a thing.' Harry's expression changed. 'You are a fool, Abdhi Missir, and fools suffer the consequences of their choices. Fools are born to suffer!'

There followed days and nights of monotonous rain.

'Dear Lord,' Mother said, sighing heavily, 'if it goes on like this we'll have a really big flood, a disastrous one!'

And the Baghmati swelled angrily over its banks and spilt out over the land.

The four-foot-high bund that enclosed our compound, fortified with shisham and teak trees, to keep out the waters of major floods, was breached as this almighty flood came spewing out of the Baghmati. The unchecked waters surged into the compound, and that was the end of our beautiful garden. Man & Co. sat on the front steps, staring stonily at the cruel wash-away. Trees and shrubs were visible only above two feet of water. Of the shorter ones, there was no trace at all.

One step at a time the water rose, till it reached the veranda's edge (three feet above ground level) and we were completely marooned. The house seemed afloat like Noah's Ark; and a variety of rare species, mistaking it for such, made a beeline for this refuge in the waters of doom, only to be received into the front or back verandas with a clout on the head, for this ark had problems enough.

We had clapped our hands and jumped with glee when the floodwaters first surged in, wading up to our knees, splashing each other and pushing reluctant dogs off the steps. But with night coming on, the mood changed. Reggie and Lenny, far away in boarding school, were not here to make light of the encompassing darkness. Vague fears began to creep upon us, and the smell of rot, decay and wet dogs drove us into Mother and Dad's bedroom, where we faced cigarette smoke.

We sat crossed-legged on the enormous old beds, raised high on their lion-pawed legs, and said the rosary together. It came out like the monotonous chant of monks, backed up by the bullfrogs' awe-inspiring blasts. And after every decade, a lizard from some dark corner of the ceiling churned out a satirical tch-tch-tchuk.

Kalri on a bamboo mat, rocked back and forth, with the child Chatter Cat struggling to get free from her clutches. 'Hay

Missbaba! What oh what is written for us? What will happen now? Will there be another earthquake?'

'Another earthquake! Jesus Lord! Don't talk rubbish, Kalri.'

Yet, there were other fears in the hearts of the grown-ups, and they passed an anxious night, creeping along the veranda's edge with lanterns, in crumpled clothes, with furrowed brows and empty stomachs, whispering and checking out the water level with sticks, while we slept soundly.

And our prayers were heard. The flood never climbed the top step to sweep through our home like a marauding army.

'Wake up, wake, wake!' Kalri was shaking us gently. 'Come see what's happened outside, oh my God!'

We shot out of bed and flew, slipperless, into the veranda. And behold! The water had receded leaving behind a scene so enchantingly strange to us. Oblivious to the damage, to the devastation of our once-lovely surroundings, we saw only change—an expanse of water to paddle in and glorious gleaming silt, smooth as satin under our feet, squelching through our toes.

'Lovely! Lovely!' we screamed at it all.

'Lovely? My blasted foot!' Dad exploded from scarily near. He was moving sullenly about in his gumboots. 'Look what it's done to my rose bushes!'

True. Some of the smaller ones had completely disappeared.

But this was not a time for regrets; it was the time for action. Strange botanical and zoological things had been delivered up from the Forbidden Kingdom, Nepal, for our scrutiny. Sleek, long-limbed leaping frogs, bereft of cover, were easily captured to compete in exciting flat-races. They leaped swift and elastic, flying sometimes straight at the spectators' faces.

And, as if our day of thrills was not quite full, distant cries trumpeted the discovery of some fearsome creature of the Terai, trapped hopelessly in powerful currents and washed ashore— never more to roam in jungles wild.

'Come, brothers, running, jumping! A wild animal—big as my hut!—baap re! See with your own eyes!'

Everybody streaked off to look upon the remains. It was never seen as tragic. The wild animal, in this case, had been an old tiger, and the resulting scuffle with knives for tiger fat made a jigsaw puzzle of the valuable skin, much to Dad's chagrin.

Wild pigs, forced out of their haunts in search of higher ground, went through thick and thin—thick brush, and the thin walls of a man's hut as he squatted, stirring his curry—before it was cornered and brought down with spears and lathis. A wild boar could be divided into a hundred portions. It was the flesh of their dreams, grilled in its own fat with turmeric, mustard and fierce red chillies. A feast washed down with country arrack.

But these major floods brought misfortune too. Standing crops, livestock and often entire villages built on the banks of the river were washed away. With merciless regularity, cracks appeared in the banks, widening rapidly. Wider and wider, till a mighty chunk of earth tore away and splashed into the ravenous waters, with whatever stood on it. Day and night, the river devoured its banks. Biting, sometimes left, and sometimes right. 'Flee, brothers! Pick up your bags and flee! The river is cutting this way!'

But for Abdhi Missir darkness had come to stay. He sat distractedly on his charpoy at the khariyan, his dark-chocolate cheeks wet with tears.

'What troubles you, Abdhi Missir?' Mother asked him.

'Missbaba, it is like this,' he said, standing up painfully. 'Kethar Ojha has slapped a case against me for recovery of dues! It is actually Harry sahib but Kethar Ojha is his tool. The paper with my thumb impression was for dues to the kothi, long ago, Missbaba, before the earthquake, in the time of your honourable mother. They have tampered with the document. Kethar is very skilled and experienced at such tricks.'

Then he sighed, looking away from her. 'I cannot tell you how, but I have displeased Harry sahib, and he threatened me. He said, before this year is up, my home in the village will be completely razed and his tobacco fields will flourish where it now stands.'

Abdhi Missir's voice broke. 'Hay, hay, Missbaba! Harry sahib is such a powerful person, how can I stand up to him? I am only a poor man.'

'Come, Abdhi Missir, take heart,' she said. 'Powerful he may be, but with God's help we will see how he carries out his threat.'

Games of Chance

The Banswari was a bamboo grove beyond the graveyard. Though scarcely fifteen acres in size, it presented a world of mystery. Rows of massive bamboo clumps grew fifty to sixty feet high into the sky. Up there, the tapering branches leaned over, intermingling to form vast, green tunnels below, where the filtered sunshine fell through, pale golden-green on smooth grey earth carpeted with crisp, khaki leaves. There was a silence here, broken only by the scuttling movements of little creatures: birds, squirrels, civet cats, a mongoose or a porcupine, going briskly about their small-scale pursuits.

There was a reason for this silence, in a land of sound.

A very old peepul tree stood in the middle of the Banswari. It was one of the oldest ever known and so immense that if fifteen men surrounded it with fingertips touching they still wouldn't enclose it entirely, Foster said. But of course, no one had ever tried. It was not a tree that encouraged any familiarity. We considered it from a safe distance.

'Oho! Babalog!' He shook his head in anticipation of trouble. 'Let it be! Let it go! What do we want here? Cluck-cluck!' and a weary sigh.

But we stood our ground. 'We'll look from here, Foster.'

Smooth little mounds of earth at its base had been splashed

Sylvia Dyer

over with red powder, flowers, or blood, by Hindus who worshipped and offered sacrifices here during the hours of daylight. This tree, they said, was possessed by a very powerful Devi, a spirit that filled most people with the jitters, while it did Mother the favour of protecting her bamboos from nocturnal thieves—for night-time in the Banswari was the most 'never-never' time of all.

But to us, the Banswari (in the hours of daylight) was a secret, green wonderland where we went, when pushed by the power of curiosity, in defiance of our keepers and our own secret fears.

'Afraid?' Abhinandan laughed. 'People will be afraid of anything! Spirits, wild animals, other people ho ho ho! Even their own shadows! Fear without good reason is madness that can kill you. And when with reason, it must be put to good use.' He regarded us with something like a twinkle in his eye. 'Are you afraid?'

We nodded with a soft and sheepish yes.

His face broke into a rare, warm smile. 'But then . . . you are only children!'

The Banswari was one of his favourite haunts. It was his casino where he played his great con game, just for fun. The track from the station, for villages in the north, skirted the Banswari, and here he lay in wait for those who had a yen for gambling—and there were many.

It was a tricky game with three cards, placed on the ground, side by side. You had to pick up any card, make a note of it, and replace it. Abhinandan shuffled them in clear view of those present and put them down as before, for you to point out your chosen card to win, or lose. Such simplicity appealed to these simple-minded folk and they were easily lured into wagering just about anything they had with them. An umbrella, a penknife or even the pumpkin they were carrying home for dinner. They sat cross-legged on the smooth pressed earth, each taking his turn. At first, their confidence was allowed to soar. They quivered like brown jellies in bottled anticipation, grinning at each other and their little heaps of winnings. But then the tide turned. Heaps diminished like gravy in a sieve, till even the family pumpkin was gone; and that was no laughing matter.

'Gone, gone, the damn pumpkin! My father will have my head for dinner.'

But one day he met his match: a spirited young thing, who walked with a swing of the hips. She was different. Her eyes outlined with kajal looked boldly into his eyes, and she settled down among the men. They looked at one another smirking, while her fingers moved stealthily, first to her eye, and then to the card of her choice. Nobody noticed the act, or the tiny black mark she left on the card. She won a basket of brinjals, a fish, a cake of jaggery and finally Abhinandan's Made in England umbrella.

The game stopped. Abhinandan stared into space, the muscles of his jaw working. Then he examined the cards and looked up. For just a second their eyes locked; then she was up and running like a hare. She had played with fire. And now the answer was flight without looking back—for every second counted.

But there was no pursuit.

'Hey! Stop! Stop! Smart chick!' He stood up, shouting after her, 'Come take your winnings! Take the whole confounded lot for outsmarting this owl.' And he doubled up wheezing with laughter, for he was a chain-smoker (a rotten habit picked up in jail). But she wasn't coming back for anything.

He sat down and started shuffling the cards.

The daroga was always bad news, and that travels fast—in those days faster than the daroga himself. He had barely alighted at the Dhang railway station with his khaki constables armed with dandas, when the news spread like wildfire, to reach any Scarlet Pimpernel or hardened scoundrel he was seeking. With a little bit of luck they made it to no-man's-land and the Nepali border, scarcely two miles away, as the crow flew or the fugitive fled. It was not only a sanctuary in this real-life game of chor–police. No-man's-land was a lawbreaker's paradise. Illicit liquor, opium and ganja were traded freely. Here Muslims fell upon the 'sacred cow' (banned in Bihar) for the taste of good, hearty beef, and outraged Hindus fell upon the Muslims for the taste of vengeance. All this terrible activity put the limbs of the law in a spot where they had no foothold.

In those days, police dogs featured not even in police fairy tales. They had only their own noses and simple methods of extracting the truth, like the British boot and the desi danda, with which the police often made a breakthrough. One good swipe aimed at the soft parts brought tight secrets spilling out like seeds from a ripe pod.

'Who was seen washing out his bloodstained shirt in the river on the day of the riot?'

'Who was shouting, "Maro, maro! Kill, kill!"'

Names spilled out, one by one. Every swipe brought more information; and it burst out that Abhinandan, whom the daroga was forever seeking, was at that very instant playing his three-card game in the Banswari.

For the first time in his life, Abhinandan was taken completely by surprise. One moment he was shuffling cards with a carefree ho-ho-ho! and the next, he was looking up into the bloodshot eyes of the daroga. A small police force stood between him and no-man's-land to the north. So his only chance of escape lay across the Baghmati, half a mile away to the west.

He was up in a flash and running with the law in pursuit; and as they burst from the Banswari into open ground, they were followed by men, women and children, all avid seekers of real-life drama. Their numbers multiplied as they pushed forward accompanied by pi-dogs, yellow with black eyebrows, black with khaki eyebrows or whatever, but every single one rounded off with a ringtail.

From time to time the daroga spun around and barked at them. They jerked back like a flock of birds repulsed by a well-aimed stone; then back they came, every time.

It was the worst season for flight, but the going was rougher for the police force ploughing through waterlogged paddy fields, in boots that betrayed them into the sticky predicament of beetles in jam. Paunchy and overweight, the daroga pressed on. He could never hope to catch up with Abhinandan, and lacked a service pistol to fire at his swiftly advancing legs and slow them down. His sweaty, nut-brown cheeks puffed out hot, dismal air, while far ahead Abhinandan reached the banks of the Baghmati. For one brief moment he hesitated at what he saw before him, then he leaped into the angry flood.

A string of goats tied out to graze by the riverbank looked up and saw the army of humans and dogs with the police party in the lead, bearing down on them. They tore up their stakes and dashed away bleating manically, before the crowd fetched up to collect thickly along the bank and stare, lips compressed, while Abhinandan, striking out for the far shore with powerful strokes, was caught in the current and borne swiftly downstream. Twice he vanished momentarily from sight. Each time the police let out a cry of gladness, and then again, a curse when he reappeared.

And then he was gone.

'Looks too good to be true,' the daroga grunted, 'let's wait a bit . . . just to make sure this is the end of that thorn in our backsides!'

Surly grey clouds hung low above them, heavy with rain. The pi-dogs in the watch party had rendered themselves extremely unpopular, sniffing at dhotis and snarling at one another, while the minutes stretched on and people strained hopeful eyes for sight of Abhinandan, tossing on the river's angry bosom, for he was a man popular with the poor. But sight of him, there was none.

'Gone for good!' The daroga turned to leave. 'Well, at least he was a courageous so and so.'

He frowned down at his khaki uniform splattered with muck, and his boots caked with the stuff, up to his knees, and spat out his disgust with a savage 'Thooooo!'

Just then a constable pointed at the far bank, where only the keenest eyes would have seen a solitary figure, wresting itself with the utmost effort from the water's edge, and he cried out, 'Look! I see a man.'

The daroga spun around. 'Quick! Quick! My binoculars,' he snapped.

The force stared at him. 'They are round your neck, Daroga sahib.'

With trembling hands, he jerked the binoculars up to his face and focused, just in time to see the man he was looking for draw himself erect on to firm land and give him a mock salute.

The daroga winced and looked stupidly at the crowd. And then he looked down, where a ring-tailed pi-dog was sniffing his boots. He let fly a sideways kick and cursed the world and its disgusting creatures. It began to drizzle hard.

For days this escapade was a thrilling topic of conversation. In every village, at every community gathering under peepul trees, spiced-up versions of the story were rolled out with adoration, and little boys frisked around mimicking the record-breaking swim across the Baghmati.

'What a senseless thing to do!' Mother said irritably. 'Was he facing a death sentence?'

'No way.' Dad screwed up his mouth. 'He was charged with leading a riot. But you should know the blighter by now, girlie, he did it for a bloody lark.'

Meanwhile, Harry was in the process of settling his score with Abdhi Missir. It gave him a grim satisfaction that the case had come to the court of the SDO, a man with whom he was on fairly good terms. He felt certain of victory.

Bachoo the Barber

We had no hairdressers, no beauty parlours. When our hair needed attention, word was sent to Bachoo Hajam, a village barber who lived three miles away, and he arrived at a brisk trot.

He was the best in his trade, and a hairstylist, you could say, though everybody regarded him as slightly 'touched' and a potential risk with his sharp instruments. It is true he was 'different' with strangely hurried movements in a land where time stood still. We thought, as children, that a streak of lightning had got trapped in his body. Words, too, flowed from his mouth without check like water from a defective tap, punctuated liberally with 'Ramasra se'—a special mantra he was addicted to. And all this while he went snip-snip, stepping jerkily back at intervals to gauge his artwork with a critical eye.

It was not always appreciated, as when Dad was given the hairstyle of Gama, the most famous Indian wrestler of those times. There was a beastly roar when he picked up the hand mirror and came face to face with his new image.

'Forgive me, huzoor!' Bachoo cried with a slight tremor of voice and hands that had dropped the scissors. 'But, Ramasra se, it is exactly like the photo!' He was perplexed and dismayed. Where had he gone wrong? He had seen the photograph of Gama in the *Illustrated Weekly of India*.

Parrot and Pig sat very still for him, covered up to our shins in a white sheet, as he snipped away at our hair, smiling down into our faces with sad, tobacco-stained teeth. Around his neck a string of brown rudraksha beads stated that he led a mild, abstemious life of vegetables and such, nothing that bled. White streaks of chandan lines hid the gentleness in his face, and the quick, spontaneous joy, for in spite of all his haste he would stop suddenly to stare at a plant, a bird or a strange insect. Or with intense interest at the ants busy at work. He'd look up quickly, an expression of wonder on his pale, lean face, and cry, 'Imagine that! God has made them all!'

People found him beyond their comprehension because he was so utterly in love with nature, so utterly in love with God.

Now, as he trimmed our hair in the back veranda, with his tongue rattling on, his voice suddenly grew soft and dreamy. 'I know so much happiness!' he confided. 'God has blessed me with everything. Everything but a child! In ten years of marriage, he has not seen fit to bless us with a child. Still . . .'—snip-snip—'we cannot have everything . . . Can we?' he asked, peering deep into our eyes for confirmation.

We held our tongues, because we had everything . . . We had Mother, and this whole, wonderful, glorious green world! Showers of flowers, purple, scarlet and gold standing out against a storm-grey sky, and a laughing wind springing up to blow all things off their feet. We loved being blown off our feet, and ran with the wind, our arms flung wide and the dogs racing after us. Away! Away with eyes shut-open, into limitless space. Till our mortal limitations pulled us back to earth—thud!

And here was Abdhi Missir, back from the final hearing of Harry's lawsuit filed against him in Sitamarhi, his arms also spread wide, driven by the same exquisite magic, racing down the road from the station and in through the front gates. We came face to face. His eyes were popping from their sockets while his mouth opened and shut like a giant carp straining to burst into speech, 'Jai Bhagwan! [Gasp] oh babalog, what news! The magistrate has ruled in my favour. [Gasp] Harry sahib has lost his case against me. Never has such a thing happened before. It is . . . [gasp-gasp] Missbaba's prayers! Jai Bhagwan!' He fell flat on his face in the driveway and wept like a child.

Bachoo, too, came one day with an added spring in his step. He was like a child sighing rapturously up at the sky as he walked, taking in deep draughts of ethereal air and laughing it out: 'A father! Ramasra se, I am the father of a little baby girl!' Well, it was not a boy; every man in this land wanted a male child, but so what? God had given him a child!

'Huzoor, Ramasra se, what should I call her?' he asked, snipping away at the back of Dad's big head. It was the third or fourth time he had put the same question to the back of the head.

Dad was in a frivolous mood that morning, and blowing smoke rings at the dogs. 'Err well now . . . how about Kiss-me-arse?' he said flippantly.

'Oh sahib!' Bachoo stopped his snipping and looked up at the ceiling with shining eyes. 'What an impressive name, Ramasra se! "Kisme" from Kismet, and "Aas" we all know, means wealth!'

'Oh Terence!' Mother looked crossly at Dad. 'How could you!'

But everyone else was impressed by the name, unusual though it was, and Kissmeaas grew into the child of Bachoo's dreams.

'Truly, she is my gift from God!' he told Mother softly, with that warm, glowing light in his eyes. 'What more could I ever wish for?'

There were seasons of good fortune, when cups overflowed with life's bounty.

And then there were bad ones, when they fell and cracked wide open. It was all written in the stars, they said.

Something Strange and Sinister

The floods that year were devastating. But now it was all over. With the coming of September the water receded. The transplanted paddy seedlings stood vivid green and upright, and the sugar cane was six feet high, with still another three months to go. All should have been well with our world.

But it was not.

The pi-dogs of Musahari Tola were seized by a sudden jitteriness, insisting on being let into the huts to sleep with the Musahars at night. They were kicked out with rough reprimands: 'Worthless pariahs, are you watchdogs or lapdogs?'

Early next morning, one of the watchdogs had quit and was never seen again. Slowly more watchdogs began to disappear, and always one at a time. It was a mystery in a land where mysteries were quickly cleared up.

Other villages too were in for mysterious disappearances, villages where only the upper-caste Hindus lived. Most of them owned at least one acre of this fertile land and were comfortably off. Their wives lived in purdah, seldom stepping out to work or socialize, but spending their lives as honoured housewives in their own thatched prisons, for each home had a little private courtyard with high thatched walls. Inside they ground the grain, milked the buffalo, cooked the meals and lived out their lives in cloistered contentment. In the dark hours just before dawn, proud sons of the village mounted on their buffaloes made a slow but certain beeline for our mango groves, or the adjacent fields, to graze furtively on the current crops, returning at sunrise, the riders full of song and the buffaloes full of milk for their owners.

But one morning, a buffalo failed to return.

'I tell you, brother, it has been sent to the pound!'

'The pound? But then, where is the boy? Has the earth swallowed him up?'

That evening we went to visit Harry. He had built a narrow bamboo bridge across the Mahari so he could visit us or take a short cut through Puchkurwa to the railway station. It served its purpose well enough till a bad flood, like the one we had just experienced, swept it clean away.

So we sat on our bank, and he on his, with sixty feet of water in between. It was a little more than knee-deep in most places, scarcely a setback for our usual social exchanges. His servants waded across with chairs for us, and we sat shouting at each other, above the ripple of restless, running water.

Ghogra appeared on Harry's side, in a snow-white uniform, dhoti hitched up, and a tray of fried snacks carried high above his head as he waded into the water. He had almost reached our bank when, all of a sudden, he lost his footing. His turban flew like a snowball. The eyes in the bulldog face popped, and the mouth opened. And he was gone.

A moment later he reappeared coated with grey silt, and still clutching the tray. But the fried snacks had gone to the fishes, along with the dishes. Even from our bank, we could see the irritation on Harry's face. They were from his best set. 'He is the king of idiots, this Ghogra, and such a show-off!'

Nobody laughed out loud.

The setting sun sent out a blaze of fiery orange from the western horizon as Ghogra was making his slimy way back to Harry's bank, grumbling about the upkeep of bridges, when—

'Shh!' Dad raised a hand for silence. 'Crikey! Did you hear that?'

'Hear what?'

'A call . . . I could swear I heard a strange call in the distance, bloody strange.'

Some of the servants had heard it too. 'Baap re baap! It's a bhooth—an evil spirit!'

'Spirit, my foot! It was a wild animal. Nothing from around these parts I'd say, but I'm hanged if I can place the bloody thing.' And his bushy eyebrows contracted painfully, trying to place the bloody thing.

Spirit or mystery animal, one was as bad as the other to us, and with night coming on we hurried home with goose pimples.

Lunch was over early. Bonzo sat on his haunches outside the cookhouse, scrubbing the dishes with ash. A few inquisitive

Sylvia Dyer

fowls came around to bother him, and he cooled them off with a spray of dishwater. In the back veranda Pig and his followers were cleaning his airgun with a pull-through. Narain Singh stopped to watch the feverish activity,

'I hear there are green pigeons in Bhokraha, many, many of them. And, do you know, some even sit low in the branches.'

'Hear that, Parrot? Let's go, now!'

There was a wail from Kalri.

'Take a net, Foster, to catch fish.' Fish had a powerful fascination for Pig. Foster disappeared into the house and was soon out with an old mosquito net.

'And where is that Chatter Cat?' The followers burst out laughing. 'Asleep in bed.'

'Good.'

'Another thing . . .' Narain Singh pointed down at the dogs stretched out on the veranda.

'Yes, yes! Chain up these dogs.'

Life was so simple in those days. No involved, complicated plans. No waiting for green signals or vague tomorrows.

You just went to Bhokraha or anywhere.

It was a perfect afternoon, with the scent of adventure in the air. 'Look! Look!' the followers cried pointing up to where a flock of birds circled to settle in the tallest tree. 'Harials—green pigeons!'

We looked up as we walked. It was a smooth-beaten, single-file track through the scrub. 'Baap re baap, how many!' Narain Singh exclaimed. 'Sahib should have been here with . . . arresaala kya!' He broke off hopping and swearing softly. He had picked up a thorn in his foot and sat down to remove it. We had reached the banks of the stream.

'Fish! Let's try our luck here.' Foster gave a chuckle and waded in with the net.

'Say, Narain Singh,' we asked, pointing at a red-brick wall almost completely enveloped by jungle, 'what's that?'

He was still poking at his foot. 'That? Indigo vats were there, long, long ago, in the time of your great-grandfather. Why?'

Kalri knew what was coming up next. 'Arre kya, babalog! Oh children! What vats vats! Nothing but bad, bad jungle there! Leave it! Come sit nicely by the stream. Hey Bhagwan!' She flopped down on the grass with a sickly wheeze.

'Kalri! Have we come here to sit by the stream and see visions?' we hissed into her ear, and sneaked off.

But no great discovery awaited us. There was nothing left of the vats. Peepul trees had sprouted through the crumbling walls, and banyans made pillars of their multiple roots for creepers to climb up and around, entwining arms to create living green chambers. Little, light-footed creatures scurried in and out at our approach, and a couple of hornbills flew out from a giant tree shattering the stillness with their cries.

'Come, Pig, let's see what's inside,' I whispered. 'Are you scared?'

'Of what?' He looked surprised at the very suggestion. 'There's only snakes.'

We peeped over the wall. No ray of sunshine penetrated the density of foliage. But as our eyes grew accustomed to the darkness we could make out two figures, their backs turned to us as they sat side by side on the broken stone flooring. A man and a woman both dressed in white, heads together, whispering. And as we stood there, she seemed to sense our presence, and turning her head, saw our faces. I heard her gasp.

At that instant Narain Singh's voice came urgently from where he sat on the bank. 'Arre babalog! Come away at once!' he shouted. 'Nobody ever goes there—evil sleeps in that place!'

And we turned and fled.

We flopped down panting on the bank, considering our discovery. 'Pig, did you see that man and woman? Think of it, sitting alone in a place like that!'

'Hmm. And very close. They must have been scared. You saw how she looked at us?'

'Oh yes. And I saw her face clearly,' I whispered in his ear. 'It was that Margaret.'

Pig turned to stare at me. 'You mean Harry's . . . oh?'

'Of course, silly! But the man, Pig? Who was the man?'

The shadows were lengthening as we turned homewards, and the setting sun sent dazzling shafts of orange-gold across the sugar cane fields. Fork-tailed drongos were swooping over with their jarring cries.

'Come, hurry,' said Narain Singh, 'daylight goes swiftly. In a little time it will be dark, and . . .'

He was cut short by a harsh, guttural cry, deep in the jungle. It was a powerful animal call we had never heard before. Never. And it put wings to our feet. A flock of earth-bound birds keeping pace with the home-bound birds above us—a motley flock composed of a parrot, a pig, tadpoles, a warrior, a man for all seasons and a confirmed pessimist holding her chest, speeding towards home safe home.

And there, Dad stood waiting for us on the veranda steps, arms locked firmly across his chest, so they wouldn't reach out to strike. Storm clouds covered his face and the thunder that came from his mouth was deafening: 'This loafing about has just got to stop. Do you hear me? Open your mouths and answer.'

We opened our mouths, but no sound came out!

Dawn was just breaking next day, when a woman awoke to find her baby gone. They searched everywhere, but there was no trace of the child. Soon children from other villages began to disappear. Fear spread like wildfire over the daily lives of people. They carried their children everywhere, and hurried home in groups well before sundown, the men carrying lathis and spears. More fires were lit and fragile doors fastened. Family feuds and differences were scrapped as the people became one in the face of this common enemy. Any suspicious sound or movement during the hours of darkness would trigger off a frenzy of screaming and beating on drums and cooking pots, and the chanting of mantras that discouraged the Evil Spirit—for the moment.

'This is all superstitious nonsense, Gladys,' Harry said when he came to visit us. 'It's some wild animal turned maneater.'

'Exactly what Terence said yesterday—a panther, or a leopard. It would explain the taking of dogs and children.'

A letter arrived from Harry. 'Gladys, do you hear what is being said? It's all rather disturbing. Now I'm told that the son of Ram Chalitar Singh the wrestler, a big hulk of a boy, thirteen years old, was taken last evening. The father is desperate and has sworn to kill it with his bare hands. He's set out alone in search of the animal! I think the poor man has lost his mind.' We peeped into the letter. It ended with—'More when face to face'. All Harry's letters ended this way.

'Pig! Come quickly!' Parrot whisked him behind a pillar to whisper in his ear, 'Remember the face in the vats? Think, Pig. The Man?'

'The man? Why?'

'Why? Look!'

Pig's head shot round the pillar. 'O Mother Mary!'

The sipahi who had brought the letter stood before us with an easy grace. We had never seen him this close before. He was one of nature's most perfect creations. When you studied him feature by feature, no single flaw could you perceive in the work of his creator. He was Harry's right-hand man, Mahanth Jha.

'What is it, children?' Mother turned to look at us.

'Nothing, Mother, nothing.'

That evening, as the sun set over the sugar cane fields, the hush was disturbed—only by an agitated drongo and two of our sipahis. Big Mouth and Jumping Jujube, both heavyweight wrestling champs, were moving up the road to their village with the slow, rolling gait of sailors, planting their lathis firmly before them in a three-legged walk. On either side the sugar cane stood dense and tall. They did not speak, just cleared their throats and spat, sending the spittle far ahead, to herald their approach. The path turned sharply and there right before them was the creature! Long and graceful, a sleek, tawny coat printed with black rosettes. It stood across the road, stock-still in a seemingly preoccupied manner. Both wrestlers froze. The animal turned its head and looked squarely at them. This snapped the freezing spell, and they acted with alacrity. Dropping their lathis they clung together raising a duet of hoarse bellows, that brought Dad and his .12 bore, with a score of retainers and dogs at his heels.

There was no sign of the animal. The two wrestlers were stuck together, evoking the spirits of their forefathers in this their darkest hour so far, when they became aware of a large audience.

'What can we tell you, brothers, you never saw anything like it. Baap re! That big! That long! A supernatural creature! A hundred heroes would tremble before it!'

'A supernatural creature that leaves pug marks?' Dad burst out. 'Heroic owl's backsides!'

The other sipahis roared with laughter, while the lower castes looked discreetly away, holding their tongues; and the dogs made figure eights, sniffing the earth and squealing. Then they were all gone, plunging senselessly after Dad into the sugar cane, trampling it down and causing damage to no purpose.

'Blast its guts! It could be miles away by now.'

The dogs were called back and everybody raced home, because nobody wanted to be the last.

'But where is Jackie?' Dada was asking. 'He should have returned with the other dogs.'

'He must be mooching around the kitchen,' Dad said. He walked around flashing his torch here, there and everywhere. He whistled aloud. Servants ran about shouting, 'Jah . . . kee, Jah . . . kee! Aow, aow Jah . . . kee!' But Jackie did not come. And even the next morning when people went searching, far and wide, in villages, fields and groves, crying 'Jah . . . kee, Jah . . . kee! Come back Jah . . . kee!' only silence came back to them.

Dada sat glassy-eyed in his chair on the front veranda, with the territory below it vacant. Vacant for days. His hand hung disconsolately down with nothing to pet.

We came to stand near his chair. 'Dada, don't worry, Dada. He must be mooching around somewhere.'

'Yes, Parrot. Somewhere in the Happy Hunting Grounds.'

Nearly two years of being foiled by a beast had gone by. In all this time Dad had caught only glimpses of the creature. Creature? He could almost swear, like the villagers, that it was a spirit with the damnable cunning of the devil.

Then one evening he was taking a walk along the bund of the Mahari. The sun was setting over the newly harvested sugar cane fields. He stopped to light a cigarette and looked around. There was no sign of any living creature but one—the long-sought bête noire of his mortification. It stood motionless, not quite thirty yards away, staring at him, as if it had waited for this moment. For a cliff-hanging minute their eyes met. And then it turned its head and walked coolly away, knowing that he carried only a walking stick!

'Christ Almighty! Can a man spend his blasted life with a loaded gun?' Dad dropped into a chair, staring at Mother in bewildered exasperation. 'Think of it, Glad, the chance of a lifetime bloody well lost! D'you know how many children it has carried off? Sixty-six! Yes, sixty bloody six! And all I've done about it is sit here on my arse and drink!'

Then came the end of the monsoon. Drying-up days, when the earth's sweat seeped out of its warm, moist surface to be sucked up in the afternoon air. Now nearer the upper reaches of the Baghmati, the tiger grass by the river's edge was dense and high as a warrior's eye, but there were clear, sandy patches where the fishermen, after their work was done, spread their nets to dry. A fisherman was making his way through the tiger grass, clad only in a loincloth, a fishing net slung over his shoulders, when he came to a clearing. There, on the smooth, dry earth, a leopard was stretched out, fast asleep. No seasoned hunter, but merely a plucky fisherman, he stalked up to the animal and threw his net swiftly and skilfully over it—leaping on to its body to pin it

Sylvia Dyer

down! There was a roar, loud enough to bring the entire village racing to the scene, while the leopard turned its head and bit a chunk out of the fisherman's bottom.

The creature was finally clobbered to death. But the humble hero of the incident had to be rushed off to the Sitamarhi hospital, with a partial loss of rear, and a letter from Dad to the civil surgeon.

There was great rejoicing everywhere. Drums and empty vessels got the beatings of their lives. Harry came over to drink to 'the end of the beast'.

'So, Tip,' he said brightly to Dad, 'it took a fool of a fisherman to finish it off!'

A barbed shaft, which Dad returned with his one-sided sarcastic smile. 'Well, that's that,' he closed the subject, 'and may the Lord be praised for it.'

But that was not that . . .

Shiva Majhi, a simple-minded Musahar, set out on a still afternoon to saw off the branch of an old mango tree he'd been coveting. It was a dry branch in an advanced state of decay, barely fourteen feet off the ground.

He perched up there thinking. If he sat with his back against the tree trunk sawing the branch before him in the usual way, he'd deprive himself of the three feet of wood he sat upon. No way! Saw in hand, he slithered over to the outer side. The branch began to creak ominously. And what was that crackling of leaves down below? He looked down and froze. He was staring into the flaming yellow eyes of a demon. It grinned at him with teeth like a rake. Shiva Majhi dropped the saw and screamed, clinging to the branch as it went down with a thundering crash. People came running. There was no sign of any demon.

People were troubled. 'Could Shiva Majhi have imagined the whole thing? . . . Or could it have been . . . ?'

And then one morning a bolt came out of the clear blue sky. 'Bachoo the barber has lost his child!'

It hit Mother very hard. She turned pale and groped for a chair to sit down. 'Jesus Master! Not that child!'

'Yes, Missbaba! Kissmeaas is gone! Taken last night by the cheetah!'

The child was playing out in the courtyard while the mother cooked the evening meal. Suddenly she became aware of an unnatural silence and called out to it. But there was no answering sound. She ran into the courtyard. It was empty, and the bamboo door hung wide open. Then the poor woman ran out, screaming, tearing her hair and screaming. Knowing not where she ran or what she did in that moment of terror.

All the men from the village, armed with spears and axes, set out in search of the truth. They divided up into four groups, fanning out as they moved north, south, east and west from the village, combing every inch of ground as they went. Darkness fell quickly. They lit lamps and torches, but in the feeble light of these, visibility was poor and progress became slow. Besides, they had to move with caution. Only Bachoo walked with a strange and fearless calm, till eight hundred yards north-east of the village, in a small patch of jungle, their search ended. The lanterns converged in a pool of light, so they could all see. Pushed under a thorn bush, pretty little clothes turned to bloody rags covered the ghastly remains of his precious child. Bachoo put his hands over his face to blot out the sight and hot vomit came up in his throat.

'If you must lose your child, should it be this way?' the others thought as they looked on. And the night looked on, and the stars looked on, and kept their thoughts to themselves.

Another monsoon followed. Clouds banked up on the horizon. They were superb in their varying shades of wrath at the earth's brutality. Now there was a declaration of war up in the heavens. Immense fury built up and burst over the earth with crashes, flashes and an unceasing downpour for all things below.

That August brought the most disastrous flood we had ever known. Entire villages on the banks of the Baghmati were washed away with most of their livestock. It was said that even an elephant with its hind legs in chains was borne helplessly downstream, trumpeting in gigantic terror.

The Baghmati had gone berserk, pushed by forces beyond its control. And yet, an unforeseeable blessing emerged from the wrath of the river to comfort us all. The 'cheetah' was never heard of again.

A year circled round before we saw Bachoo again. Mother sat reading one afternoon in the front veranda when she looked up, and there he was, standing silently before her. He looked different, with silver streaks in his hair and conspicuous lines of suffering etched on his face. But of bitterness, there was no trace. It wore a deep, sad serenity.

'I am sorrowful, Bachoo,' she said with the utmost gentleness, 'about your child. Oh what a cruel blow it must have been to you.'

'Missbaba,' he said softly, and his eyes were full of the old kindliness, though with quick, gathering tears, 'Missbaba, God gave her to me, and God took her.' He raised his hands, palms facing upwards in the humblest of gestures. 'What right did I have?' He smiled wistfully, and turned away to leave.

He walked slowly, looking down at the sad earth till at the end of the long driveway he came to a bed of sunflowers. They had grown tall. Very tall. There he stopped and stood alongside, cocking his head to get a better look at their bright, glowing faces, well above him.

Mother's eyes were wet. 'Just a dwarf among the sunflowers,' she said softly, 'but a giant among men!'

Lust for Land

After the monsoon came brilliant days with dazzling white clouds in a deep blue sky, a blue reflected in all things below.

The earth slowly breathed out all its moisture and sat back to dry.

All nature had to hold its breath, for the paddy was in flower. Soon ears of grain formed on the stalks, pale green and tender. If you pressed them gently between your fingertips, a milky substance popped out. The pulp soon hardened into grain, and there were golden fields, ripe for the harvest. And now, every morning, the Willy-wagtails came bob-bob-bobbing along, pecking busily at riches hidden in the grass, their long tails bouncing merrily to herald in the magnificent winter.

In this glad season Rajan Singh and Bhajan Singh set out together to visit Harry. A very rare gesture for them, this togetherness, but they had a problem of mutual interest.

Harry looked them over with an icy smile, as they settled into his best period chairs, jigging their legs ceaselessly.

'Harry sahib,' said Bhajan, his small eyes, set too close together for beauty, focused on Harry, 'we come for your valuable advice. You see there is an old boundary between our land and a plot of Missbaba's, which has shifted over the years—floods and all—trees were not planted. On measuring, we find that half of Missbaba's plot is really our land! Heh heh!'

He picked up a crystal ashtray and twirled it carelessly in his fingers, while his eyes said, 'What is this child's toy!'

Harry scowled at the hand that had desecrated his crystal.

'But,' Bhajan continued, quickly putting the ashtray down, 'we want an amicable settlement with Missbaba. Our relationship has always been good. So tell us, Harry sahib, how can we go about this—to our best advantage?' The legs stopped jigging as he waited for an answer.

Harry was thinking. The scowl had been replaced by a look of interest. 'Amicable? What are you saying! Can there ever be an amicable settlement over land, which is to your best advantage?' He gave a short, crisp cluck. A spark flickered in his eyes. 'Certainly not. Now, file another case—against Missbaba! She hates litigation as much as you love it. This alone can be to your best advantage.'

It was bad news for Mother. 'A batwara case, Jesus Lord! This could run on for years! It might just about ruin us!'

'On the other hand, think, girlie, if we compromise and give them the lion's share that they're angling for, it will press the button for a succession of claims and start a slow but certain downhill slide for us. Christ Almighty, I'll bet my ruddy arse that Master Harry's at the back of all this!'

And so it began—the financial drain of the batwara case, destined to drag on for seven years, dragging us down with it.

You couldn't have land without land disputes. Some mornings, small farmers, disputing among themselves, came to Mother for an out-of-court settlement. They squatted down on their haunches in the front veranda, backs against the wall, in a neatly packed row.

But there were those without problems or disputes, who were simply hanging around to ask her for land in batai (sharecropping). There was more land than we could cultivate ourselves. So the excess went to sharecroppers and secured their loyalty into the bargain.

Some people came with bowed heads, and joined hands to ask for a loan. Where else would they get an interest-free loan? Or one that might well be forgotten?

Mother walked off to her bedroom humming pleasantly, with the house keys jingling in her hand. She went to the big, white almirah where she kept her loose cash and flung the door open. On the inner side of the right hand door was a list of names with amounts against them. There were ticks, scratches of cancellation, and notations that only she understood. She preferred writing on this door. A notebook could get lost—not so the door. Sona Raut, she wrote. Then came a pause, with the pencil poised to record the amount, when sudden shouts of warning from the backyard reached her ears.

'Bhaag! Run fellows! It's heading your way!' With an 'O Jesus!' she slammed the door shut and stepped back just as a large cart bullock with eyes like golf balls and tail raised like a golf club charged through the bedroom, passing between her and the almirah and out on to the front veranda followed closely by dogs and cattlemen in pursuit. The invasion moved on, its cries growing fainter with distance. She opened the door, frowning. 'Sona Raut . . . what? Oh dash it!' She shut the almirah door and closed the matter with finality.

Education

Education! The dark threat hovering over our perfect lives struck.
'This loafing about all day has got to stop!'
And it stopped abruptly. In the carefree month of March we were on our miserable way. It was a long, dismal train journey, peppered with coal dust and tears.
And Lenny cribbing, 'This Parrot has the waterworks in her head.'
But Pig never cried. He was the 'Little Man', and he just got a stomach ache.

The dawn of that fateful day broke cold and clear through the compartment windows and there before us were the Himalaya, objects of transcending beauty, seen only as the insurmountable walls of our prison-to-be, coming nearer and nearer. And the train began to shriek in a sickly way.

'Move!' Dad barked at us. 'Stop moping around and get going.'

And we got going like glued-up organisms, to change our dear, familiar clothes for voluminous bloomers, black woollen stockings and other offensive stuff with a fresh hostile smell that were the trappings of the doomed.

It was all happening too fast, like the taxi that zigzagged up the mountains in an insane hurry to lob us into school. School was a massive grey stone building enthroned in the clouds with St Michael the Archangel looming out of the mist, sword in hand. Its railed-off grounds were swarming with alien beings, red-faced and chattering, in small knots or large groups, till a frightful clanging of bells shut them all up.

Where had we come?

To another planet, with a silent school parlour. Grey. There were nuns in the parlour—two black-and-white pillars with triangles of pink human face, speaking in hushed tones, like at a funeral. And suddenly it was icy cold. Ice in the heart that froze you deaf, dumb and blind.

And now, they were standing up to leave.

'Goodbye my little darl—'

'No, no!' We flew at Mother, grabbing fistfuls of dress that could not be freed without the loss of silk.

The pink triangles were clucking in distress. 'Dear! Dear! It's always better when the fathers bring them. Oh dear!' They said, one with an English accent, and the other with a strong German one.

Dad was looking up at the ceiling. Mother was bearing up very well. No quivering breakdown of facial muscles, only the wet, red-eyed look. Her handkerchief was soaked through.

She had come to a decision. 'Maybe . . . tomorrow, Sisters?'

'Very well then, tomorrow.'

The Sisters agreed jointly. Their eyes turned heavenwards; soft, white hands appeared to make graceful arcs of regret in the air. Their heavy rosaries jingled. There was a smell of fresh linen.

Tomorrow! The heaven-sent gift of a tomorrow. We were racing back to the taxi, our blood circulating brisk and free. And tear-washed faces grinning all the way to Granny Corbett's Boarding House.

After one or two more 'tomorrows' it worked.

'Everyone goes through it,' Dad comforted us. 'Know how you'd end up without school?' He brought out his handkerchief and blew his nose like a trumpet. 'Like the Musahars!' Sniff, sniff. 'Too bloody true!' He smiled his one-sided smile. 'Make up your minds to like it.'

And we did. You can like almost anything, if you make up your mind.

We returned from school for the winter holidays with brand-new ideas and missionary zeal. Touched by the fire of the early Christians, we tried to convert Foster in the green seclusion of the cassia tree, preaching to him and the dogs, on overturned flowerpots. They had to listen to Bible stories with some fancy touches of our own. We played it by ear, and laced it with feeling. And over the days we watched him 'softening up'—till finally he confessed that he was converted!

Our first convert with a 'but'.

'But, babalog . . .' He swallowed hard and his Adam's apple rose and fell woefully. 'I do wish to be a Christian but it will make problems too big for me. My family will disown me. The village will turn me out and I'll be an outcast for the rest of my life.'

'Oh hell, Foster, we can't have that!' We sat, baffled and defeated.

Then Pig sprang up and began to waltz around, with the dogs staring curiously at him. 'You know what, Parrot?' he cried. 'The

Baptism of Desire! He can have the Baptism of Desire!'

'Yes, Foster! You can be a secret Christian.'

'A secret Christian?'

'Yes, yes. In your heart! Sit down and cover your eyes with both your hands.'

'No! No! You are going to squirt water in my ears!' he cried.

'What rubbish, Foster! It's something very nice this time. Just wait and see!'

We ran through the garden to a bed of spider lilies, and were back with the best and purest we could find. We stuck it behind Foster's ear.

'There, Foster.'

His eyes opened up and moved sideways to get a look, and he grinned sheepishly at us.

'Now you're a secret Christian. Your desire makes you pure as this lily. If you die now, you'll go straight to heaven and be with all the angels. Foster, pray you die now.'

'What? Die now?' He stuck his dismayed tongue through the gap in his front teeth.

'Never, Foster! We were only fooling! Come, let's hold hands and jump.'

We held hands with our secret Christian, 'Jump, jump, sugar lump!' and jumped ourselves breathless.

A good bit of our days were spent in our front veranda. Mother sat reading the *Statesman* (it was always yesterday's) that had just fetched up. Dad was stuck in the crossword puzzle of an earlier paper with a low wall of dictionaries and encyclopaedias around him. On days when he didn't go to court this was his daily challenge, with the precincts of his labours filled thick with cigarette smoke and explosive coughing.

He looked up irritably. 'Never any peace! Now what the hell is this?'

A small procession was coming through the front gates: men and women, but in the lead was a woman in an old, tattered sari and three little children who clung desperately to a bowed and emaciated buffalo. They stopped at the base of the veranda steps, just in front of Mother.

'Missbaba,' the woman joined her hands, palms together, 'I come to beg your mercy! My buffalo had broken free during the night, and your sipahis caught it grazing in your paddy field. I found them taking it away to the pound. Huzoor, I know I should be punished for this, but I am a miserable widow. Ay Bhagwan!' She covered her face with both hands. 'I have not the money to redeem it. Look at us, Missbaba—at what we have come to! This wretched buffalo is all that we have.'

A miserable widow! A widow in this country walked the earth alone; she had no protector, no breadwinner, no partner in life for the rest of her days, for a widow could never marry again. She might be better off dead, in this land where a woman without a man was considered fair game by the majority of men, and shunned by a society that believed she was responsible for her husband's death by having in some way incurred the displeasure of the gods. In an existence that seemed like a lifelong penance, she dressed in the plainest of clothes, and walked with her head bowed down, on a level with her destiny.

It all came over Mother in a rush. 'Very well then. It is all right. You can take your buffalo and go,' she said to the woman.

'But, huzoor . . .' the sipahi, spoke up, 'this is the third offence. I feel she should be taught a lesson.'

'There are many who should be taught lessons, and for far greater offences, like certain thieving sipahis, and waah, they go scot-free. Enough now. Take them to the khariyan and ask Abdhi Missir to give her five maunds of paddy. She will be more watchful in future, I have no doubt.'

The sipahi's mouth fell open. 'Give her five maunds of paddy?'

The woman's mouth too fell open. She stumbled up the steps and threw herself at Mother's feet, weeping in big, gasping sobs, for a hundred long imprisoned sorrows had been freed in this one moment of kindness.

Mother turned around to see Abdhi Missir. 'Oh Abdhi Missir, you're here! I just told them . . . '

'Yes, Missbaba, I have heard.' He had been there all the time, watching the proceedings with his peculiar frowning smile.

'You must think that what I have done doesn't make sense. But God has given us so much, and this poor woman—she has nothing.'

'I know, Missbaba, it makes perfect sense to me.'

On one of our daily rounds we got a crazy idea.

'Foster,' we said, 'take us to see the poor widow's hut and the starving, miserable buffalo—'

'Oh baba!' He sighed. 'How on earth will we find her hut among so many?'

'Come, Foster, we can search!'

'Puckry village! You will not find it pleasurable!'

'Foster, we do not go for pleasure.' And we set out.

We found ourselves lost in a maze of narrow, beaten pathways snaking through the village, followed closely by snotty, grinning children and pi-dogs. We passed reclining bullock carts, their shafts pointed like guns at the cloudless sky, and came suddenly upon a charming, green arbour on which large, round ash gourds sat heavily, sprinkled over with nature's powder. Inside, a buffalo lounged languidly chewing the cud, its jaws swinging from side to side, indifferent to the pestiferous flies. But as we drew near, its bloodshot eyes rolled and it hissed rising in ponderous disapproval at our clothes and alien smell. And we fled as it snapped its rope and charged. Shoes caked with mud, chaff and buffalo dung scarcely hindered our headlong flight to we knew not where, with followers screaming, and Foster cursing that he lacked a lathi to break on its snout. We found ourselves in the Banswari. Here we stopped, breathless among the brooding bamboo clumps and flung ourselves on the smooth beaten earth, shaking with laughter. Till Pig's hand touched something moist and sticky.

'Aaaa! What's this?'

It was a wet, purplish patch on the grey earth. Foster crouched down to examine it.

'Hanh!' he said, cleaning his finger on a leaf. 'It's blood. Look, here too is blood, something killed!' He was frowning now. 'Yes . . . leading this way.'

And as we followed, so intent was he on the blood trail that he never realized he was leading us towards the Tree of Evil where they offered their bloody sacrifices, till we were almost there. A clump of people stood staring down in horror at what was in their midst, their faces twisted in revulsion. Some of them broke away to spit while others flung stones at a couple of dogs nosing around.

'Aaaa!' our followers cried racing forward. But Foster held us back firmly.

'What, Foster! Why can't we go too?' we shouted, struggling and using our elbows to shake him off.

'Babalog, it's not good for you to see everything,' he explained with a troubled face. 'The youngsters have gone and we will learn soon enough.'

And soon enough the youngsters were flying back, eyes straining from their sockets. 'Baap re baap! We saw it!' they cried, tongues falling out, 'Sukhesar's son! The one you call Shorty. It's his head! Chopped clean off and left on the altar of sacrifice.'

'What a ghastly end,' Mother said. 'Poor Sukhesar! I always had a dreadful feeling about this wretched affair.'

News of the horror spread in a cloud of dark whispers. Foster looked grim and had nothing to say, at least to us.

Christmas Time

Christmas time had come and the house began to bulge with guests. The overflow went into compact little tent houses borrowed from 'Hawwn', the Raja of Sheohar, where the men were lodged. Each had two rooms, a bathroom and a veranda, set up on the east side of the house, while in the west a large shamiana was set up to become our dining hall.

The domestic staff worked flat out during those days, though for us it was unadulterated fun. They too had fun, showing off their special skills.

There was much coming and going between the two houses. Harry's house was overflowing too. He had Dorothy and Ernie, along with his own friends whom he had asked for Christmas. His favourites were from the Belsund Sugar Factory. The Belsund Sugar Factory in Riga was not where you think. It was only six miles away from us. Our sugar cane had been going there ever since it was built for James Finlay & Co. Now its manager was a European Jew named Jacobs. Harry had made a hit with Mrs Jacobs, a plump, elderly person who baked pastries fit for the gods. Some of these divine creations arrived regularly from Riga for Harry and were rapidly demolished by Parrot and Pig.

And now for the arrival of a celebrity from our eastern parts. Raghuni, his broad face inscribed with the lines of a life deeply lived, and flowing, shoulder-length hair that was uncommon in those times, had arrived with his troupe and stood beaming at us through limpid brown eyes. He was a playwright, actor and comedian, even a composer of ballads. Raghuni & Co. were a special Christmas-week attraction ever since I can recall. The troupe consisted of three musicians, with a sarangi, dholak and harmonium, and a dancing boy who did his utmost to pass for a girl, keeping the audience charmed, while Raghuni got set somewhere out in the darkness, for his various acts.

The show commenced soon after dark. The stage was our front veranda, spacious enough to accommodate sipahis, servants and their children in the wings, while chairs were arranged in the drawing room with its doors thrown wide open, so we could watch the show with the houseguests. Two Petromax lamps blazed, with a stunning brilliance and a steady hiss.

The dancing boy appeared on the stage slim as a reed in garish and sparkling regalia. He shuffled forward with a challenging look from glittering snake eyes, stamping his ghungrooed feet. A quick flick of his wrist sent a gauzy pink veil over his head. He clapped a hand over one ear, quivering and gazing up at the ceiling, and with a startling suddenness burst into 'Hhyynnh!' This tuning up was repeated till he hit the right notes. Then he was off and away in a shrill nasal tenor belting out ancient ballads that went breathlessly on as he lurched back and forth like a restive beast with a chained hind leg. Till he was exhausted. Now the tabalchi revved up, striking his tabla with sharp, rhythmical strokes, sucking in his lips and jerking back his head. The harmonium player closed his eyes and swung his head like a revolving table fan. Moans of ecstasy seeped from his mouth. The veranda spectators huddled together, wrapped in dusty coverings, heads covered against the icy night, eyes glittering and mouths agape. The smell of cattle, woodsmoke and damp straw clung to them.

Then suddenly Raghuni emerged from behind the chrysanthemum pots, dressed as Yamdoot, in black cotton rags, his face smeared with charcoal and painted with white streaks, carrying a stick with a red rag dangling from the end. The red rag, he announced, represented a palki which would bear the souls of the just, like royalty. But the foulest form of transportation awaited the wicked. Trussed up in putrid rags they would be dragged by a single sinful leg into the underworld. This concluded with a dreadful 'Aiyy-nn-nh!' as he lunged at the veranda spectators.

Next morning, the garden in the surrounds of the veranda resembled the scene of a lathi charge, with overturned pansy boxes, broken chrysanthemum pots, and low-growing plants trampled into multicoloured chutney.

Mother surveyed the scene in sore distress, drumming her fingers on her thumb. 'O Jesus! My poor chrysanthemums! I've had enough of this madness,' she said for all to hear. But the madness went on for seven nights. By then, everyone had had enough.

At the close of those winter days, we gravitated to the drawing room. With Dad at the piano, everybody crowded around to sing community songs, bursting into 'Happy days are here again'. Dad would be pink with pleasure, stars in his blue-grey eyes, and his rich, powerful voice drowning out the cares of life. And since a good many had done their schooling at North Point, Darjeeling, these sing-songs always wound up with the grand old school anthem, a stirring thing that filled us all with glorious fizz: 'Hu-rrah for our home in the moun-tains'.

During quiet winter afternoons the rockery was a romantically sequestered spot that attracted city people like Dorothy and her lovers. Almost every year she gave her current husband the slip, and appeared in Dhang with a dazzling wardrobe and a current lover. Lovers in Dhang were as safe from the outer world as eggs in styrofoam boxes.

Love! There was more of it in the evening in the drawing room—true romance, as seen on the silver screen. The bewitched lovers stood leaning over the piano, one on either side, fingertips reaching out for each other, creeping nearer and nearer, till they touched and curled and became one in a clasp of love, as they sang to Dad's bold accompaniment, 'Give me your smile, the love light in your eyes/Life could not hold a fair-er Par-a-dise!'

Dreamy eyes lifted from the keyboard, met, and locked. 'Give me the right to love you all the while!' Their voices had fused. Hands, eyes, voices! This was love! And we were witnessing it from ringside seats—till suddenly it was knocked cold by a shout from the chair in the corner, 'Ho! Ho! Ho! How nice, how nice!'

Dorothy's frequent changes of heart gave Harry the jitters. When his equilibrium was shaken up he was a remarkably changed man. His face twitched. There was a tremor in the hand that held his whisky in the evenings.

'Gladys, I can see it coming again. Divorce. She sheds her husbands like a snake sheds its skins!'

Talking of skin, nobody had ever got under Harry's skin like Dorothy and Ernie, whom he had come to love like his very own children. So life wasn't such smooth sailing for him, either. He gave, and he got.

Abdhi Missir said it was the inevitable work of karma.

Our guests were exposed to rare ministrations, like a daily massage for men only, first thing in the morning. Mr Foley had arrived the previous evening on the 6 p.m. train, for by now the number of trains had increased excitingly. He'd travelled all the way from Calcutta, changing trains three times en route, keeping a sharp eye on coolies who vanished with the luggage, and with the perilous Ganges paddle steamer crossing ('Travel at your own risk') added to the thrill of journeying to Dhang.

He lay in a trance-like sleep in his bedroom. Foley was a pencil-thin man who had to sit tight in a strong wind. Once, when we had taken him for a duck shoot on a windy day, he was blown off the boat, as he stood up to get a better look. It was a fearful thing to fall backwards into the dark, weedy waters of a jheel, but he was fished out by alert fishermen, alive and gift-wrapped in weeds.

He was now wrapped in a cosy quilt, when the door burst open and Ghogra swept in with the palang-ka-cha (bed tea). Ghogra, who prided himself as a masseur, got down to business right away starting from the foot end. He dived under the coverings seizing Foley's big toe, and jerked hard—*crack*. There was an instant cry followed by the sounds of a scuffle.

A head with puffy eyes appeared, like a rodent from its burrow, and Foley shouted, '*Chhoro, chhoro, pagal kahan ka!*' (Leave me, madman from who-knows-where!) But Ghogra would not leave off. And so ensued a weakening scuffle with more cracks. Laboured breathing and a long-drawn-out 'Aaaaah!'

His bedroom by now had filled up with witnesses and fidgety dogs. Ghogra had stuck to his business and cracked every single toe. The quilt had slipped down to the floor. Foley lay still and exposed in his striped pyjamas with hands clasped together on his chest and eyes closed like the laid-out dead. It was an alarming sight.

'Father of all asses! What have you done!' Dad seized Ghogra's coat front, ready to shake him, when Foley's eyes opened. He looked radiant.

'I say! It feels *bloody* good!' His eyes beamed energy.

Ghogra, released and honourably acquitted, put on his best martyred air. His nose twitched. 'Sahib, your bath water is becoming cold,' he announced to the ceiling, and made his exit in a huff.

When Abhinandan came to visit us he was never empty-handed. Usually he carried a fish, but sometimes there were more exciting things like parrots from the Nepal Terai, a tortoise, a peahen's egg, a young porcupine or even a baby otter. Now he turned up with a pair of puppies.

'Christmas present,' he declared.

They were Akhtah hounds, originating from a place in north Bihar, claimed by the know-alls as 'aristocratic canines' once favoured by the Mughals. An Akhtah hound was a long, sleek creature with short, khaki hair, charcoal-grey cheeks and eyebrows, a long, whiplike tail, and a notably deep chest with 'no stomach at all'—an altogether military-looking creature, like a cavalry officer with stiff, waxed whiskers.

The puppies came in loose skins with melancholy eyes and big paws. Their little black mouths surmounted by prickly whiskers had the smell of fresh toast when we picked them up to kiss and cuddle them.

'Not too much of all that,' Abhinandan said. 'They have to grow up tough.'

In time, these Christmas gifts grew into hugely disappointing shapes, named Brutus and Sheba. Brutus was a surly, unmanageable brute that killed every goat he caught grazing in our fields. Complaints poured in; compensations mounted up. And Brutus would stand no correction. He was the only living thing that growled back at Dad. 'Brutus! Jesus wept! Why did we give the ruddy dog a name like that?'

The situation grew grimmer till one day he snapped at Dad's hand, taking off a bit of Irish skin, and that was positively the end. He was banished to the Sitamarhi mela and 'lost' there.

There's no record of this powerful dog's activities at the mela, but finally he made his way to the law courts, where he padded about, snarling at pleaders and litigants. But finally, 'O Gord!' a pleader recognized Brutus. 'This is the dog from the kothi. It must have been bloody stolen away from there!'

And Brutus was back again in Dhang, but with a hangdog expression. He knew he was an outcast from Puckry kothi, and settled down to the life of a vanquished warrior at Harry's khariyan, under the sinister eye of Kethar Ojha.

Parcels arrived on the two o'clock train. Man & Co. went with pink railway receipts to inquire after them, carrying them back on their heads. Parcels of various sizes, packed with Christmas gifts, confectionery from Firpo's, and other things to make our senses reel with delight. Rich plum cakes with thick almond icing, with borders of crystallized fruit and flowers, and in the centre, a chocolate Santa slouching under the weight of a mysterious sack. Fruitcakes were baked at home. Many pounds, with many hands to help and hinder, and the dogs under the table, waiting for a windfall. Appetites were roused by the bracing cold, the excitement in the air and the power of pervading aromas. Hillocks of bread poured out from the oven and vanished like magic.

Sylvia Dyer

The garden was a feast of colour, and teeming with brilliantly plumaged birds. Bulbuls whistled the sweetest airs, and even spoke in tongues. They perched on our windowsill and cried, 'Put on the radio.' It was quite distinct and unmistakable. When we switched on the radio, we got the war news on BBC. 'All is quiet on the western front,' it said. But the men in the drawing room were never quiet, thirsting always for war news and alcohol. Both sparked off arguments among the elderly, in a smoke-filled room.

One day, a tractor arrived. Tractors had been making an appearance now, in big city showrooms. Dad had ordered a Fordson Major, and it appeared one day, with a dark, fierce-looking driver whom Lenny promptly named Bug-rat. This Bug-rat drove straight to the khariyan and got stuck in the threshing of paddy. He was a man of action, unlike the idle Dhangonians. Work that took all day for a score of bullocks was over in a wink with Bug-rat and his tractor. Those who witnessed this astonishing feat fell back, one upon the other as if struck by a bomb blast.

'Ay Bhagwan!' they cried. 'It is a God!'

'City people are damn smart,' Lenny told us, 'but they can't tell a bull from a cow! They only know machines.'

And then it was Christmas Day. The fattest among our watch geese (picked out by Mohan and Smallie Jim, the cooks) and turkeys that had drunk vinegar the previous night were roasted up, with stuffings to remember. A leg of ham, come all the way from Firpo's in Calcutta, was boiled in Tennant's beer. There were many kinds of cheese, potted meats and superb pork products, vegetables fresh from the garden, and fruit from the hills. And Abhinandan, if he happened to be a 'free man' at the time, would turn up with a couple of mahseer, to be cooked whichever way we pleased. There was Firpo's plum pudding, confectionery and all the other goodies unimaginable in this far-flung wilderness. Wine flowed freely, men argued and told tall stories, and sometimes corny jokes that were met with silence. Then quickly, Parrot, Pig and Chatter Cat were tickled in the armpits to produce the necessary laughter—it was such a thing in those days to be polite!

Abhinandan, all dressed up for Christmas, in the best Maithili Brahmin fashion, took up his position with the table servants, scrutinizing our guests in their fancy paper hats. He would come up later with uncanny assessments of their characters and backgrounds from these brief studies. They in their turn grew curious about him, asking, behind their napkins, 'Who is this extraordinary-looking man?' Nobody was told the truth, lest they choked on their turkey.

After lunch came the feeding of the poor at the khariyan. Little children and old people, no matter where they came from, were given a good feed, followed by the most thrilling event of the year—the wrestling matches.

These matches were like the world heavyweight championships, and had been a special Christmas treat, since the days of J.R. Tripe. People walked miles to see physical giants like Amrit Lal Jha (who had once fought a bull) performing in the akhara. There were lesser mortals like some of our sipahis who excelled themselves, but it was Mahanth Jha, Harry's right-hand man, who conquered hearts. The crowd pressed forward to get a better look at this apparition of physical perfection that wore an expression of serenity and gentleness that did not belong in the akhara. There was a gasp of awe and admiration: 'Look! Look, brothers, this is a god!'

Christmas dinners were always at Harry's. The best brands of liquor flowed around. Dada knocked back the whisky so fast that Dad watching him with rising gall would suddenly go 'pop'. He would jump up, snatch away Dada's glass and fling the contents out of the window.

'Dad, that's one too bloody much!' with a hiss and a glare. 'Christ Almighty! Will you never learn!'

Ernie walked home with us. It was cold and windy outside; we shivered and caught hold of Ernie's strong, warm hands. Ghogra carried a Petromax lamp high above his head like the Statue of Liberty, and the sipahis clanked their lathis as they went, warning off any wildlife lurking in the adjacent cane fields—though there was warning enough by voices raised in argument, in lusty song, or in sad, slurred speech.

'Oh!' Ernie said, diving into his coat pocket, 'I almost forgot! Here's something for you two!' He brought out a wristwatch for Pig. And for me, a little gold locket engraved with a design of the rising sun.

'Keep it forever!' he said, softly.

'Do you have a small picture of you?'

'A picture of me, eh? How would you like it—with my rat face, goat face, or iguana with a forked tongue?'

'Umm . . . your plain face will be just as nice!'

He laughed. Then suddenly he was serious and I caught a flicker of pain in his eyes. 'You deserve someone better, far better!' he said, looking away.

Far better? . . .

The next day at the khariyan, there was the great athletic meet of staff and retainers, with a variety of races for domestic servants and labourers, of whom the Musahars were the most fleet-footed and the people of Puckry, most flat-footed. A three-legged race, a tug of war and a hundred-metre dash were reserved for the sipahis. These heavyweights rolled like solid rubber balls, some of them stubbornly inseparable from their lathis.

Last of all was the disastrous dog race. The dogs, dressed up in our old clothes—knitted bonnets and booties, and even shorts with a hole for the tail to come through—were spurred into making for the winning post. Instead, dog turned upon dog, ripping the ridiculous clothes off one another. Playfully at first, but as some fangs bit deeper, the mood changed and they had to be doused with buckets of cold water. It cooled their tempers but put a damper on their Boxing Day.

Shikars

Preparations had begun for the annual shikar. Sometimes it was at Bikhna Thori, but more often at Baghaha. Both stations were on the fringe of the Terai, where the railway came to a dead halt in the face of impenetrable jungle. The train that travelled this route carried very few passengers, and with all things being favourable, moved twice a week, with a tumultuous hissing, clanking and spewing out of soot to achieve a top speed of ten miles an hour.

An advance party set out on this train to Baghaha supervised by two sipahis, who sat with the engine driver, and a wagonload of Musahars. They had arranged themselves among a formidable range of paraphernalia such as tents, mattresses, thunderboxes, crockery, cutlery, canisters of ghee, dry rations, bottles of booze, and a buffalo calf (included as tiger bait) squeezed in snout to mouth with the Musahars. As the train drew into Baghaha whistling tremulously, they leaped out to their business of readying the scene for our arrival, hacking down trees for a clearing in the jungle with a strong, circular stockade in which they pitched the tents—ours on the innermost side and theirs dangerously near the entrance, where they might have been the first to be seized by the leg.

Harry never favoured shikars, preferring to stay home, with a clear field for the pursuit of his intrigues. But then, Ernie and Dorothy's decision to join us with their current lovers turned his soaring spirits into sawdust.

'So now, Gladys,' he said with a sigh, 'I hear she's joining you with this new fancy of hers,' eyes weighed down with anxiety, 'and what—what if that husband of hers finds out? A military man, they are so sharp, heaven help us! Anything could happen! She doesn't think, stupid girl!'

But Harry's words, repeated to the 'stupid girl', only brought peals of laughter. And the shikar party moved off in Mr Cooper's saloon, with tiffin boxes, cooks, sweepers and other all-purpose men.

Cooper was a big, hearty Englishman, with twinkling blue eyes. He was an engineer on the railway, and one of the best shikaris this side of Jim Corbett. He had an adoring wife. A big-made woman with a radiant baby face and tight curls, who loped after him cooing 'Dair . . . dee!' and never let him out of her sight.

It was a merry, moving picnic that took five hours to cover fifty miles, and could be stopped anywhere. When the train came to a halt, the cookhouse workers went into action. Eggs, cutlets and parathas sizzled by the railway track on a fierce charcoal fire, while Foster ran for boiling water from the engine, and made tea.

Our hosts Bhayaji and Laloobhai, two local zamindars who were Dad's friends, were waiting for us with three large shikar elephants that chomped on banana fronds, swinging their trunks dangerously, while the men shook hands and got chummy with one another.

Early each morning they were off on these elephants, returning at sundown with an assortment of game, strung on bamboo poles or stuffed into gunny bags. It was a great challenge for the cooks, carving carcasses, stirring roasts and grinding masalas, and the smell of food travelled far into the jungle. The men, dog-tired, threw their sola topis in the air and plonked down on wooden benches to drink by the roaring bonfire that blazed in the centre of the enclosure all night. The nights were very cold, and everybody needed to warm up, while stunning pegs were poured into glasses, and stories grew taller with every passing drink. Bhayaji and Laloobhai, big, dark, mellow men with droopy eyes, glowed with pride as their Holland & Hollands were passed almost reverently around, to be admired, and even fondled. The Musahars, who filled in as beaters, were grinning inanely after a stiff shot of country arrack. A couple of drums appeared and there was a staggering song-and-dance display for our pleasure, till a very meaty dinner was served piping hot. And then it was time to retire.

Inside the tents, there was a rough-and-ready scenario, with mattresses set on beds of straw and lanterns that burned stoutly through nights of snoring, giggling, whispering, while outside, the jungle was wide awake. But far away Dorothy's husband, the 'military man', had heard rumours of the most disturbing kind. He tore himself from the war front with his service revolver, and a heart riddled with doubt, to seek out his wife in the jungles of northern India. And being a man with an intensity of purpose that would carry him to any corner of the globe, even Bagaha, landed suddenly like a guided missile from the war zone. It was a quiet afternoon, except for the echoing sound of Musahars chopping wood in the jungle, with eyes and ears wide open for man-eaters. In the distance they spied, crashing through the undergrowth, a pink-faced khaki object on two legs, which could only be an English sahib! And at once a sing-song announcement was relayed back to camp: 'Sahib! Ho—oh—aylun—re—hai! Oh—oh!' The sahib has arrived!

At that instant the lovers were sprawled on a mattress in their tent, listening to the war news on the radio. 'All is quiet on the Western Front,' they heard. But mingled with the crisp voice of the announcer, though in a far higher pitch, they heard: 'Sahib! Ho—oh—aylun—sahib!'

Dorothy jumped up from the mattress. 'OMYGODIT'S HIM!' For what other sahib would come like a bolt from the blue even to this godforsaken hole? 'Finished!' she cried in a small voice of dread, while the lover was running around picking up scattered clothes and stuffing them into a small leather suitcase. Gone was the quiet afternoon. George Cooper, a man who could look a tiger in the face from close quarters, was stuttering like a machinegun.

'Now-d-d-don't p-p-panic! Let me handle this,' he assured Dorothy, eyes sparkling with excitement. 'We're gonna fix a d-d-disappearing trick!' And there was action as never before in this land of stand-still to save a lover from the bite of bullets, and everyone else from a very messy situation. Even as the husband came crashing through the undergrowth in a beeline for Camp, the lover in a jungle hat was zigzagging through lantana bushes in the opposite direction, to vanish on a railway trolley with two of George Cooper's men, leaving an innocent scene with Dorothy smiling sweetly for her husband and the service revolver.

But the 'military man' had smelt a rat that had disappeared mysteriously; and there was warfare in their tent with the flaps down. It concerned the discovery of a man's grey, woollen sock under the mattress. The aggrieved spouse was in no mood for socializing, and they packed up and left on an elephant, in an atmosphere of gloom.

Stop moping. Tomorrow we're having a beat, so be ready, all of you!

'No bloody fears, count me out.' This sharp, high-pitched utterance came from Ernie's Calcutta girlfriend. She was terrified of elephants and liked the jungles even less, with its leopards and tigers. Understandably, she couldn't be left alone in camp, with cooks and carcasses, so Mother opted to stay back while we were off on the elephants deeper into the jungle, towards the foothills, where machaans had been set up at strategic spots. You just had to step off the elephant's head, and tickety-boo—you were on the machaan, cunningly camouflaged by foliage. Dad was camouflaged even more cunningly, in his pull-all-over-and-under.

He looked at me. 'Hell of a shindy you kicked up over coming out! Now that you're here, get one thing straight, girlie,' he said with a nice sniff (he was in a mood of joyous expectation), 'if you want to stay on this machaan, not a move, not a squeak—get dat?' He pulled out his handkerchief and blew his nose. 'Blast this cold. Or deh ole gays up—udderstood?'

'Yes Dad.'

Musahars and local tribals, called Thaaroos, were already

crashing through the jungle, hammering on empty vessels and emitting primitive cries. We could hear them coming nearer. As they drove the animals towards the machaans the air got charged with suspense. Even highly strung men, like Cooper, froze into the vegetation with a remarkable control over themselves, and Pig and Parrot froze as the reality of 'face to face with Mr Stripes' hit us. Through the trees we could see Ernie and the boys on another machaan. Ernie had not frozen. He curled his fingers to make binoculars of his hands, and looked at me. He put out his tongue.

Now, small creatures and large birds broke through the scrub, cautious and soundless: a peacock, a mouse-deer, and a sounder of wild pig. The men held their breath and their fire because it was Mr Stripes they were sweating for. Then suddenly we heard the crackle of dry twigs, a quicker movement in the tall, dry grass—a flash of orange passing through, with black stripes, moving in a straight line for our machaan. Cooper nudged Dad and winked. Nearer and nearer. Now fifteen yards away. Dad's rifle was pointed just right, his cheek tight against it, finger on the trigger, the big head of a tiger appeared . . . then all of it! Majestic and terrifying at the same time, it stood, looking left and looking right, but not up at us.

Dad's greatest moment had come!

And then it happened. The gun barrel jerked suddenly upwards with a 'Haaaann choooo!' One of the biggest sneezes of his life! Like a bomb blast in the silence. The tiger whipped around and was gone in a flash.

Mr Cooper just stared with a wide-open mouth. It was all over.

Those who were 'bloody lucky' got to see the Big Cats. And those who knew that a tiger wasn't something to be sneezed at, bagged one. That's the way it was.

But were they defeated? Three days later, during lunch, a couple of tribals drifted in with information. A tiger had killed a village buffalo. 'Two to four days back. Maybe.'

'By jeepers! I bet it's the same one that got away in the beat!'

Cooper stuck into his wild boar roast while his wife watched him with doting eyes. 'But Tip, figure this out. Four days ago? It could be miles away by now.'

'True, George, but dammit—it's worth a try!' Dad rubbed his hands briskly together. 'Two of us'll sit over the kill. You never know, we might be face to face with Mr Stripes again! Yippee!'

And they were off on the elephants with some servants and shikaris, taking essential supplies.

We were left in camp with one cook, ten Musahars and a .12 bore gun. It was delightful, having little adventures with the Musahars who were quite at home in primeval forests like this. In the evening, they entertained us with their animal tales of imagination and exaggeration. But there was a change in the entertainment programme, the second night.

The usual racket ceased, and we were just dozing off, when, 'Shh! Did you hear that?' Heads popped up from quilts. It was the sound of wood being sawed—very near. But in the night? 'Who could be sawing wood in the middle of the night?' Mother was up in a flash. 'Quick, quick, children, the gun.'

Ernie's girlfriend let out a scream inside her tent. 'Oooo! Help me, O Jesus! I should never have come to this bloody place.' Mother, with the gun pointed forward, was moving like a hunter in a long, flannel nightie printed with sprigs of roses, out of the tent and into the centre clearing where the bonfire of heavy logs burned in a frenzy of bright orange. Nothing moved but flickering shadows in the firelight. She looked around. There was nothing inside the enclosure. Then very deliberately, she pointed the gun at the treetops and fired both barrels. Bang! Bang!

There was a stampede. Musahars shot out from their beds of straw, and the tents collapsed, trapping the rest in canvas with howls of, 'Bagh! Bagh! Save me, Missbaba!'

Mother put the gun away, chuckling softly. 'Golly! That was enough to scare it away for good.' Next morning, outside the fence in the soft, moist earth where they skinned the animal carcasses, she pointed out fresh pug marks. 'As I thought. It was a leopard,' she told us. 'Sometimes their breathing sounds like the sawing of wood. I've heard they're susceptible to bronchitis.'

The men were back by evening, and slid down their elephants, dog-tired and sweaty with no sign of Stripes or even Spots. As they straggled in, Ernie's girlfriend flew from her tent in a torrent of tears straight at Ernie. She pummelled his chest. 'Take me back now!' she screeched. 'I hate this bloody shikar thing!' He looked at us embarrassed. 'Now!' she screamed, and raced back to her tent.

'Crikey!' Dad threw his sola topi at an empty chair. 'What a bloody day! Those Thaaroos were talking pure crap. Round and round all day, and not even the tail end of a tiger. And then, early this morning . . . ' he groaned, flopping down heavily, 'sitting around with mugs of tea—too piping hot to drink—you know how you sometimes get this feeling something's watching you? It was one of the blasted elephants waving its head at us. Something must have sent it off its nut. And before we knew what, it charged! Christopher Columbus! Luckily the nearest hut was close enough, and we shot in like greased lightning, six of us!' He paused, lit up a cigarette and blew a cloud of smoke at us.

'But was that all? Hell's bells no! There was its bloody big nut stuck in the doorway—groping about with its trunk for us. And us pressed flat as chapattis against the opposite wall. Ernie, poor fellow, was the nearest! We were yelling like the devil's aunt! Till—guess what?' Dad's eyebrows shot up as he looked around at his spellbound audience.

'What?' we yelled together.

'A little nipper, barely a foot off the ground, comes pelting along, screaming and swearing at the blasted thing, yanking at its ears and lashing its head with a twig! You hear that? A twig! And what do you think it does? It turns its big arse around and moves away like Mary's little lamb.'

Meanwhile, Harry had been playing his favourite games at home.

Sukhesar met us at the station with a glum face. 'Huzoor,

Harry sahib's servants have cut down thirty-two shisham trees on our bund, fringing the Mahari.'

'Cut down our trees? Is this true?'

'Yes Missbaba, and carted them away.' He drew in a deep breath for the delivery of the final stroke. 'While your presence was away, the government land measurer was called here to re-measure that area. He declared that that entire strip falls into Harry sahib's holdings. What could I do, Missbaba, in your absence. I was helpless. Harry sahib's Musahars were ordered to cut down the trees and push back the bund to a new boundary line. I never saw them work so fast.'

This called for an immediate visit to Harry's place.

'Really Harry, this is preposterous. The boundaries were settled in 1934, after my mother's death. If it has taken seven years to discover the mistake, you could at least have waited a few days for my return.'

Harry listened patiently, like a much-misunderstood man.

'Calm down, Gladys. I tell you I knew nothing of it, till afterwards,' with a hopeless gesture of innocent hands, 'it was this Kethar Ojha, I had to pull him up.'

'Pull him up? After so many of my valuable trees were pulled up and carted away! Jesus Lord, where will all this end? If it ever does!' Tears of rage sprang up in her eyes. 'I'll tell you something, Harry. Even Kethar Ojha—that notorious cut-throat—would not have done this to me, unless you put the knife in his hand.'

Harry winced and his face flushed darkly. 'You see, Gladys, the government surveyor has approved the new boundary line. Maybe you'd like to take the matter to court?' And he smiled, cool as a cucumber.

'Maybe I will! Who would doubt that you bribed the wretched man?'

Mother did the half-mile walk back in a few minutes, and sat down, breathing fire. 'Never an end to it! He knows only too well that I can't afford another case!' Her handkerchief came out, and she blew her nose with fury. 'Oh damn this nose!'

'And he knew nothing?' Dad snarled. 'Perhaps we can believe that! He wouldn't let his right hand know what his left was doing. My blood boils! God's truth, girlie, sometimes I'd like to get my hands on his throat.'

And he was not the only one. Abhinandan, sitting cross-legged on the veranda floor, was gritting his teeth and scowling up at the ceiling. He had been a witness to the whole shocking drama.

'Missbaba,' he said softly, 'through these many years, I have watched Harry sahib. He has tried in so many ways to break you and you never retaliate. He will go on destroying you, and laughing at what he thinks is your weakness. There will never be an end to it. Never till he has destroyed you.'

He stood up to leave after this outburst and suddenly his jaw began to quiver. 'Missbaba, if you would only let me . . .' he drew the edge of his hand sharply across his throat.

For a moment she stared at him in shocked disbelief. 'How dare you suggest such a thing!' she flared up at him. 'Violence is all you ever think about! If he has to destroy me, then let him destroy me! There's a God above us for vengeance.'

Pin-drop silence. He could see that he had gone too far, and turned a dusky red with his eyes fixed on the floor.

'Missbaba,' he said flatly, 'your God has no vengeance!'

For a long time, there had been no communication between Harry's place and ours after this last painful episode. Then, one day Harry came limping across the Puchkurwa, dogged by a couple of his bodyguards. It saved him the three-mile drive by car which was a long, circuitous route, and despite all precautions he always got covered with dust.

He had come to discuss the most important topic, harvest. Casual, just as though the crushing loss and bitterness had never occurred.

But there was frost in the air.

'A good harvest this year,' Harry said, watching Gladys's face.

'We've done even worse than last year.' She looked away, irritated by the barbed statement.

'Because half your income is being harvested by your sipahis. Everybody knows, but you!'

Now he sounded very concerned. 'Where, I ask you, is the need for Tip to be running to Sitamarhi day after day? Morning till evening he is stuck there while income goes down the drain."

Gladys was doing a bit of deep breathing. 'I've sacked two of my sipahis,' she said coldly.

'I know, I know, Gladys, but there will be others! Thieves of the first water! Thieves everywhere!' he burst out, in feigned concern. 'Tell me, how can you run a place like this without supervision, personal supervision? Never heard of it!'

Dad was livid when the matter came up between them. 'Master Harry thinks he's bloody smart! Why do I run, day after day, to the Sitamarhi court? Why am I an honorary magistrate? Why? Christ Almighty! Glad, don't you people realize that times are changing? This position gives us some security. More than anything at this present time, we need security.'

And he was right. Dead right.

PART 3

1942: The Great Change

It was 1942. Times were changing and so were people. Hatred for the British suddenly flared up and spread like a bush fire, even to the back of beyond, where most people knew not that the world was round, but now learned enough history to hate the British and anything even remotely connected with them. The atmosphere grew ominously charged, building up for the coming storm.

Darbhanga was one of the worst-affected areas. Groups of students swaggered about, arms flailing in the air, red paan-stained mouths shouting, 'White dog, quit India!'

It was written on the walls, compound walls, building walls, latrine walls, even in cowsheds, these smouldering words of expulsion were written in dung. Every Indian was ganging up against the British, who had had it too good for too long.

Even Chatter Cat caught the mood, marching about with a bamboo stick on his shoulder, shouting, 'Inquilab zindabad!'

As if alarm bells had gone off everywhere, the Europeans and Anglo-Indians in isolated spots began gravitating to large towns and cities. People were on the move with their precious belongings, while terror-striking rumours flew from mouth to mouth.

Harry let out a mocking laugh when Mother left too. 'Ha ha! Let them show the white feather—running to Samastipur!' ('Showing the white feather' was one of his favourite expressions of derision.) 'What will happen?'

So when it happened, two people were caught out in the cold— Harry (who didn't want to show the white feather) and Dada, who hated the town and its people anyway, both clinging stubbornly to the belief that the black clouds would simply roll away.

But there were guardian angels.

'We must make haste and flee from here!' Abhinandan appeared before Dada, slumped in his chair on the veranda.

He looked up in shock. 'Huh? Flee from here! How?'

'You will have to become women,' he was told.

'Women! Christ Almighty! Why women? Have you gone mad?'

'No Buddha sahib.' Abhinandan squatted down by the chair and his voice came in a whisper, 'If you wish to save your skin, you will also have to change its colour. You dress up not for a pagal nautch [fancy dress ball] but for a game of life and death!'

He glanced furtively around. 'We pass through some troubled villages. Last week they caught the Anglo-Indian police inspector, Waller sahib, tied him up in a gunny bag and set fire to it. Did you know that?'

Dada's face went red, but he was silent.

'Oh dammitall! And how do we go?'

'By the light of the moon, in an ordinary bullock cart drawn by common bullocks.'

'Lord bless us!'

Harry too had become aware of the situation and its imperative needs. Mahanth Jha was the next to appear with an urgent note from him.

'It is all arranged,' Harry wrote. 'There must be no delay. We leave tomorrow at 3 a.m. sharp. Nobody should know about this but the trustworthiest, like the bearer of this note. I don't know if we can trust this fellow Abhinandan, he has no love for me! But the whole thing is his idea and he has much influence in these parts. Hope he's not up to any of his tricks. But we're in this together and he will not want any harm to come to you! Well, we must hurry. Time is running out of our hands and we must be gone before word gets out. More when face to face.' He concluded, in his customary style.

A bamboo frame was hurriedly fitted over an ordinary village cart and covered over with coarse, soiled sheeting.

'We will bring you white cotton saris to wear and conceal your faces, just in case. You will also have to shave off your moustaches.' Abhinandan chuckled softly.

'No, no! This is going too far! We will need to look like men when the British Tommies pick us up.'

'Buddha sahib, that will be the least of the hazards you will face.'

It was August, a month when floods worked out their crafty schemes for the toppling of mankind. Rugged dirt tracks rose steeply, and then dipped, veering away to left and right, a deadly test for a village bullock cart on narrow wooden wheels. If it overcame this trap, patches of soft, sucking silt waited wickedly, a little further on.

Harry and Dada, wrapped in saris, clung to the side rails as they were bounced and lurched about inside the cart, while Ghogra drove skilfully (he was a man of many skills, though he had not learned this particular one from the ICS). Abhinandan, Narain Singh and Mahanth Jha walked alongside, dressed humbly, so as not to attract any attention. They gripped the cart rails on either side, to steady its tottering progress, swearing at Ghogra. Ghogra swore at the dragging pace of the country bullocks. He had not bargained for this kind of excitement and wanted it over fast. Harry and Dada cursed softly to themselves in the fetid and steamy interior.

'Harry boy, how with all your private eyes and ears did you get into this tricky situation?'

'We make our mistakes!' Harry snarled back. 'We make our mistakes and we pay for them!'

He brought out a handkerchief and wiped the sweat from his face.

'Harry boy, I never thought I'd see you in a sari!'

'Man alive! Why don't you just shut up.'

'Sorry, old boy! Oh dammitall, this blithering thing keeps slipping off my head! How the devil does one keep it from unravelling?'

'How the devil would I know?'

'Got a drink on you by any chance?'

Harry looked at Dada in weary disgust. 'Ghogra's put some brandy in my attaché case and there's water in that flask.'

Dada reached eagerly for the bottle. 'Good stuff. To hell with the water!'

'Holy saints!' Harry hissed out. 'I don't grudge you the drink, but is *this* the time?'

The moon had disappeared and an angry dawn was breaking greyly. The cart lurched, swayed and struggled on with the escorts pushing from behind. Then it began to rain, and an immense choir of bullfrogs struck up a gloomy chant like a requiem.

They came to Gharburra where the road snaked through the village. It was a troubled village, with murderously anti-British sentiments. As they entered, ring-tailed pi-dogs streaked out at them snarling as if they'd sniffed out treachery. Abhinandan hissed and dismissed them with a sweep of his lathi. They passed on, between mud huts with smoothly plastered walls. Some were illustrated in red paint with prancing elephants, and stick figures with sly eyes, on horses.

Then a man recognized Narain Singh. 'Where to, brother?'

'My mother is seriously ill. I'm taking her to the Sitamarhi hospital.'

'Hai, hai! At a time like this! There's trouble there, brother, a troop-train full of white soldiers with trigger-happy fingers on their accursed guns.'

'We have to take the risk,' Abhinandan cut in, 'life is a game of risks, is it not, brother?'

'So it is. It is.'

The rain had ceased, and it grew brighter. There were waking village sounds: buffaloes, goats, bawling infants. A patch of water came into view. The road here was almost submerged. The cart moved forward sluggishly and sank into the mire. The bullocks strained every sinew to get it free. 'Move! Move! You husbands of prostitutes!' Ghogra screamed at them. He pushed forward, striking their starved posteriors with both his feet. The village spectators rallied around to push.

But despite all the effort nothing was budging. Then a strange thing happened. A drowsing pi-dog, suddenly triggered off by the commotion, darted under the cart and bit the bullocks' legs. They reared up and jerked forward. The cart rocked drunkenly and it moved. Free! Free, with its dark secret. And away they went on wings of angels with never a look back.

A troop-train was standing on the railway siding, with British Tommies everywhere. Harry and Dada quickly shed their oriental trappings, emerging into the most glorious daylight, like moths from their drab chrysalises. They were greeted with a cheer. 'Nice! How nice, how nice!' Dada cried in relief. And it was nice, all right. But Harry had to live with what he considered the worst embarrassment of his life—especially when 'face to face' with Tip.

Meanwhile, in Samastipur, every European and Anglo-Indian had taken refuge in the Bengal & North Western Railway Institute, convinced of an imminent mutiny-type of attack. The halls of merriment were now filled with anxious mothers, wailing babies, cats, dogs, parrots and little boys who fought mock battles among themselves, dodging through the rooms with toy guns. Their only protection was the AFI, an auxiliary force made up of their own menfolk, commanded by non-commissioned officers of the British army. There was a shortage of arms and ammunition, so everyone who possessed a weapon of any sort had to produce it.

Mother brought out her .12 bore, and sadly took stock of the ammunition. 'Bullets for human beings! What have we come to! Terence, I can't believe this is happening!'

Day and night the rhythmic outburst of slogans came to them from afar. A litany of 'Murdabads' and another of 'Zindabads', but mostly, 'White dogs, quit India!'

It was like the river gone mad. Everyone was jumpy, expecting the worst from the other side, particularly after the incident at the level crossing. A British troop-train had unwittingly made things hotter for those imprisoned in the institute, when troops had opened fire on an angry mob all set to detain their train. That day a memorable drama had been played out, with hundreds braving bullets for their freedom.

Fakir Mohammed our tailor, who lived just a stone's throw from the scene of action, was a petrified witness. 'Bullets flew like hail!' he told us. 'Some so close to my head that my hair curled!'

And it stayed that way. We saw it for ourselves, when he came to measure Chatter Cat for a new herringbone suit: 32"–33"–34". His hands shook while taking the measurements, as he recounted the experience. 'It was a frightful way of getting a permanent wave,' he said.

After the tragic incident, the troop-train had moved on, but the folks in the institute remained to face the resulting music, with nights and days of torment for 'White dogs' and even khaki-coloured dogs, like us! However, the joint-family lifestyle contributed its varied distractions in this ghastly furnace of suspense, like alcohol and forbidden love by night, scandalous gossip and bitter disputes by day. But greatly moving were the times when they shelved it all to join together in prayer: fervent, tearful, persistent prayer that made its way to God's heart.

And they were spared from the big showdown.

The situation settled down like a raging fever gradually cooling off, and the family returned to Dhang.

'You silly goats!' the boys wrote to Parrot and Pig, for by now they were finished with Goethal's Memorial School. 'You really missed something!' And Mother. 'Thank God you were safe in school, my darlings; things were just dreadful!'

By the end of November, when we were home for the winter holidays, things were as good as ever for us, but not for Dada. The remaining years of his life were closing like a book. Page after page of work, read, eat and sleep— smoking and whistling through it all.

Parrot and Pig stood observing him: slumped in his armchair, gazing into space, already in another world, the space under the chair filled with emptiness. He knew it and felt it. An old man with a wound that was draining his life's sap away, the wound of a lost love—the unquestioning, unconditional love of a dog that never reproached. There were older, deeper wounds that he never ever spoke of. Just smoked them away. Just whistled them away, like his favourite song. 'There's a long, long trail a'winding into the land of my dreams/Where the nightingale is singing, and a white moon beams/There's a long, long night of waiting, until my dreams all come true/For the day when I'll be going down that long, long trail with you.'

For the first time we realized that Dada was old. His mind began to wander hopelessly. Even during serious discussions at the dining table, he'd chip in with remarks quite off the point. They came like howlers out of the blue. But the grown-ups were not amused, and some would turn and stare at Dada quite irritably. 'Dad, you've caught the bull by the tail!' his son burst out, flushed with embarrassment. But Dada just parried with 'Nice! How nice, how nice!'

Then there was the business of his bedroom lamp. He had grown abnormally concerned about it, as though his life depended on the thing. As if he secretly believed that when the light went out, so would the spirit from his frail, old body. Special care was taken to see that it was in good working order, with oil sufficient to last the night.

By the next winter he had become irritable, complaining of the cold and shortness of breath, and the new doctor with a gold tooth and gold-rimmed spectacles was called from Sitamarhi.

'An enlarged heart,' he declared, his stethoscope making its routine journey over the heaving chest, 'and, of course, old age.' Then, looking up at the rafters in the ceiling, 'It's all in God's hands!'

But age had not withered his appetite for food. He began to snatch goodies at the dining table. Big helpings of jam and crisp, white khajas dripping with syrup went down his food pipe before Pig and Parrot could get at them. So when Dada began to have stomach aches nobody was overly concerned.

'Come now,' Dad measured out a dose of Eno, 'just down this and go to sleep. You'll be right as rain in the morning!'

A wind from the north sprang up and rapped on the windows. The nightwatchmen in the veranda shivered, and curled up more snugly in their homespun coverings.

About 3 a.m. one of them knocked on Mother's bedroom door. 'The lamp,' he said, 'has gone out in Buddha sahib's room.' Servants dashed in to rekindle it. It must have been the wind, they said; it had been blowing hard all night. But it wasn't. The oil had finished and Dada lay very white and still. His eyes were half open and his mouth frozen in a slack circle, as if he'd left this world, whistling. Whistling his favourite song . . . He had taken the longest trail of all.

He was put quietly to rest in the family graveyard, in his best navy-blue suit, and pure white spider lilies.

'Don't be sad, Piggy, up there he must be watching us and saying, "Nice! How nice, how nice!"'

Comings and Goings

Warm winds began to blow as the days moved into March, racing mercilessly to the end of our annual winter holidays. Each year, as school time drew near, grey ghosts of misery began to hover around us. We were engulfed in a crushing sadness, a gut emptiness, watching the big, black trunks slowly fill up with odious school uniforms while Fakir Mohammed worked flat out on the hand-operated Singer sewing machine, on the back veranda floor. The dogs were sprawled around looking bored. They yawned in a stifled desperation, so widely that they could have dislocated their jaws. The dogs knew everything.

Pig and I sat on the veranda steps, staring sightlessly at the garden. Chumra came and sat on his haunches alongside us. He gave me a silent sideways look, as though he knew there was a problem, painful and deep, that couldn't be discussed, and closed the matter with a comforting lick on my ear.

'Live each day like it's your last!' Pig said in a hollow voice, hammering in each word, like nails in a coffin.

'What are these hard words, Piggy!'

'Hard? They were Lenny's words, when we were having chhota-hazri.'

He said, 'Take it like Abhinandan in the lock-up!'

And so, the years passed with his comings and goings. One day he was here with a fish, and the next he was gone like a spirit. And no talk about it.

We were back again for the winter holidays, when Harry's car followed by a trail of dust drove in one morning with the top of Rama's head just visible behind the wheel. Harry eased himself out of the back seat, a beaming Harry, because, thanks to the handsome contribution he had made to the war fund, the British had bestowed on him an MBE.

He was in high spirits. 'Gladys, wild geese! They've been sighted on the Baghmati, near the bridge. If we want to get a shot at them, we should set out soon.'

Gladys was taken by surprise. 'Wild geese, but we're out of petrol, Harry! Chamanlal's gone for it on the morning train with Terence.'

'What does it matter matter, Gladys. There's more than enough room for us and the children in this car. The boys can follow up with Ernie, on their horses.'

It was a good ride on the District Board Road to the Baghmati bridge, a long stretch with a fine surface. Years ago, we used to race along this stretch of road with Ernie and the boys, or at least we tried. Pig on his one-eyed animal, and Parrot on a rickety museum piece. And there was Ernie cantering up the centre road. Such a pleasing sight, the big grey horse and rider! Particularly the rider. We ran to him, with a scream, 'Ernie!' That smile!

Those mesmerizing eyes! When they looked into the wide-open windows of your simple, green soul, you could be done for. But this was not the time for reminiscing.

'Come, children, we must lose no time!' It was Harry's voice.

We were bundled into his car with the boys riding behind, tearing along the District Board Road. Narain Singh stood on the footboard, gripping the window frame with both hands, face screwed up against the wind, and clothes flapping violently.

Mother disapproved of this mode of travel for them, but the sipahis looked childishly disappointed; it gave them an undreamt-of thrill—after a lifetime of bullock carts—and gradually the objections were overruled. So, from his upright position, Narain Singh was able to see what was coming. And he cried out in alarm, 'Oh rok re!'

Rama's little feet moved fast. Clutch and brake. His mouth moved faster. He jerked the steering wheel to left and right. The car swerved crazily. We braced ourselves for it. It was a ditch, three feet wide, cut right across the road. There was a bang and crunch of metal. Smoke, dust and hot water. Narain Singh flew like Superman through the air. We were shaken like pegs in a box, while Rama of the cleft palate lifted up his head and let out a piercing, nasal howl.

Life is full of ironies, and often unfair. While cuts and bruises were distributed liberally among the sound, the only serious injury struck the man with the cleft palate. Rama had fractured his leg, and was doomed for the perilous ministrations of the civil surgeon in Sitamarhi. Then there was the horse that had been following the car, too closely. Ernie, down on his knees, was examining its foreleg. His face went white. He ran his fingers through his hair and pulled.

'Oh damn!' he said bitterly, and there was a black fire burning in his eyes.

Harry looked at his car. His face turned a dull purple. 'So, it has come to this! Well, we will see who is responsible. They will not escape, I promise you!'

It was the work of some goondas from a nearby village. All through the year, people looked forward to the Christmas wrestling matches. And this year, there had been none.

'Cowardly jackals!' The Harpur Rajputs were up in arms, itching for a good fight. 'Come brothers, let's take the hides off these scum—their own fathers won't know them.'

'Enough! Enough! No skulls will be cracked open.' Mother cooled them off. 'We can't take the law into our own hands. This is a matter for the daroga.'

'Still . . .' She sighed, as we made our way home in the tyre-cart. 'I can't believe this! After all these years . . .'

'Times are changing, Gladys.' Harry scowled. 'People are changing. Who knows what else will change?'

Who knows, she wondered as her eyes fell on the shisham trees, lining every road and ridge—beautiful and enduring sentinels of territory. And she was thinking . . . These things will never change.

The big grey horse was limping painfully along. We followed in single file. The funeral before the death. A watery-orange sun was dipping down behind the Banswari. You could smell sadness, soaked in the air. And feel the silence in your bones.

'Tell me, Reggie, what's happening? Where're we going?'

'It's a funeral. The horse is going to be destroyed. Its leg is broken. And look, Parrot, you don't have to come!'

'Destroyed! But why? Can't it go to Sitamarhi like Rama?'

'Because a horse is different. Take it from me and shut up or you'll only make matters worse! He loved the horse, and now he has to destroy the thing he loved with one bloody shot.' Reggie sounded gruff—too gruff for Reggie.

He turned to look at my face. 'Ah ah! What's this now? Really, you girls! Is this anything to bawl about? Here. Here's a handkerchief.'

It was when the mustard fields were in full bloom, the evenings spiked with plaintive dove calls and an almost unbearable sweetness in the air that I cried, not for the horse, but for Ernie.

Everything was so exquisitely sad by the banks of the Mahari that day that you had to cry, for someone, for something.

The horse stood alongside a deep pit, to make its burial easier, for the Musahars who had dug the pit were debarred from touching the animal once it had become a carcass.

For a moment, Ernie stood stroking the horse's head. It blinked and looked at him with dark, liquid eyes, and tears slid down its smooth, grey cheeks. I saw the glint of water in his eyes and looked away, so I wouldn't make it worse. There was a muffled shot, and the horse fell back with a heavy thud into the pit.

Then it was all over.

Wrapped up and put away forever, in silence.

Nothing but silence from Ernie as we walked back home, and he had eyes only for the earth he trod upon.

'I'm going back to Samastipur,' he declared, not looking at anyone at all.

Independence

The war was over. Independence was in the air. It brought both jubilation and dismay—depending on which side you were on. Among the Anglo-Indians it set off a restless, troubled movement between country and town.

Harry, these days, was a frequent evening visitor. There was a different mood and a different kind of dialogue to be heard now.

Dad, back from Sitamarhi on the 6 p.m. train, brought more distressing news every day. 'Independence is all very well, but trouble, I can tell you, is brewing up all over the country.' He paused to light a cigarette, waved the flaring match about and threw it out of the window. 'Sure as God made little apples—split in two, it will be!'

'Heaven only knows what that will mean.'

'It can mean only one thing, girlie. More blood will flow.'

'O Jesus Lord! And what about the Anglo-Indians? How will it go for Anglo-Indians?'

'Many of them speak of going back "home"—poor pilgarlics—a home they've never set eyes on. Yes, masses of them are packing up to leave. Believe me, things will be bad here. They're saying it's bubbling up like oil in a cauldron! 1942 all over again, I'd say worse! This time it'll be Hindus versus Muslims.

'Don't say that!'

'Girlie, it's the plain and simple truth.' Dad blew out a stream of smoke.

A letter arrived for Mother from the British High Commission in Calcutta. She read it over several times in growing distress.

'Listen to this: It says I'm to proceed with my family to the UK. They can no longer be responsible for us after Independence.'

'Well, Glad, we should have known it was coming. But the UK?' Dad poured himself another drink. 'It'll be no fun, take it from me! Do you have any idea what conditions are like there after the war? Bad as we can imagine! And are you used to housework, girlie?'

Mother simply sighed.

'And their winters! Oh crikey! Dark at four, with cold that freezes the marrow in your bones. No sight of the bloody sun either, just drizzle-drizzle till it drives you mad. Can you take that kind of life?'

'So then, what can we do? Where do we go? This is our country, our home, the only home we've ever known!'

'True, Gladys,' Harry who had been listening intently, fired the final shot. 'But when the ship is sinking? Gladys, you'll get a good price for your property. Have you ever thought about East Africa? Yes? Well, life there is very much like this, a beautiful country and you'll still have plenty of servants.'

'I agree, Harry, but to uproot ourselves for another land, another people, another life! To start all over again, at this age? No thanks, Harry. I'll take my chances, like you. This is where I'll live and die!'

Literature on East Africa poured in with enchanting pictures. Kenya? Uganda? Which?

Neither. We would stay right here and go down with the ship. Servants, dogs, bullocks, cows, geese, Muscovy ducks, bachelor turkey and all!

It was over too for Ernie's bachelor days. He was finally caught and marched off to the altar.

Panther White the fleet-footed, who had preyed upon womankind right through the war years, while men were busy on battlefronts all over the globe, was now a captive, like a maneater that is finally trapped.

Harry was pleased. 'The boy is settling down at last. All this running around madness, Gladys. All my money thrown about like paper will end. Heaven be praised.'

And there was a great celebration at the Planters' Club. The Muzaffarpur Planters' Club was one of the oldest in India. It stood by the shores of a lake with perfect lawns sweeping down like green carpets to the water's edge. Water lilies covered the surface and well-fattened waterbirds drowsed in the shallows. From the far shores, dhobis could be heard beating clothes with a zeal that gave them a brilliantly white, though short, lifespan.

The club had a vibrant life, subdued by day but riotous by night. In a large billiards room, where magnificent animal heads loomed out from the walls (prized trophies since its earliest times), you could hear the gentle clicks and tuk-tuks of cues on billiards balls, from silent tireless players with eyes only for the balls.

There was the bar, small and cosy, where bachelors with smouldering eyes gazed over the rims of their whisky glasses at young women. And where the financially hazardous custom of

Sylvia Dyer

'sab se poochho, drinks all round' made, as time went on, bigger and bigger holes in members' pockets. But for the present it made life a madly merry thing, merry enough to toss one another into the shallows of the lake.

Then, there was the Snake Pit, a nice glass chamber, where the older ladies collected to knit and spit venom, watching the 'deplorable behaviour' with narrowed eyes of suppressed displeasure.

A large dance hall came to life in the evenings with a piano on a little stage and a parquet floor that went bounce-bounce when they did the La Conga. One long wall was covered over with cartoon sketches of pig-sticking scenes, and the other with immense gilt-framed mirrors wherein you could see yourself in a new evening gown, jitterbugging with a reckless partner.

Over the years, we had 'suffered' going there, as one of the sacrifices made by children for peaceful coexistence with parents. But growing up had brought about a sharp reversal of leanings.

Now, there was a grand celebration. Harry had splurged. Everyone of any importance was there. It was packed tight with guests from far and near, and a band that was hired from Calcutta.

Even Abhinandan had invited himself to the wedding. All dressed up, he was quite spectacular. People turned to stare at him, standing on the fringe of the crowd, taller than all the others, with his arms folded across his chest and head held arrogantly high, watching the guests and the proceedings with a keen interest. He had a secret admiration for the British that stopped short at some of their customs and social practices, as now, when the dancing started.

'Dhath teri!' His eyes opened wide with shock. 'What is this? You call this dancing? One man's wife and another woman's husband stuck together, and moving!' It drove him outside to spit out his disgust. Then he was back to ask, 'What sort of dance is this?'

'It's the dance of the British,' the waiters told him. 'It's called ball dance.'

We saw very little of Ernie after this celebration. He was stuck with his wife in the Samastipur house and lost to us forever.

The years of childhood had slipped away, and we were finally done with boarding school, when Abhinandan came again to visit us. He found us sprawled like basking lizards in easy chairs on the front veranda, passing our time in the slothful manner of drones.

Pig was back on vacation from Faraday House in London, where he'd been sent to fulfil Harry's dreams that Mother had got infected with. But they were not Pig's dreams. And Abhinandan sensed it. He sensed, as he sat watching us now, with those keen, penetrating eyes of his, that we were, perhaps, dreamless people. That all we would ever amount to was worthless mediocrity. I saw it in his face. No lawyers to defend him, no doctors to mend him, no great engineers he could brag about.

Now Rajan Singh, with his long dreary face, came to visit Mother.

'In the early hours of this morning,' he said with a troubled frown, 'there was a dacoity in our village! Kya baat hai, Missbaba, such a thing has never happened in our village before! And a most peculiar business it was. Only one man's house was attacked, Harry sahib's manager, Kethar Ojha! And well planned too. The night he was on duty at sahib's khariyan. They came with their faces masked, bound all the family members to the central pillar of the house and left without a sound! Even the village dogs raised no alarm! But Missbaba, after all this trickery, what did they take? Nothing at all! The loot was strewn all along the path leading out of the village. Why? The poor people ran about like rats at a feast, picking up cash, gold and silver ornaments, for the house had been stripped of everything. But what could the dacoits have gained for themselves?' he asked, looking at her very shrewdly.

'It was no ordinary dacoity.'

'So you agree, revenge was the motive! Kethar, we all know,

has harmed so many people, but always the poor and the timid. So then, Missbaba, who among these miserable wretches was daring enough to have carried out such mischief?'

Who? She had guessed. But let the answer come from him.

'I'll tell you, Missbaba,' he whispered. 'He who many regard as the champion of the oppressed, Abhinandan Jha! He has paid back Kethar Ojha, in one lump sum, for all he has done to these poor wretches with Harry sahib's blessings, of course!'

'That's all very well,' she said with a sigh, 'but with Harry sahib's blessings, I fear he'll have to pay a heavy price for this service.'

Yet another monsoon was upon us. From the wide front veranda we watched the rain come pelting down. Days like this drove us out from the gloomy indoors.

Kalri, with her face furrowed even deeper from years of looking on the darkest side, squatted near Mother's chair. 'What rain, what rain, Missbaba! What, oh, what is written for us?'

And then like an answer to her question we saw Sukhesar coming up the drive with his dhoti hitched up, the rain hammering with furious feet on the umbrella he held with his only hand. A cotton covering tucked under the stump of his other arm clung wetly to his shoulders. He often went to Sitamarhi with cash and documents needed for our never-ending batwara case, and returned on the 1 p.m. train.

He came slowly up the steps, wearing a stony expression. Ever since his son's ghastly death, he had worn it like a mask.

'Missbaba, there is bad news,' he said, 'Abhinandan has been arrested. There's a charge against him for murder!' Looking sharply around, his voice dropped almost to a whisper. 'There's talk that it was engineered by Kethar Ojha, with inspiration from Harry sahib. It seems that Kethar Ojha made convenient use of the dacoity committed in his house to snuff out one of his own enemies and plant the body at the scene of the crime. So when the dacoity was traced to Abhinandan, he was charged with the murder of this man as well. Witnesses were bought and primed to make it look like premeditated murder.'

'As I expected!' Mother stood up. 'I'll take a walk across to Harry's.'

Mother pulled on her gumboots, took a strong umbrella, and set off down the centre road with Narain Singh in tow.

Harry was at his desk, going through some papers. He looked up in surprise. 'What, Gladys—in this rain? And you look upset! What's happened?' He got up quickly to offer her a chair.

Mother sat looking fixedly at him. 'What's happened?' she repeated. 'Abhinandan has been arrested on a charge of murder in the first degree!'

'Well, Gladys, is there anything so unusual about that? You know as well as anybody what a reputation the man has.'

'Cleverly spoken, Harry! Frame a man with his reputation. And yet, who was it that risked his life saving yours during the 1942 disturbances? Lord Jesus! Some people have such short memories.'

'I see . . . But why flare up at me, Gladys? How do I come into it?'

'How indeed! We don't have to search in a haystack for the truth. It is out all over. They are saying it was all nicely fabricated by that favourite of yours—your left-hand man for all purposes sinister, Kethar Ojha! He too has a reputation.'

Harry leaned back in his chair, hands together, fingertips touching.

'Kethar Ojha . . . I see . . . He is to blame for everything, because people do not like him. Do you think that Abhinandan has no other enemies—a man like him?' He paused, and his left eye began to twitch. 'I'm told he even threatened to cut off my head! Mine! You might not have heard this, Gladys,' looking pointedly at her, 'but I did! I have my ways.'

'And I have my answer!' She pushed back her chair and stood up quickly to leave. 'I must hand it to you, Harry! Between you two beauties with your wizardry, you'd kill a flock of birds with one stone!'

Harry had gone to Calcutta. Margaret, his mistress, sat at the entrance of her little house, thinking.

A cold, moist breeze sprang up, stirring the leaves of the champak trees, and the birds to exuberant twittering. As clouds sped across the sun, shadows appeared and ran along the ground to vanish in deep greenery. And suddenly a drop of rain fell, and another, followed by the sharp pitter-patter of rain feet.

Mahanth Jha walked briskly along the Mahari bund and crossed over to the rear of Harry's compound. He looked around cautiously; there was no one in sight. He walked along the hedge of chameli bushes, and into Margaret's little house.

She looked up and saw him. Her eyes went wide and her hands flew to her mouth to stifle the cry. 'You must be mad,' she whispered, drawing him quickly inside, 'mad to come here in daylight.'

'I had to! I had to see you!' he said. 'It is all over! He knows about us.'

Harry's right-hand man! In all his life he had wronged no one but Harry. Overcome every snare the devil had set for him, but this one because that's how life is, with its wily little tricks. He was an honourable man but it was his heart that had betrayed him.

They looked wordlessly at each other and the blood drained from her face.

'I must go away, and quickly,' he told her, 'for both our sakes.'

She turned slowly away from him. 'So it is over!' Her voice broke. 'I always knew, some day it would be so!' Then, swinging round to face him, 'But where, now, will you go?' she asked quickly.

'I know not where,' he answered her, looking away into the misty distance, as blank as the future. There was a time-tempered sorrow in his face, for he had sorrowed long over the perfidy of their relationship. 'But it is best that you never know.'

'Never know? Then . . . we will not meet again? Not ever?'

He turned his head, and their eyes met. 'No, not in this life,' he said sighing, 'but in some future life we will be together, proud of our love, not this sneaky relationship of lies and deceit.'

'Not in this life,' she repeated, dragging out the words of this death sentence. And then she smiled sadly. 'If that be so, I'll wait for you,' she whispered, 'I'll wait forever!'

'And I,' he said, 'will love you for a thousand lifetimes!'

Her arms reached out for him, hot tears trapped in the dark lashes, to hold him, to feel him against her for one last time.

But he drew quickly away. 'No! Stay there, my love. Just that way that I might hold this image of you in my heart till I die.'

Then he turned quickly, and was gone.

It was a fine morning, dry and crisply cool, with the crows calling in the special way they reserved for these days. From where we sat chatting in the veranda, we had a clear view of the driveway and beyond the gates, left carelessly open, to where the dirt track to the station turned and was lost to sight. Someone was coming in through those wide-open gates. The dogs having met and sniffed him out to their satisfaction were trotting alongside. He must have arrived on the one o'clock train; we could hear it whistling at the station.

Dad put down his newspaper, frowning, as the man came hurriedly up the driveway. 'Something's wrong, sure as God made little apples!'

'Huzoor,' he cried breathlessly, 'there is very bad news! Abhinandan has been sentenced to death!'

'What? To death?'

'Ji huzoor, I was there. I saw it all. The courtroom was packed full; they had expected an acquittal. Witnesses had lied and contradicted each other. So the sentence, when it came, was a terrible shock for everybody. Such a drama was never seen before. Two of his nephews who were sentenced along with him just dropped like stones on the courtroom floor. Abhinandan went mad with rage when he saw them fall from fright. He flew at them and kicked them back to consciousness. "Cowards!" he shouted, "If we must die, let us die like men." There was silence in the courtroom. But what happened next, they never expected at all. He picked up one of his khadaun and made a sudden charge for the new magistrate, shouting, "Death for us, so let it be. But for you—son of an owl put here to dispense justice—take this from me and wear it like a medal on your chest," and he flung the khadaun with perfect aim. Baap re baap! Such cheering and confusion filled the courtroom. I thought, now there will be a riot. But the police quickly closed in on him and took him away in chains.'

Mother's face had grown very pale. 'This is an ugly business,' she said, tears springing up in her eyes. 'Very ugly indeed!'

'Master Harry's work, of course.' Dad flicked his cigarette at the box of grinning pansies. 'They'll have to go in appeal.'

And then, the voice of Kalri, 'What to say! All bad, bad things are happening Missbaba, anywhere everywhere! Even Mahanth Jha has disappeared.'

'What did you say, Kalri?'

'Yes Missbaba. Gone. Nobody knows where! All the village people are talking and saying such, such things, oh baba!'

It was a Friday, and we ate our dinner that night in silence—thinking about the man who brought the mahseer, and was going to be 'hanged by the neck till he was dead'.

'Mother, do you know, Abhinandan once told us that as long as he lived we would never have another dacoity here. Why? Did we ever have one?'

It was late. The dinner table had been cleared, and Mother had dismissed the servants who were hanging around. But we often sat put, chatting comfortably.

'Oh! Have I never told you about it before?' She smiled. 'It was a long time ago, after my father's death, when we had all come from Calcutta to live here, and I was just a little girl. Harry had gone to Assam to buy his elephants. He did it once in two or three years, but it took quite a few days each time. So the old lady'—Mother often referred to her mother as the old lady—'Rosie and I were alone. I tell you, we were taken completely by surprise, because they came, not at night, but in the afternoon when there were no watchmen and all the servants went home to the village. Only Ghogra—he was scarcely eighteen at the time—was pottering about downstairs, while Nagiya and Kalri were out on the terrace. Suddenly we heard this atrocious hammering on the front door. Ghogra came charging upstairs, in a panic. His eyes looked like organ stops. "Daku log! Baap re baap! What will we do, Memsahib? So many of them, they will butcher us all, ayyyh!"

'"Shut up you fool!" the old lady snapped. "Quick! Take this child downstairs, then out from the back door, and run as fast as you can to the village. Raise an alarm. Bring help for us, soon! Run now!" So he put me astride his hip and ran. Even in those days, though he was strong as a bull, he was such a goose, trembling with fright, and his legs so wobbly it was like riding a sickly goat. He ran till we reached the village, where, my word, he set up such a howl, it was heard in Harpur village!

'In the meantime, when the racket had settled down, the old lady had walked into the living room with a revolver in her hand. My! My! Rosie and Nagiya were flat on the floor, while six or seven men were moving about the room. They had wrapped the ends of their turbans over their faces, so they wouldn't be identified. O lordy! Furniture was smashed, objects lay scattered everywhere. She had barely taken in the scene when someone looked up and saw her standing in the doorway. Immediately he shouted, "Bandook re, chheen re!" And before she could pull the trigger, a lathi blow struck her head from behind. She blacked out. What she remembered next was Rosie shaking her frantically. "O my God, Aunty! I thought you were dead—all this blood! Quick! Let's get the hell out of here, while they're busy." But the old lady could scarcely move. So Rosie caught hold of her feet and dragged her with all the strength she had, leaving a trail of blood all the way; through the dining room into the back veranda, down the steps and out to where the gardenia bushes had grown into a dense, entangled mass. And then they heard the cries, the distant cries of many men drawing nearer. And at the same instant they got the smell of smoke and the crackle of burning thatch.'

'Burning! Why?'

'This is how dacoits used to operate those days. After every dacoity they set fire to the place. Most verandas in those days had a thatched roof covered over with tiles. Thank God the Harpur Rajputs—there must have been a good number of them—came swarming around and put out the fire. But the dacoits had got away with what they could carry.'

'Then why did the Rajputs shout from far when they could have come quietly and caught the dacoits red-handed?'

'Well, for one thing, scaring them off sooner gave them less time for mischief. You know, they hadn't managed to break open the steel safe, and some of the silver tied up in bedsheets was left lying on the front veranda. But what mattered most—lives were saved, for the old lady and Rosie might have been found and killed by that time.'

A solitary figure was making its way across the fields, westwards to the Baghmati, visible clearly even by the light of a waning moon in her snow-white sari that glowed like a luminous thing. She moved with purpose, though glancing back over her shoulder as if she expected to be followed. Was she? She couldn't see; her vision was blurred with weeping. How many days? Did it matter? She would never see him again. Only the image remained of his face with that last shattering look of anguish! It would not go away. She could not weep it out.

And Harry sahib, her master? He had finally learned of her perfidy. And how? Nobody would have betrayed her secret, because it was also her lover's. Who would betray a man as well loved as Mahanth Jha? But then, there were times when hatred overruled all other considerations. A long-suppressed hatred of her—it was Ghogra!

She stood by the riverbank drained of all emotion, enveloped in silence and emptiness. The cry of a startled waterbird made her turn around. A sudden flicker of hope in its dying embers. Maybe he would come. But her heart didn't quicken for it knew too well, it could never be.

The soulless night, and the hush of death.

'Not in this, but in some future life,' he had said.

It wasn't him. It was the sound of a drunken fisherman on his way home from the illicit liquor market at the border that had alarmed the bird. He stopped transfixed on the narrow path that zigzagged along the riverbank, obscured by tiger grass, for what he saw barely fifty yards ahead knocked him cold sober, and sweat seeped from the pores of his body. The misty white ghost of a woman stood gazing down at the water. And as he turned to run, he heard a great splash. His screams tore through the night like a drunken siren.

Kalri sailed into the room with her mouth open. She burst into speech.

'What to say, Missbaba!' Early in the morning, it was still dark then. 'Ay Missbaba!'

'Kalri, pull yourself together and speak clearly.'

'The fishermen—they ran fast, fast when they heard such night-time shouting. Hay, hay! Too late! She was drowned in the deep side! All the fishermen brought the body out. Oh ho, Missbaba! Mud, mud all over! And her mother searching half the night in what all places. When she found her, she was a corpse.'

'Who are you talking about, Kalri?'

'Hay, hay, Missbaba! It is Harry sahib's Margaret!'

'Dear Lord! These things are coming thick and fast.'

Harry was back from Calcutta in a highly agitated state.

'Drastic changes, drastic changes are coming, Gladys, some good, but more bad. Disastrous, I would say!' He brought out a handkerchief and wiped his face. 'And we cannot fight them.

It is the end of zamindari. Our villages will be gone. You can imagine what that will mean.'

She sighed over her untouched food. 'There were rumours here too, but I had hoped it was only idle speculation. God knows how we will manage without our labourers.'

'Yes, only heaven knows how! There'll be problems we've never faced before. And furthermore, I don't want to frighten you—the ridiculous land ceiling! Thirty bighas of land per person. With only seven members in your family, it can beggar you, Gladys! Fortunately for me, I have the major part of my assets in shares and bank deposits. But you, you will be hit hard. Sell! Sell whatever you can, while the going is good! Soon the government will be down on us. They're paying a miserable compensation for land they will take away. And who knows if that will be paid even in our lifetime.'

'Far worse than I expected.' She took a big gulp of water. 'We can only hope and pray.'

'Yes, Gladys. Storm heaven with your prayers!'

'Of course. How fortunate for you, Harry, you need no prayers at all,' she said a bit irritably. 'By the way, your man Mahanth Jha has disappeared! Where on earth could he have gone? Surely, you didn't dismiss him? He was the best you ever had—a model of honesty and integrity, such a rarity in these parts.'

'No, no, Gladys!' Harry put down his spoon and fork. His face flushed and he frowned down at his chicken curry. 'I was away in Calcutta, and when I returned, he was gone! Left without a word to any of his people.'

The last words trailed off, scarcely audible, and she saw in his face an expression of intense pain. Suddenly it struck her, for the first time ever, how blind she had been to the sorrows of this man! She simply put her hand over his, and said, 'I'm sorry.'

A Festival of Affliction

The sun was sinking when an elephant's shrill trumpeting broke through the stillness, accompanied by the rhythmical ting-tong of a heavy bell swinging from side to side as it drew nearer.

Mother came out on the veranda. 'It's Hawnn,' she smiled, 'on his way to the Baghmati.' For November had come with the most important Bihari festival called Chhatt, a time when Hindus bathed in the rivers of the gods, for healing.

The Raja of Sheohar, whom we called Hawnn, visited her usually about this time for old times' sake and settled his large frame tightly into a chair.

Mother smiled at him. 'It is good of you to come.'

'Madam, how can we forget old connections,' nodding sweetly, 'when we know that your grandfather and my grandson were truly great friends,' he said to her in a great mix-up.

They smiled at each other. Little pleasantries passed, in slow motion, back and forth. Brief observations on the weather, the agricultural yield this year, inquiries about health, children, animals, birds, etc., and finally, 'What can I do for madam?' There wasn't anything.

Then with a reminiscent smile and a deep breath: 'Hawnn . . . to come back to your grandfather! Should I tell you, madam, he had a kind heart under his fierce exterior. Hawnn . . . My father told me an amusing story about him. He said that once a Hindu bride was being carried to her husband's home in a palki. She was weeping aloud, very loud, as is our custom. Hawnn. But then, the British knew so little of our customs! Your grandfather heard the noise. It must have sounded very terrible to his ears. He stopped the marriage procession, and ordered the carriers to take her back to her father's house at once!' His large frame

Sylvia Dyer

shook with laughter. 'You can imagine, madam, what confusion that must have caused.'

Then, as the thought of present afflictions crossed his mind his laughter drained out and he frowned. 'Have you heard, madam, they speak of zamindari abolition. How can they do this? We will fight! Darbhanga has already taken the matter to court.'

Mother shook her head sadly. 'It'll be heads against a stone wall.'

'So, you too think that way. A great misfortune!' He looked down at his hands. 'We have no skills to earn a decent living. It will be the end for us.'

Our batwara case with Rajan and Bhajan, inspired by Harry, was over at last. It had dragged on for seven long, ruinous years. The court decided what we could well have done between ourselves, and without the astronomical costs.

Harry had tried in so many ways to wreck us. And largely, he had succeeded. Now, it seemed, life was breaking him.

'Gladys,' he said one day when he came to visit, 'I have to ask you a favour. I hope you will not find it in your heart to refuse me.'

'Now what is this enormous favour, Harry?'

'Sell me a little piece of land alongside your family graveyard.'

She looked at him in surprise. 'Alongside the family graveyard?'

'Yes. You see, Gladys, before long I'll be dead, and I want to be buried near Rosie and my mother.'

'Dead, at your age? What rubbish, Harry! Besides, God forbid should that happen you are family and have every right to a place inside the graveyard. You don't have to pay me for something like . . . Good Lord, what made you think of something like that?'

'Gladys,' he leaned back in his chair, looking ruefully at her, and said, 'I think of all that's happened in these past years. I can't pretend I haven't harmed you again and again. Can you find it in your heart to forgive me?'

'Harry, the past is finished and done with. Let us not talk of this again.'

He drew out a handkerchief from his pocket and wiped his face. 'You don't know it, Gladys, but I'm a sick man, a very sick man.' He sat, palely slumped among the roses in the rose-patterned chair.

Gladys sat thinking. How Harry has changed in this last year! No more fuelling of ruinous litigation. No more chopping down shisham trees or demolishing boundaries. No more intrigues.

'You children had better run along and pay Harry a visit.' Mother frowned at us from over the newspaper. 'It's been some time since you last went.'

'Come, dress up quickly, we're going to Harry's place for tea.'

'You dress up, Parrot,' Lenny said. 'I've got to take over from Reggie at the khariyan.' Since Dada's death Reggie and Lenny had taken over the affairs of the khariyan, with Abdhi Missir and Sukhesar.

Another lecture awaited us at Harry's place. This time it had switched from wealth to health, and it started as we sat down at the tea table.

He couldn't wait. 'Your health is your most precious possession. Remember that, children.' Harry was droning away dreadfully, while we stared at the small iced cakes and Jacob's Assortment biscuits, and Ghogra poured the tea.

'Remember this,' we were jerked out of our cake-study, 'you can have all the wealth in the world, but without health, you won't enjoy a pice! You can have the world's best cakes on your table, but you cannot take a bite! No pleasure is pleasure any more.' He sighed heavily and the light in his eyes went out. 'You will just suffer and suffer, body and mind. You can run to Calcutta. You can fly to London. The best doctors can't cure you. No amount of money can save you. Children, take this bitter truth from me and hold it in your memory!'

Never in all these years had Gladys discouraged us from visiting Harry, knowing well that we brightened his days.

Months before the event, he called his carpenters. 'Cut down that old shisham tree from behind the garage. Lop off the branches, and let the trunk lie in the rain and sun to season. Next year we should get good planks from it.'

'Ji huzoor,' they agreed, 'good for the new tyre cart.'

'No. I had not that in mind. They will be good for my coffin.'

Immediately, Ghogra, who was pottering about with a duster in his hand, covered his face with the duster. 'Ay Ram! If you die, sahib,' he wailed aloud, rolling his one uncovered eye at the ceiling, 'what, what will become of me?'

Harry turned irritably on him. 'I have provided for you, gutless goat, so cut out the melodrama.'

Kethar Ojha became sick too, with a mysterious stomach affliction no vaid could cure. It left him with little desire for food and less for mischief. There was peace in Dhang for many a poor man.

A Time to Die

It was late summer, and an unusually hot day that drove people indoors. Sweat poured off the punkha coolie as he pulled at the rope of the drawing room fan. The dogs let out little moaning growls and flopped down on the veranda floor with the muffled thud of dead flesh. Even vociferous summer birds like the brainfever bird and the koel seemed to have lost their voices. Still and silent it was, that day.

'Such heat, O Lordy!' Mother stood up suddenly. She picked

up a fly swatter and knocked out two persistent flies. 'There's sure to be a storm,' she said, walking out to the east end of the veranda to take a look at the sky, where angry clouds were banking up on the horizon.

Then she saw a man running down the centre road that cut across Puchkurwa.

'What is this now, I wonder?'

He was drenched in sweat, and breathing hard. 'Huzoor, Harry sahib is sick! Very sick!'

'O dear God! Has anybody gone for the doctor?'

'Ji huzoor, he has come. And even the Padre sahib.'

'I'll be there immediately,' she said quickly. 'You children can follow.'

And she was gone.

The room was dark. A little sunlight spilled in from the only open window. Our mission priest sat by it, looking out; his well-weathered face was expressionless.

We saw him every month, when he arrived on a bicycle from the Morpa Mission, six miles away, to say Holy Mass in our dining room. He was a hard-headed philosopher and dispensed comfort in one great, hard-hitting shot: 'Whichever way you take it, you've got to take it!'

Mother sat by Harry's bed while we stood behind her chair, with Chatter Cat fidgety and stiffening with fright at the sight of Harry's face. It was a mask of pale ivory with a tinge of pale green, and the eyes sunk deep in shadows. The nose was pinched and beakier than ever. A sparrow-hawk. A bird of prey that had showered material gifts on us—tea parties, dolls, bicycles, gold bangles, chocolates when we fell down and bled. Adult conversations. One who had mattered much to Parrot and Pig was now dying in the guise of a perfect stranger—with a cold, stranger's look in his eyes—Death.

Ghogra was flat on his face, wailing aloud and beating the polished red cement floor with his forehead.

Sylvia Dyer

And so this life of Harry's ended. Dorothy and Ernie were away in Europe. In fact it was a month before they showed up to collect their sizeable inheritance.

Reggie, Lenny and Pig along with a few Christians from the Morpa Mission carried the coffin that Harry had prepared for himself, a year before. It was a long haul down the centre road from Harry's house to our family graveyard. Ghogra staggered alongside, wailing and beating his barrel chest with audible thumps while the accompanying crowd sniggered.

We buried Harry alongside his sister and mother, as he had desired. There was no visible emotion, anywhere, as the priest recited the burial service; but as his last remains were being lowered into the grave, Ghogra lurched forward, his face covered in tears, crying out in a broken voice, 'Sahib Huzoor! I'm coming!' But strong arms jerked him back, while people turned and looked at each other, speaking with their eyes.

Yes, it was a performance that would be remembered, but Ghogra was perhaps the only one who really loved Harry.

Mahanth Jha was never seen again. The police, with all their danda-power, were unable to trace him anywhere; and it became one of the unsolved mysteries of Dhang.

Meanwhile, Abhinandan was languishing in jail. They had appealed against the magistrate's verdict, but his misbehaviour in court had further added to the charges against him.

Now Dad spent every day in the Sitamarhi court. It was becoming a necessity for 'prestige' as the eco-political situation pushed us steadily downwards. He drank thirty cups of tea and returned every evening fagged out. He sat at the dining table, smoking and poring over the *Statesman* crossword puzzle.

'Is there any news of Abhinandan's case?' Mother asked one evening.

'I hear it's gone to the high court.'

'Then, Terence, how d'you think it will go?'

'If there's a retrial he should save his neck, though he'll be stung on the second charge of assaulting the magistrate. Anyway, it could take years.'

Another year moved on, with its season of leaf-fall that left the trees stripped bare to the merciless sun. It was a wonder how this harsh experience brought out the most gorgeous blossoms of summer.

That night was one of the loveliest I can remember. The moon with its undeniable magic drenched our world in silvery light with soft velvet shadows to create a beauty not of this world. It filled my soul with a strange longing, for I knew not what. So I just went for a walk with my grey velvet shadow. The sound of soft panting made me turn around. Chumra was following me. We both stared at the moon.

'Chumra,' I bent down, pulling his loose, hairy cheeks as far as they would stretch, and planted a hard smack on each, 'Chumra, you mad dog! I love you!' He licked my hand with his rough tongue, and we walked on, regardless of Kalri's wail from the front veranda

It was our last walk together.

The opera of summer birds commenced early. In fact, the koel and crow pheasant could never wait till dawn. As it grew brighter, more and more birds joined in, and finally the brainfever bird. The dogs awoke and stretched lazily in the heat; and then the nightwatchmen, who had slept soundly. The doors of the henhouse were flung open, and noisy poultry streamed out. Voices buzzed. There was the bustle of another day, breakfast with its delightful smells, and dogs slinking in to sit under the table. But where was Chumra?

Man stood on the veranda steps. 'Come,' he said in a low whisper, and he led us through the garden to the cassia tree. Chumra lay dead. His body was stiff and cold, with his wide staring eyes covered with flies. It must have been that way for hours. Close by, Man pointed out the remains of a snake, bitten

in two. He crouched down, spreading out the hood with his fingers to show us the spectacle-like markings of a cobra. 'Hai Bhagwan! He had no chance this time,' he said, shaking his head sadly. 'Grown too old, too old for this game.'

We buried Chumra right there, under the cassia tree where so often we had sat together, sharing my feelings. And the wind sighed, and blew down a drift of blossoms over his grave.

And now a whole way of life was ending. The British were winding up their affairs in India and the Bihar Light Horse had a winding-up party at the Muzaffarpur Planters' Club.

Dad had been a member of the Bihar Light Horse for many years. It was an auxiliary force, composed of planters, civil service officials like judges and magistrates, and a sprinkling of British boxwallahs (gentlemen of commerce), all troopers under the command of a regular army officer holding the rank of captain. They were sober, respectable men. But when they got together with the planters, it 'brought out the worst in them', according to the Snake Pit ladies. The planters had always been a wild lot, rendered so by the harshness of a lonely and hazardous life in the far-flung hostile wilderness. They met life head-on, and lived it hard. And when they met at the club, they drank hard, swore hard, got high and fired off a few shots in the air, like pressure cookers blowing their valves. They played rough and crazy games that made them extremely unpopular with those who sat coiled up with their knitting in the Snake Pit.

The club that evening was brilliantly lit and buzzing with chatter. Maharajas and rajas, everyone who mattered was there for the farewell, in blue patrols, dinner jackets and evening gowns with dazzling jewellery. After a long meandering speech weighed down with alcohol and tears, priceless old pieces of silver were presented by office-bearers to themselves. They were leaving and they would not leave without the silver. It started with the colonel who took the biggest cup, staggeringly heavy to carry, even if you were not drunk. But as this impressive prize distribution progressed, a murmur of disapproval was building up among the members. It erupted in the loudest 'boooooo'. And then things went quite out of hand. Spoonfuls of soufflé flew across the room and soon grew into a full-fledged pudding fight with more than enough pudding for all. Cleverly, the band struck up to create a distraction, and people left off to sing aloud, flushed, reeling and spotted with dessert, merrymaking with hearts a-breaking.

Spirits flowed down aching throats and damask tablecloths, drowning sorrows, for the bottom had fallen out of many individual worlds.

And a man was crawling under our table in search of something: Dentures? Car keys? A glass eye? A gun? There was no telling, till he was drawn out by his coat-tails, with, 'Wh-wh-what the hell do you think you're doing down there?'

A bewildered face, red and watery-eyed, appeared from under the tablecloth. 'I'm lookin',' it said sadly, 'just lookin' for yesterday.'

Mother

Mother, who cared for every living creature, cared so little for herself. Even alarming symptoms were dismissed as 'nothing at all'. So her illness was diagnosed too late; and the surgery for breast cancer, performed in a Patna hospital, was not a success. The surgeon told her so. The malignancy had spread too invasively to be contained. It was a death sentence she accepted with silent resignation.

For the first few days following her return home, she would sit in her armchair on the veranda, oblivious of the summer heat. Sit for hours, staring into the garden, looking at her cassia tree, something she'd had little time for before. Covered over with masses of blossoms, it had become a vision of surreal beauty, like

Sylvia Dyer

a rose-tinted cloud that glows from an enchanted light within. And then one day, a change came over her. She brought out her sunshade and began to walk; and Pixie, who had spent the better part of ten years sitting under her chair, got up heavily and followed her everywhere with droopy eyes and floppy ears that swept the ground, leaving a twin trail in the dust. She walked about her beloved garden where the birds sang with euphoric abandon, and butterflies fluttered drunkenly in the hot sun. And through every room in the house, sadly pensive, discovering little things she had never noticed before. One day she found a scrap of paper on her writing desk, a crumpled scrap with a few words scribbled on it. She sat down, smoothed it out and read slowly:

Oh sugar-coated days,
Your sweetness filters still
Through nights of tears, incipient fears
That life is but a sugar-coated bitter pill!

'Yes,' she said, looking up at me, 'life can be a sugar-coated bitter pill. We are born with the taste of sweetness in our mouths, and then, as life moves on we begin to taste the bitterness—some more than others. But it is something we have to take, to finally realize Paradise! The Hindus have an explanation for all this pain, in karma. Man must pay off his spiritual debts, incurred not only in this life, but in previous ones before his essence is pure enough to be absorbed into the Infinite. This belief settles many bewildering questions about this world's sorrows.' She sighed. 'We say why is life so unfair? What have I done to deserve this? Why are innocent children born afflicted? They have an answer in karma. We have our own beliefs. But whatever they may be,' she said with a smile, 'if we can take it without growing bitter inside us, then we have moved on, like homing pigeons, closer ever towards God, each in his own way, on his own assigned journey.'

Then, 'No, no! No tears, my darling.' She took my hand tenderly. 'These sorrows pass. And pain, actually, is brief. For what is a month, a year, or even a lifetime in the vastness of Eternity?'

As winter approached and the days grew shorter, her steps began to drag. Then the disease invaded her spine and she could no longer move from her bed. She would never get better. We could only watch her dying, inch by inch.

I walked out to the veranda. Reggie was there, sitting on the steps. 'Come, sit here.' He patted the cement floor alongside and I sank down, with my legs turning to jelly.

'There are things we cannot change,' he said softly. 'This wonderful thing we call life comes into this world with one leg tied to death. I'll tell you something, Parrot. Never be afraid! Fear goes through you like acid. It can destroy you more surely than the object of your terror, and that, believe me, makes a difference to the final outcome! Don't think that because you're afraid, because you pray yourself to a standstill, life will let you off the hook. So stand fast and face it.'

I looked slowly up at Reggie, and in his gentle eyes I found a new kind of courage.

Soon, Mother's lovely face was so swollen and distorted you had to look again to know it was Mother and, as the days dragged in an endless monotony of pain and pills, her voice too was lost. Kalri sat all day and night by her bedside. She could do little else. Her heart, she said, was breaking in little pieces.

Then one afternoon, a tall, familiar figure we had almost forgotten stood in the doorway of her room. His short-cropped hair was flecked with grey and his lean, hard face palely drawn. It was Abhinandan! After five years, he had finally been acquitted by the high court and released from prison.

'What news?' he had rapped out, alighting from the train at the railway station. 'Tell me, what news is there of the kothi?'

And when they told him, he was struck by a strange emotion, a fear that was overwhelming, for it was a thing that could not be tackled by violence. He just froze where he stood, staring at them with the eyes of a dead man.

And now standing in the doorway his shoulders sagged, and suddenly cracks appeared in the armour of his face. And then tears, rapid tears sliding unashamedly over his rugged cheeks, to drip on the floor. He didn't even try to brush them away, this man of steel and gore, to whom tears were as anomalous as snowflakes in hell.

And he was moving forward to the foot of her bed, whispering in a hoarse voice, 'Missbaba, is this Missbaba? No! I cannot understand your God! This should have happened to me—a thug, a murderous brute as you once called me. That would have been justice. But you, Missbaba, you are a saint!' And his voice broke as he cried out, 'Ay Bhagwan, strike me down, for in spite of knowing you I have lived the life of a monster.'

There was silence, deep as the ocean. Then slowly, Mother's pale lips smiled at him; and her eyes were smiling with the light of a profound wisdom that seemed to put, in the simplest way, life and death, and the ceaseless tyranny of human suffering—all in their fitting places in Eternity.

And Abhinandan covered his face and went away weeping.

The Last Sands

Many trees shed all their leaves towards the end of winter and the onset of summer. Every day a warm wind blew across the land and the leaves danced their dance of death. In batches they fell to the earth, never more to dance. The trees were left bare, their stark, forlorn nakedness a sight not to be looked upon. Bereft, but only for a while. It was just the cycle of nature and not the end. For there is no end.

But it was the row of old shisham trees that puzzled us, as we stood with Sukhesar watching them from the khariyan. This could well have been the very spot from which the sadhu had observed them, a hundred years ago ... Something was missing now. Something we had long lost track of.

'Why, of course, it's the flying foxes!'

'My God! They're gone! Every single one!'

'I have been marking this for some months now,' Sukhesar said. 'They could see the great change coming. They had nothing to stay for!'

And it had come. An ill wind had blown away the flying foxes and the fragile paradise we knew, once upon a time. The magic spell of a hundred years was broken and the last sands ran swiftly out with changing times changing the face of everything. Land reforms had fragmented large estates and land in excess of the land ceiling had been acquired by the government for a pittance, breaking the back of every big landowner.

'Hawnn,' they told us, 'wanders aimlessly about his palace grounds. He hasn't changed his clothes for days, and speaks only to the walls.'

Everywhere, the orchards were slowly disappearing to be replaced by paddy fields, and magnificent old trees that had withstood the onslaught of countless storms came crashing down by the act of a single axe, for the small buyer had discovered the market value of timber. Ancient boundaries, along with their rows of shisham trees, those once-invincible guardians of territory, were levelled out, rendering it all into a flat and featureless landscape.

Sukhesar stood in the doorway clearing his throat to attract attention. Dad looked up from his crossword puzzle.

'Huzoor, we have a problem,' he said, 'there will be no coolies when we take out the tractor for ploughing tomorrow. The Musahars are all gone! Run away to cut wood in Assam!'

'So it has come! Well, it had to happen, sooner or later.' Dad flicked his cigarette out into the garden carelessly. He had stopped shouting. He was in the habit of saying, 'Let tomorrow come, tomorrow we'll see what can be done.'

And as the days move forward, darkness comes for everyone. Kethar Ojha has turned into a withered tree, the skin stretched like yellow parchment over his ribs. There is cancer in his stomach. Every day he empties his food into a hole in the ground for Brutus (the dog who would bow down to no man), now the bowed beneficiary of Kethar's charity.

Land is changing hands almost every day at the registration office near Dhang station. Brutus accompanies old friends on their way there every morning—something to do, something to break the dreary monotony of old age. And one day he doesn't make it back home. He lays his large, bony frame down under the khushi Ojha peepul tree, and dies.

And that's how Ghogra goes a couple of months later. He drops there on his return from the registration office, gasping and clutching his chest. The onlookers stand by, unmoved. They mistake it for his best-ever performance. All they know is that he has willingly traded the land Harry gave him for his lifetime. He just transferred it to Ernie for a lump sum of money. Money! But to the rural man land is life, and money, just fancy paper that is soon gone with the wind.

And now Man, with nodular leprosy, has come to say his last goodbye. His face, as he looks at us, is already dead.

'Don't worry, Man,' we try to reassure him, 'it's not so bad. You'll get the latest treatment and you'll be back with us before you know it.'

'Yes, babalog.' He swallows hard and his eyes glisten with banked up tears, for he knows, and we all know, the truth.

Foster is blind, and has to be led about by his grandchildren, and Kalri is dead. She died suddenly of a stroke, soon after Mother's death.

But all sorrows, like joy, pass away—and we can hold in our

hearts only that which we wish to. So, if I close my eyes, I can fly backwards over the years that changed the face of all that we once cherished, past the denudation and deposition of time's tears and laughter, back to the years of the flying foxes and the sugar-coated days of childhood!

It's so simple. Just press rewind . . . and there . . .

It's early December. Pig and Parrot are coming home from school on the 2 p.m. train, chugging through green, green groves and golden paddy fields ready for harvest, heads stuck out of the window, divine Himalayan wind in our hair with a generous mixture of railway coal dust. While Dad, in a tweed jacket and flannels, stands with the carriage door drawn back, sizing up the prospects of a good sugar cane crop.

Dad draws deeply on his cigarette and flicks it out. 'We're in,' he says, as the train trembles and slows down, and the engine gives a shriek of joy as it pulls into the pint-sized railway station under a royal-blue tin board that says DHANG.

And then we hear it. Shouting like the last day on earth. Sipahis and Musahars like a swarm of bees surge in through the open doorway and windows, before the train can stop. They're salaaming and grinning . . . Muddy Musahars pounce on our luggage, big school trunks, canvas bedding rolls and baskets of hill oranges.

'Oh babalog, babalog! It's been such a long time!'

'Too long, too long!' we shout with arms spread wide, tearing down the steep railway embankment to where the tyre cart, hitched to the famous Chinamen-pair, stands waiting, all set with deckchairs. Bullfrog and Snouty flash us dazzling white smiles from gleaming black faces, as they sit holding the bullocks' tails, ready for take-off.

'Bad floods again this year.' Narain Singh rubs his shaved and oily head. 'Arre baba, flowed away with the roads—jiggered up the car! Chamanlal is in Sitamarhi searching for a new axle!'

'Hee hee! But news, tell, tell, what news?'

'Good, always good! Wild geese back on the river! Abhinandan Babaji home from the lock-up!'

'Like us!'

We leap into the cart.

'Move!' Bullfrog screams, catching the bullocks' tails and away we go, deckchairs leaving the deck, bump-bump along a rough track, its potholes cunningly concealed in weeds. Up and down, through chequered fields with clumps of toddy trees, past sugar cane fields and mango groves. And now, the road is fringed with straight, young shisham trees, their slender trailing branches covered with little coin-shaped leaves. A fitful breeze from across the river stirs them suddenly to life; and as they dance, the sunlight catches their lacquered faces, and for brief moments the trees are covered with shimmering coins.

Then the track turns sharply to show gates flung wide open.

Pig's fingers pull my hair. 'Look, Parrot, look! Oho you fool! You're always dreaming!'

And there before us, set in a kaleidoscope of colours—is Home!

Bullfrog and Snouty shout, 'Howw . . . Howwww!' They yank the reins taut. The bullocks' heads jerk backwards. The cart lurches and slithers to a stop—and it's a time for flying through the air . . .

The dogs leap at us, mouths pulled back in toothy grins, spittle flying free, pink tongues shooting out to lick our faces.

And there, midway up the veranda steps, under an archway of climbing roses, is Mother, smiling. And her eyes are wet, giving her a watery vision of a Parrot and a Pig, home from the hills. Chatter Cat clinging to her hand, points excitedly at us, while Horsey takes a welcoming leap at Dad's chest, muddying his shirtfront.

Dad roars like an alligator.

Dada shouts, *'How nice, how nice!'*

Lenny and Reggie give us a big wink and their faces are

beaming, like seraphim. Ernie curls up his fingers to make binoculars, and looks at me. He sticks out his tongue.

All the servants stand ranged behind. Everyone we ever knew and loved is there. All set for a group photograph of radiant faces, a picture for all time, with the afternoon sun at just the right angle.

'Smile everyone!'

'Smile!'

'*Click!*'

Sylvia Dyer

Acknowledgements

My gratitude goes to my daughter Marilyn without whose enduring support, encouragement and help this book might never have seen the light of day. To my loving, supportive family, my son Lance, daughter-in-law Zoe and granddaughter Amanda. My brother Leslie, his late wife Sybil, and his daughters Gladys, Ingrid and Jennifer.

My gratitude also to my ever-helpful nephew Darryl D'Monte. To David Davidar who gave me hope, guidance and invaluable help. To Peter Moss my friend and adviser. To my very dear Shireen Vakil, Jean Simeon, Achal Ahluwalia, Winston Machado, Shikha Mitra, Sabita Burges and Cyrus Sataravala, who in various ways have assisted me on the journey of this book. To my patient editors Ravi Singh and Jaishree Ram Mohan.